If You Want To Know

...

Just Ask!

LJ Bremer

Linghwa Books

If You Want To Know...Just Ask!

Cover design by LJ Bremer.

This is a totally human creation. Absolutely no part of this book has been created by AI.

First Edition

ISBN: 9781739886547

DEDICATION

For Seran, my twin flame.
Thank you for coming into my dreams and waking me up.
Thank you for being in my life – and remaining with me throughout everything we have endured.

I might not fully understand what is going on or know what will happen next – but I do know that I have loved you throughout eternity and will love you forevermore.

Thank you for helping me heal.
Thank you for bringing me back to life,
Thank you for returning my dreams to me.

We are one soul living as two: our souls entangled and our destinies intertwined, woven into the fabric of reality. It is more than a single red thread of destiny connecting you and I together, but the tapestry of life and all the souls and all the threads that have us woven together.

I love you.
I have always loved you.
I will always love you.

If You Want To Know...Just Ask!

CONTENTS

Acknowledgments

My eternal gratitude to Jane who has been supporting me for many years both spirituality and as a dear friend. Thank you for sharing this journey with me, and for being an integral part in this book becoming more than unpublished anecdotes and typos.

My journey would never have begun without the fantastic support from my lecturers and mentors at university who have always supported and championed my work and pushed me to challenge myself in so many ways. So much of my creative portfolio that has developed throughout my time at UWTSD has overlapped with my reality, and I am so grateful to Lyndsy and Laura who have supported me throughout my studies and have helped me make sense of my creative works and of my spiritual journey that are unequivocally entangled to one another.

I have been blessed to have some truly remarkable lecturers during both my BA and MA course who have worked wonders on helping me to improve and develop my writing in different genres; and also allowed this book to come to life which is culmination of my academic and esoteric journey to this point in time.

Thank you to Elin for being a fundamental part of my journey and for contributing a part of your story to this book. Without the many conversations we've shared, I would likely never have accepted the reality of the twin flame connection or allowed it to grow and develop.

Thank you to my soul tribe for being there for me throughout the many ups and downs of this journey too. Thank you for allowing me to indulge in the euphoric moments of connection as much as the occasional wallowing in the doldrums that comes with dark night of the soul. I am honoured by the friendship we share and to have been able to develop myself spiritually with the guidance and suggestions from you all.

Finally, the greatest thanks goes to my parents who are sadly no longer with me. I would not be here in so many different ways without their ongoing love and patience with me throughout my life. I have been able to explore my spirituality and my beliefs to greater depths than many thanks to their willingness to listen, their insight as both parents and as psychiatric nurses, and their individual curiosity to the overlapping subjects.

They were my anchor to life and reality which can so often be unbearably dark, they were my light and my hope through the night, and it was with their support and encouragement that I could brave the greatest step of my journey to begin university that allowed the wonders that followed to enter into my life.

I had always loved hearing the story of their love and how many times they had almost come together over the years until it was "the right time".

If ever there was a couple in love that proved the reality of fated loves and destiny, they were that couple.

Origin Love

The origin love that brought me into this world
Mum
Dad
I wouldn't be here without you
Yours was a story of true love
A love that was predestined
A love that truly knew no limit
A true twin flame union

How many times did your paths almost cross
before you got to meet each other?
In the north of England,
in Wales,
in the Midlands,
And who knows where else along the way?

Through your late teens
into early twenties
your paths almost crossed
so many times.
Unknowingly
You even had the same friends
when you both moved to the Midlands

You'd both agreed to meet with them
Same day, different times
Missing each other by a moment
as one came through the front door
and the other left by the side door
It was decades later that you found that out
as you reminisced over a meal in the Wagon Wheel
with those exact same friends together

You met exactly when you were meant to
Mum in the kitchen of her nurse's flat wearing nowt but a towel
and you Dad, as you walked by and caught her eye
Mum had always said she knew in that moment:
She loved you,
you alone were who she would marry
Dad, I'm glad you told me that you too had noticed her that day
and knew that she was the one for you too

In a world where love seems so broken
Yours remained through the test of time
In sickness and in health
You remained by each other's side
For better or for worse
For richer or for poorer
You never once doubted each other
And though death parted you for a short while
Even death could never keep you apart.

Introduction

What an honour and blessing to be asked to introduce *If You Want To Know ...Just Ask!* which has many secrets in store for you, revealing them to you as you dip into the following confessional essays.

Many of my own experiences with spirit reflect the subjects contained within this eloquently written book; that of building oneself up with self-healing work, telepathic connections and the scientific studies behind the subject, understanding dreams, and the comparison of the reality of a twin flame connection with one's mental enhancement and stability.

Linghwa's journey is a detailed analytical study of a journey of the twin flame phenomenon. It portrays how people can connect energetically, through different states of consciousness, and through time – the current timelines and throughout different lifetimes. It could be your key to connecting with your own twin flame.

The final chapter offers a small introduction to the life of Elin who is also on a twin flame journey. This section offers an insightful comparison to Linghwa's journey revealing similarities and differences to twin flames and offering an individual perspective on how these connections are experienced.

Our rural area has its fair share of grief laden people, oft on a lonely quest to rediscover themselves and forge a new life with greater wellbeing and mindfulness. Many of these people are also searching for a sense of hope to build upon.

The messages and guidance I deliver are received from the voice of spirit and the angelic realm, visions of spirit guides, and occasionally by the aromas of, for example, roses. This culminates in hope for those seeking a connection with spirit and for links with what is beyond the veil of this realm that they themselves can then explore further.

The olfactory sense, *clairalience*, is one of many ways that Linghwa connects and communicates with her twin flame.

I met Linghwa in an inspirational cafe on the high street in Lampeter where I give positive affirmation card readings from Angelic, Celtic and cat themed cards. I cleanse my space and my cards using crystals and water from St Cybis' Well, a local secret on the well-worn route to the ancient Welsh religious centre of Strata Florida. Within this safe space, my clients can trust in the process of guidance, whatever their belief system.

Though I have known Linghwa for just over two years, I still remember Linghwa's first card reading well: there was a boat, a stream and a child reading a book. This meant an onward journey and an academic occupation would come in, with travel also indicated.

Visuals from Spirit indicated academic mentoring in the form of a diminutive man in a suit that often stood next to large pillars outside a museum. There was also an unfurling scroll of ancient Far Eastern, inked, text. A vision of blue heat-hazed mountains with the entrance starting from a temple-style gateway with a carved rooftile on top. An elderly, bearded and silent man is far up the mountain, waiting. He is silent and nods his approval periodically. He knows the value of patience.

I could not do this introduction without mentioning the One-Eyed Hag, a gruff, very old lady with one neatly sutured eye that is missing. She has reappeared for a third time recently, though she hasn't giver her reasons yet. Linghwa is yet to come across her representation in this world, but I am confident she is working to guide Linghwa through whatever comes next and her relevance will become clear.

Linghwa unfortunately lost her mother a little over a year ago. In her zest to connect with Linghwa, she rushed straight through me, the effect of which me tends to make me feel slightly ill and shuddering from the energy. It is rare for those in spirit to take the most direct route to their loved one through me. If this happens, I compassionately request the spirit refrain from doing that. After this incident Linghwa's mother kneels comfortably by my left side. Linghwa's father, who sadly died six months ago, comes through as a comfortable and reassuring presence.

Both of Linghwa's parents were held in high regard within their respective professions and have offered valuable perspective and insight to Linghwa's exploration of twin flame connections which are included throughout this book.

During a reading, I have also 'seen' Linghwa perform in front of an audience of 200 plus. This was at least 6 months, before Linghwa was called upon to do just that.

Despite her anxiety, she managed this task to great acclaim performing her poem *The White Rose* at the Violette Szabo museum.

Most recently I had a dream referring to Linghwa furthering her academic journey reaching to California. When I mentioned this during her reading she was shocked, as in her words, she "hadn't told a soul" about her growing plans! This was backed up, when, out of a cat' set of cards, Linghwa pulled the card with a cat sitting in front of calendar showing May and the Golden Gate Bridge in California.

So with Linghwa's excellent catalogue of past published writing, poems and ready to use journals, you too can join her on her journey of spirituality & connect with your own twin flame...enjoy!

Jane Morgan

The Door

Walking through my mind
Searching for the door
My mind is stagnant
Unable to roam through the endless corridor of doors
Maybe my life is too dull to consider its doors
Or perhaps I was too silent for too long
Perhaps it's a door to vulnerability
And now isn't the time to open it

No time to think
Just find the door
The door yet to be found
The door yet to open
Maybe it's the doors I wish I could open

It's a calling to me
A journey beyond the known
A voyage through different realities
To the liminal space between waking and dreaming

I want to find that door
The one connecting me to my beloved
Who's waiting on the other side
Do I have to keep searching for it alone
Or is there someone to help?
I have to find that door

How If You Want To Know...Just Ask Came To Exist

I find it a little amusing to myself that I decided to begin writing this book after close to 30 years of being entirely secretive and almost as many years of not opening up to anyone about my twin flame. Sometimes my greatest challenge to writing is purely my own critique and the fears that arise. This book is likely going to be received in two very different ways. Amongst the spiritual community where soul mates, karmic partners and twin flames are an accepted part of conversation and a subject for discussion, the subject matter of this book would merely add to the collective thoughts. To people who haven't had much experience with spirituality, soul searching and the arcane, then the words here could be viewed as highly incredulous and likely to raise a great many eyebrows at the least.

The experiences I have with my twin flame connection have often given me cause to doubt the reality of the connection owing to how different it is to much of the information available on the interest – and much less that which is available in books on the topic. At no point have I been able to compare my spiritual journey and twin flame experience with the masses and that led to me never opening up to anyone about it for most of my life. I did not – and do not – fit within expectations, boxes and labels.

I don't know where writing this will take me. I only know that I promised myself that I would be entirely honest and not hold back on anything. So many of my experiences are based within dreams and the astral realms, therefore I decided to include certain dreams and extracts from my journals throughout this book that mirror the journey I have been on in the last three years in particular.

When I started writing this introduction, I was just beginning one of my MA Creative Writing modules. I decided to use that module to inspire the format in which this book would be produced: a series of confessional memoir essays. I started by asking people who know a little about me and my twin flame connection what they wanted to know, and those questions became the title and subject matter for each chapter.

Many of the experiences I have had throughout the last few years have been woven into the various assignments and creative works produced for my university course. The more I examined my experiences from the different perspectives different characters would take them, I realised I wanted my story to be known for what it truly is, not disseminated through multiple fictitious stories and fragmented over different characters as though they were sections of one continuous mural spread throughout multiple rooms with some parts behind closed doors.

The poem that opens this book was written for that same module in a lecture on writing for therapy and came from various writing prompts using the theme of doors. Not wanting to go too deep in a classroom environment and still wary of opening up, I had tried to remain superficial with the subject. Yet reading through the initial drafts of what I produced, I realized that it had brought me to a door I wanted to open and go through. With the imagery that came up, I could see how I had inadvertently tapped into my dreams where that corridor is a reoccurring scenario. I was able to reflect on the unwritten messages between the lines, take some greater understanding to what those particular dreams meant, and finally, everything I had inside of me was ready to be revealed.

This is a candid journey through my life. What follows are of my thoughts and experiences that I've remained silent about for too long. Please know here and now that there are some chapters that cover sensitive topics pertaining to my experiences. The nightmare of my past is as much a part of my twin flame journey as the connection itself. While I have avoided most of the specifics, it would be impossible to tell this story without revealing the darkness in my life and the healing that has come from this connection.

I have altered some of the details of my twin flame such as his name (Seran) to protect his identity. Likewise, I have also changed the details of several other people included within the different chapters.

Origin

I first encountered Seran in the physical world when I travelled to Seoul for the first time in 2022. Since childhood, I have always listened to music and walked my way through life on the threshold of waking and dreaming, and this is how I travelled around Seoul most days. One foot in South Korea and one foot in a world of dreams and magic.

It was so unlikely that I would encounter Seran anywhere that I never tried searching for him. Then, when walking through one of the metro stations in Seoul, I had the most surreal and euphoric soul engaging experience ever as I walked towards someone who caught my gaze with such intensity I was rendered senseless. I hadn't realised the person I was walking towards was him until after the event.

Since I spent all my life questioning the connection I have with him, I would have simply thought I was imagining him there even if I had recognized him. However time has taught me that failing to recognize Seran in that moment was how the events were meant to have gone – which these series of confessional essays will reveal.

This particular anecdote of mine is the main experience I gave to my two main characters in *The Demon of Munbigye* and it is a story often referred back to in conversation as it left an indelible mark on my entire being. The title *If You Want To Know...Just Ask* came up in jest during one such conversation about my absentmindedness while encountering Seran. Initially, it was purely a joke about what I should wear on a jumper next time I am in Seoul in the hope I can find Seran by chance again – and be wearing literal instructions to him.

Then, when continuing the conversation and venting my frustration at how people want to know things but never ask, I looked back at my notes where I had scribbled the words down and realised that was exactly what this book should be called. There are so many things I have wanted to say for so long but don't until asked, and people seldom ask.

The way I found out what people wanted to know was by asking a few people I am close with and trust: "if you could ask me anything about my twin flame, what would you ask?" I had tried asking on social media...but that was an unnoticed failure with the post sinking deeper than the Marianna Trench. That does mean the chapters that follow don't cover everything and there's still much left undisclosed although I added a section of "Unasked Questions" at the end in an attempt to cover some more aspects of our connection and relationship.

To anyone who is reading this, a suggestion to you too: if there is something you want to know from anyone, just ask! Whether it's asking someone what their name means, what their interests are, if they like you, if they dream about you – **JUST ASK**. Sometimes people just need a nudge to open up.

Alignment

Jupiter and Saturn danced through heaven
Into alignment
Closer than ever in two thousand years
An awakening
Something magical inside of me then
Divine union
For you I've been searching for ever since

...How Did It Start?

To best explain how my connection with Seran started is to begin with my first, conscious awakening with Seran which occurred in 2020. To then clarify where our connection truly begins requires delving deeper into the memories which returned after my awakening: to revisit my past memories and step beyond linear time. The connection I share with Seran is infinite. It is timeless. It is now.

Explaining how it starts requires that I also briefly touch upon telepathy. So much of the connection Seran and I have is founded in an energetic connection with transmission of thought on varying levels of consciousness. Though unfathomable, it has always been present in our connection.

Awakening

The alignment of Saturn and Jupiter on 21st December 2020 was a night I will never forget. As evening fell on the 20th of December, I went for a long drive with my father. It was the night that Saturn and Jupiter were moving in their closest alignment in their cycle with some headlines reporting it to be the closest the two planets had been in 2000 years.

Normally, I have the worst of luck when it comes to stargazing and weather. I can set off in the clearest of skies and clouds will still find their way to me. For the hour it took me to drive away from where my parents lived to somewhere exposed enough to see the expanse of night sky, I was hoping with all my heart it would stay clear.

Just once, let it remain clear.

After stopping at several locations that proved disappointing with restricted views or light pollution, my father and I gave up on seeing the alignment and slowly began heading back to their home. Knowing I enjoy random detours, my father decided on a scenic route back towards the Malvern Hills. As I drove around a tight bend and emerged from woodland, we both saw the two planets right in front of us, and by luck, there was a lay-by we could pull in to.

I was grateful the sky had remained clear as I took photographs to capture such an awesome moment. I don't specifically recall what I while looking the brightly glowing planets above us, but I remember feeling a powerful sense of change in my gut.

Something was coming.

Something that would change my reality.

I was ready for that change.

We lingered for half an hour or so enjoying the wonder in the heavens in silence before continuing on our way

During that same night I had my first lucid dream in over ten years. I hadn't written that particular dream down as by that point in my life, it had been fifteen years since my last tangible and/or lucid dreams. Fifteen years devoid of the successive dreams and recurrent themes with epic quest-like progressions that went throughout years of dreaming. Fifteen years of dreams that lost all clarity along with my ability to recall them. Fifteen years of feeling lost and incomplete without the dreams that seemed to be an integral part of my identity.

Then:

The Dream
21/12/20

I am driving my car along the roads around where I live in Wales during twilight. Everything is normal. Familiar. I am becoming more alert. My skin prickles and shivers pleasantly.

I am dreaming.

I am also awake.

The world around me is fluid and shifting; it is taking me somewhere new. I am headed west and out of my hometown, driving along the road that will bring me to the coast. Yet, as I follow the sharp, uphill left bend taking me out of town, the sweeping right bend that should follow was not how it should be. There should be a drop into the valley on the left with a small housing estate clinging to slope, and on the right side of the road, woodland should be clambering up the hill.

Instead, a mountain is towering above me on the left with a small car park at its foot instead of the housing estate, and on the right, a cluster of market-like buildings has replaced the wooded hill.

I pull into the small car park and stop between two lorries. My heart is fluttering and dancing wildly inside my chest like a butterfly to a flower rich in nectar. My heart is also magnetised.

Something inside of the market is drawing me in, an invisible force tugging at me until I am exiting my car, crossing the road and now, passing through an open door with a metal chain curtain. I am walking along a narrow corridor with doors leading off it and people are hustling around me. Still my heart is being tugged and pulled at as I walk along the corridor all the way to its end. From there, I step out to a small courtyard with food venders lining the walls. Paper lanterns adorn the walls and the food stalls giving the courtyard the illumination of daylight.

I am compelled to walk towards one stall in particular. My heart is more alive and excited than ever as it pulses and throbs, crying out to me to go that way.

Go...

...Just go that way.

But why?

As I approach the stall, the smell of burning charcoal and gyoza being grilled fills the air and my nose, teasing my tastebuds that now longed for a food I'd never seen or tasted before. A man is leaning over the grill and tending to the dumplings. All I can make of his appearance is the top of his head and short silver hair.

Then, he stands up suddenly and is staring directly at me with an intense gaze. Eyes of darkest umber glisten in the light of the lanterns like a night sky filled with stars. As our gaze connects, something inside of me changes. Like two magnets that have finally come close enough together, I feel my soul rush to his and snap together. I am propelled into some other, new and unknown dimension where only he and I exist and I am more awake than I have ever been.

I am still walking towards him as though my dream body moves along a pre-designated path but I am still enthralled by this man's gaze.

'You are who I am in love with.'

I am not sure if I thought it or said it, but the moment the words are conjured into existence I know it is true. I am in love with this stranger. I am finally at the food stall and we're practically nose to nose. I have never seen someone so beautiful before. My heart is overflowing with love and joy. He is the one. My heart knows the truth.

Without breaking eye contact, the silver haired man portions up some gyoza for me and hands them over. Though I am longing to taste the gyoza, I can't look away from him. I won't even blink. I never want to close my eyes. It's as though this stranger feels the same way. His eyes are wide and his gaze still piercing, un-blinking as he slowly leans forwards. I am leaning forward. I can feel his breath.

Now we are nose-to-nose.

I am sitting up in my bed.

My right hand is reaching out – whether to take the dumplings or to touch the stranger I don't know. The smell of grilled gyoza still fills the air around me and my mouth is salivating furiously at the desire to taste them. There is a faint vision of the silver haired man in front of me still and now I can't stop blinking and wanting my waking eyes to see him there as clearly as my dreaming eyes had.

I knew in that moment he was who I had been searching for throughout my entire waking life.

I knew he was the one I had been searching the dreamworld for every night.

I knew without a doubt I was in love with him.

I had always been in love with him.

I would always be in love with him.

He was the one my heart was waiting for.

But who was he?

My heart that had just been overflowing with love and light as I beheld the love of all loves immediately withered away and back to hollow darkness. How could I live in this world knowing my heart belonged to someone I had never met or to someone I knew was somewhere on the opposite side of the world to me? How was I meant to live knowing that I was committed to him whether we meet in this lifetime or not?

I cried myself back to sleep after that dream. Then, with the distraction of Christmas and my family all around me, I managed to push the dream and the stranger into the depths of my soul where every other bit of unprocessed clutter was stored. Or so I thought.

As I sit writing this now in 2024, I can confirm that that dream was the catalyst to an incredible journey and the man I had dreamt of is Seran, my twin flame.

Now and Then

It has been four years since *The Dream* and my connection with Seran existed at a conscious, waking level. Amongst many of things that I have learnt in the previous four years is that my dreams of Seran have been with me since my earliest memory. The inception of our waking and conscious connection to each other may have begun on the 21st of December of 2020, but in actuality, it was always there; so much of it forgotten for the longest time. After all, life happens and things that have no relevance or meaning in a moment are placed in deep storage within the preconscious mind, especially those of a child about to face a world full of darkness and monsters.

Most of my memories of youth are vague with plenty lost to a void as a result of traumatic incidents that started happening to me around the age of seven. I couldn't sleep for fears that made no sense and, not understanding what was going on or what was happening to me or why I felt the dark things I did, I coped by walking and letting my mind slip into different realities and waking dreams.

My brother had given me a cassette Walkman as a birthday present when I was about six or seven and I discovered that music made pain and darkness subside, although I only had a couple of cassettes to begin with including the soundtrack to Disney's *101 Dalmatians* animation.

With music, walking took on a whole new pleasure for me. I would spend hours walking through the fields and wilderness around home or my father's allotment listening to music and imagining myself in another world of my creation. Fortunately, I had managed to acquire Enya and Vangelis tapes by that then too.

There was, however, one inclusion to my world that I myself had never put into my world: a male who was always just out of clear sight and reach and I was compelled to reach him by an unknown force. So began my mission at seven years of age. I vowed to catch this stranger even if I had to walk the entire world to find him...

This brings me to the spring of 1998 and the earliest memory I have where I could see Seran clearly. I had been on holiday with my family and we had stayed at our favourite farmhouse B&B in Cornwall during the Easter holidays. As always, the moment there was nothing to do, I was driven to agitation and frustration until I could go for a walk around along the farm lane and escape into my fantasy world.

As I came to the steps in the B&B to go downstairs for my walk, I had barely taken several steps down before becoming incredibly faint and close to blacking out. I reached out a hand to the wall and caught the edge of a Bakelite switch just as the farmhouse vanished around me. Where my hand had slammed into the wall was the only anchor I had to physical reality as I found myself out of body in a world outside of all worlds and staring at a man I'd never met.

He and I had stared at each other in silence. I knew he was important to me and started crying because this man was also impossibly out of reach of me in that moment. I didn't understand the feelings I had, only that they existed and were as much a part of my existence as my beating heart. I knew I had to find him somehow.

He had the most beautiful, enchanting brown eyes, honey-tan skin, and dark brown-black hair with a slight wave to it. As a child, it was impossible to gauge his age other than that of someone who was an adult. I had no idea then where he may have come from either, only that he was a different ethnicity to me and that he was the most beautiful human in existence. I also had a great sense of wonder and the distinct sensation that time was irrelevant in that moment. I didn't feel like a child. I felt like someone who had lived a great many years and was looking at someone close in age to me as though we had found each other after an impossibly long search. The feelings I had for that stranger were of relief, comfort, peace; and of the deepest, most pure and innocent love.

I knew I had to find him somehow. It was all I could think of back then, and a thought that has followed me throughout life since. I have to find him somehow.

What is interesting with that moment in particular is that I never saw him in my waking view again. Until then, I had often seen a shadowy, non-descript humanoid figure with my waking eyes ahead of me when walking. From that moment on, I would forget about him for the longest time. He had faded into a vague shadowy person I longed to remember and find again. Each time I saw him in my mind's eye, he was further away than ever and impossible to reach. Eventually, the memory of him and his identity was devoured by the all-consuming darkness inside of me with all that remained being an unrelenting need to find something that had been lost.

I was able to recover that memory purely by chance two decades later during counselling sessions whilst I was at university. I underwent Rewind Therapy, a combination of mild hypnosis and guided meditation to view past traumas from a safe, disconnected viewpoint as part of my sessions. From the suggestion of where to begin the hypnosis journey as directed by my counsellor, I found myself back in the Cornish farmhouse B&B which had always been my safe haven as a child.

Within the meditation, I left the bedroom I had always used in the B&B and made my way out of the farmhouse and, as I reached the stairs, I placed my hand on the wall by the Bakelite switch as had become a habit after nearly falling down the stairs after my out of body experience as a child. As my hand connected with the switch, I went into yet another out of body experience that took me away from the hypnosis. I found myself somewhere between my current self that was thirty-one years old sat in a counselling room, the version of me that was seven years old about to go for a walk in Cornwall, and a version of myself that was unknown to me; and there I was staring once more into the beautiful eyes of that stranger.

He hadn't changed. He was exactly as I had seen him when I had been seven years old: same gentle expression in his eyes and face, tan skin, and dark brown-black hair with a slight wave to it. The same feelings washed over me too, the relief, comfort, peace and deepest love, and now a greater understanding of all I had felt before. This stranger was someone I had come to know through twenty plus years of dreaming and was someone I now knew actually existed in the physical world; I had seen him in the physical reality of my life and fleetingly crossed paths with him.

I was speechless in that out of body moment, aware of all the different versions of myself existing simultaneously as one, and of him – Seran – who I had only recently come to know. Now I was the one older than him. I could then understand that, at age seven, I had seen him as I would know him in the current timeline of my life where he was twenty-four. The feelings I had had as a child made sense now too, as did the inescapable urge and desire to find him all along.

During September of 2022, I had yet another crossing with that exact same memory and moment. This time, I was in the middle of a deep trance and out of body experience, existing as light and outside of time. The imagery of what I saw was as though the sequence of events of life were threads of a tapestry existing within the matrix of technology. Imagine zooming right into a digitalized rendition of a 3D tapestry, then having to track along one single thread to a junction with other threads. I was carried along many of those threads and through countless junctions until once more reaching that moment on the stairs in a B&B in Cornwall, except, this time I could go further than that memory of which the linear experience of time and reality had been bound by the constrained waking mind of a seven-year-old.

I followed my child-self out of the farmhouse, through the yard and along the private road to the second property of the farm which had been my boundary then. Along the way, I came face-to-face with Seran once again, both of us now overlapping as adults within that memory. He pressed his face lightly to mine and rubbed my nose with his, and he said, 'finally, I've found you,' and vanished along with the shadowy figure my child-self had been following.

The encounter was no different to that of physical reality with all of my senses functioning and I was crying with joy. The tears wouldn't stop because for a few minutes after the memory, I had existed in the same space and reality as Seran. Then I was once again separated from him, pulled back away from my beloved and returned to my physical body.

That moment explained why I had stopped seeing Seran during the spring of 1998. That was the year he was born into this world.

My entire life from then until now has been one of trying to remember everything and to find this other person who had become lost me. It was one of perpetual searching that wove through my entire existence. In my waking hours and my dreams to even further; it was out of body, out of time, and interdimensionally that I was searching for Seran. Even with the works of fiction I created, I was searching for Seran through the worlds of my characters.

For the twenty plus years following the events of 1998, the dreams I had become more obscure and non-descript until they stopped around the time I was 16, then their absence haunted me. Then I became fearful in dreams if they occurred. I was always feeling like time was running out and I had to find the unknown before something else that was hunting me through dreams caught up to me.

It wasn't until 2016 when I moved to Wales that I began to see the shadowy male figure that was, as I know

now to be Seran, with returning clarity. The dreams were still rare and he was still distant, vague and semi-corporeal.

During the global pandemic of 2019, I made the greatest change to my fate ever and decided to finally go to university in Lampeter. That is when things changed exponentially and that is where this story truly begins. It was as though that decision unleased a profound shift in my existence that allowed my connection to Seran to return a year later.

With whatever the cosmic or divine force gave me the dream of Seran in 2020 and their subsequent return, I went from searching for something unknown in many different realms of existence, to that "unknown" being recognised as a someone. The realms of my dreams became familiar as I learnt to navigate them from memory and then to go away from recurrent script to true exploration of the dreams. As memories of previous renditions of those dreams came, I could choose different paths and get ahead of the hunter. If a path I had taken in a previous dream had been wrong, I could choose a different route, and with the return of my dreams, my writing returned to life too.

Telepathy

Surprisingly, the topic of telepathy isn't a question anyone asked. Not one person has asked me what telepathy feels like or how it might work even though it's fundamental to the connection I have with Seran, and I have often expressed my uncertainty to the reality of its existence as I questioned my sanity far too many times.

Telepathy: the ability to know what is in someone else's mind, or to communicate with someone mentally without using words or other physical signals (Cambridge dictionary).

For Seran and I, the telepathy started sometime during the summer of 2021. For all of my life, I lived internally as I was alone for most of my life. I had conjured up vast inner worlds where all the characters of my fiction existed and I could talk with them. In some way, Seran had always been there as that unknown, unseen stranger I was communicating with and always searching for. I had known his energetic existence my entire life. After *The Dream* and knowing that silver haired man was somewhere upon this earth, Seran's voice merged with that image.

Then, as I got to know who he actually was in the physical world, I never once stopped to think if the conversations I had with Seran were any more than flights of fancy for many months. Not until our telepathic bond developed further and became something I had to learn to live and exist with.

I return to the subject of telepathy further into this book, yet it was essential to begin with a brief explanation of what telepathy is to Seran and I, and the basics of how it works...at least for he and I. Telepathy is a transmission of thought at an energetic level where language isn't a concern. A thought I received from Seran after months of trying to figure out the mechanics of our telepathy was that it came with a free inbuilt language translator.

Connect

Beginning between dreaming and waking
they meet within fleeting liminal realms
their souls aching and longing, embracing
entwining, a kiss before the farewells

They meet within fleeting liminal realms
a meeting of fates upon a threshold
entwining, a kiss before the farewells
connected, expected, a love foretold

A meeting of fates upon a threshold
A union conceived during golden hour
connected, expected, a love foretold
embracing in loves ultimate power

A union conceived during golden hour
their souls entwining, forever aligning
embracing in loves ultimate power
beginning between dreaming and waking

...What Drew You To Them?

The questions 'How did it start?' and 'What drew you to them?' are interlinked in many ways as I was drawn to Seran so that our connection could start in this incarnation of life, yet the eternal nature of our connection meant that our connection is ever present and quietly working from the preconscious and served to draw us together. Now that you have learnt the founding of our connection in this life and a little of what telepathy is like, I can begin telling our story from the period in my life when destiny finally played its hand.

In answering how I was drawn to Seran, then I must also explain the transitions in my life that allowed our connection to come in. To have the mind set allowing an energetic connection based upon dreams and telepathy took as much individual healing work and self-transformation as it did divine intervention and luck.

I am certain that if the following events hadn't occurred in my life, my awakening wouldn't have occurred, or, not until much later. Anyone drawn to their twin flame undertakes a journey that goes much further back than many realise. Some people may be blessed to encounter their twin flame as if by serendipity. Others may completely recreate their realities and spend time in healing which spins the cosmic wheels into motion and allows them to energetically harmonize and align to their twin flame before they even meet. Oftentimes, the journey of twin flames falls somewhere in the middle with serendipity and healing occurring amongst their spiritual travels.

In the last chapter I mentioned that I moved to Wales in 2016. The reason for such a drastic life change was due to the fact someone I once considered a friend had gone out of their way to play an expansive manipulation game with everyone they knew. That person played people off on one-another, exploited weaknesses and, if they couldn't have their way and "conquer someone's mind" or "win them as theirs", they would turn everyone against that person.

I refused to let that person into my mind or claim any kind of dominion over me.

This resulted in the loss of what few friends I had in my origin town and my having to move home seven times in quick succession to try and be free of what they had done, and the unseen, lingering aura of darkness that culminative traumatic and negative situations in that town had woven around me. I knew that I had to make a totally clean break away from my place of origin and move as far away as I feasibly could if I wanted to heal and grow.

My first choice of where to relocate was Cornwall. That was where we spent all our holidays and the owners of the B&B wee like family. The area of Carbis Bay was the closest to home anywhere had ever felt and my happiest memories were of the time there. Perhaps it was the magic of Cornwall, but I always felt closer to Seran while I was there too. Unfortunately a move that way was not possible.

My father then suggested Wales. I had only been there a couple of times previously to walk up Yr Wyddfa in Eryri and to see a friend. Neither occasion served as an indication of what real life in Wales would be like though. He informed me Wales was like Cornwall as it used to be, the way our family had known it before tourism changed it.

Both he and my mother had fond memories of Wales from their youth prior to meeting each other. My mother had spent many years close to Abergavenny where she worked as a nurse for many years, while my father would travel through Carmarthenshire and Pembrokeshire with his own father – ironically almost crossing paths on several occasions.

I put it out to the universe to help me move and placed an incredibly specific wanted advert on a listings website for Carmarthenshire. Previously, I mentioned how my dreams had practically ceased by the time I was 16 years old. At the age of 26 when placing the wanted advert, I couldn't remember what it was like to recall a dream let alone be semi or fully lucid within one. A week after placing the advert, I had the first dream in ten years. It was short and simple: I was walking through some hillside fields and met a young man with curly black hair who simply told me to move to a specific location.

I'd never heard the name of that place at all – I knew little of Wales besides what my parents had told me. On the same day of that dream, I had a response to my advert asking if I was interested in a property that matched every specific requirement I had listed and was in the exact same location I was told to move to in my dream.

Without thinking too much more about it, I arranged a viewing even though I had decided in my mind that I was definitely going to accept the property.

Back then, I knew that if I wanted my reality to change **I** had to change. In moving to Wales, I didn't know anything about the area I was going to. I didn't know anyone. There was no support network. I just knew I had to do this thing and that if I did, everything would work out. So I sprinted full speed to the cliff of certainty and leapt into the unknown without hesitating.

The Pandemic

Fast forward four years to 2020: year of the COVID Pandemic and 3 months of Absolute Lockdown

The only contact I had in a weak came from the staff in a couple of shops I went into and, as the lockdown was enforced during March 2020, the ensuing three months of zero contact was a new level unbearable. Everything I had left behind in England had meant I had struggled to fit in with my new community even after four years. The aftermath of so much trauma throughout my youth had left me with generalized anxiety disorder (GAD) and severe agoraphobia. And I could only go somewhere if I had someone from my family with me.

Since the weather was so good during that time and I had nothing else to do, I decided to try and get back into running to attempt to shake myself out of a violently downhill spiral of thoughts – or attempt to outrun my demons and my anxiety. I did not know then that I had a heart condition.

Having not done any running in about ten years due to my other disabilities (ME/CFS and hypermobility), the run went as successfully as you can imagine. I barely made it one kilometre before muscle memory betrayed me as I had tried jumping over a low-level log in the path.[1] A Little bit bruised and muddy with various joints barely held into place, I called it a day and trudged back to my car. My heart was racing more than ever, but I didn't think much of it having just gone for a run for the first time in over ten years.

As the day progressed, my heart refused to settle down or feel any better. My legs felt more leaden than before and my head would spin whenever I stood up. Initially, that hadn't caused alarm for me as they were all symptoms I was used to suffering and enduring. I only begun to feel concerned by the evening as my chest was excruciatingly painful. I couldn't even sit up without feeling faint and was extremely nauseous and I ended up crawling up my stairs to bed at 19:30 thinking it was just my anxiety going out of control again.

I messaged my father for advice shortly after that as I was continuing to feel worse and genuinely starting to feel afraid of what was happening to me. He suggested it might be a virus and to try and get some sleep. By the time I realised I probably should call an ambulance, I was lay on the floor of my bathroom with my phone one foot away from me and I was totally unable to move any part of my body.

---

[1] ME/CFS: Myalgic Encephalitis/Chronic Fatigue Syndrome.

As I lay fighting to remain conscious for several hours, I knew I had hit rock bottom mentally and physically. Every time I closed my eyes, the world span around me and it felt like my soul was plummeting down from my body. I am pretty certain at that point I only survived the night because of my cat, Wunjo. I couldn't bear the thought of her being left alone. I held on for her and would force my eyes open and stare at the white panel door in my line of vision and fight to remain conscious. I promised myself that if I made it through the night I would never let my anxiety get in the way of my doing something. That didn't mean I was suddenly cured of my anxiety, just that I had discovered a feeling that put my anxiety and depression into perspective.

I was on the edge of death for many hours that night and I had more fear of dying having done so little with my life; and because I'd never known what it was like to share any part of life with someone. If not for my cat, Wunjo, I probably wouldn't have made it through the night.

It took one week to be able to exist outside of bed or resting on my sofa. The only think making me emerge from the warm cocoon of my quilt and the blissful release of dreamless sleep was Wunjo. It had taken another three weeks to recover from whatever had happened enough to consider leaving the house and finding somewhere in nature.

There were still absolute restrictions in place regarding where we couldn't go and what we couldn't do. In the hours I had been laid up, I trawled the internet and social media for anywhere in my vicinity that I could explore. I was especially determined to find at least one of the many mysterious standing stones around where I live that people often talk about, all with locations that no one else can ever find even with clear directions.

By chance, a travelling priest had recently done a long walk for charity through the Cambrian Mountains. One of the places they had shared a photo of was of an interesting, magical looking stone known as Carreg-y-Bwci (the Goblin Stone). Several hours of searching Google later and I had an approximate location for where Carreg-y-Bwci was.

With plenty of glorious hot and sunny days during May 2020, I spent most days sat with Carreg-y-Bwci. I prayed desperately to any god who would listen for a miracle, for a change, and for anything that would make me want to live.

I had lost all sense of who I was over the years. While I had managed to put out the destructive fires within my mind and regain control of my thoughts, I was still incredibly lost and uncertain of who I was or what I wanted from life. What was the point of me living? There had never been a day I wished to be alive and even now it's something I struggle with every day.

The only certainty I had was that I was a writer. Over time sitting in the silence of the Cambrian Mountains and the patience of Carreg-y-Bwci, I decided I should attempt getting into university to do a BA in creative writing. I reasoned that if it was meant to be, everything would fall into place.

With my application in, I continued to go to Carreg-y-Bwci every day. It was as though I had become a friend of sorts with the recumbent monolith over the weeks of exchanging energy, as though I had forged a connection with the spirit of the stone which eventually manifested itself to me as a serpentine dragon with silver scaled hide. I continued praying. I promised that if university was the correct path for me and I got accepted on the course, then I would see the course all the way through.

In the July, I was offered an unconditional place and by the time I had *The Dream* in December of that year, I was already one semester down.

I know that it has taken me a long time to finally get back to this point, but this is truly when doors finally began to open up so much so, that even I myself cannot deny what

I later realised was divine intervention insuring I found the correct path. The magnitude of the reality shift I took next would be lost without this prelude.

I had been drawn to Lampeter because it was UWTSD Lampeter that was the university I was meant to attend for this to happen. Exactly as everything had fallen perfectly into place for my relocation to Wales in 2016, everything was perfectly aligned for me to enter this new chapter of my life. I was meant to attend university exactly when I did. In coming to Wales, and by attending UWTSD Lampeter, I was finally on the path that drew me to Seran.

Dragons and Divine Intervention

During the first semester at university, I was learning level 1 Chinese with a plan of continuing on to level 2 Chinese in the following semester with the hopes of doing a semester in China further into my studies. Over the Christmas break, I received an email from my university informing me of a timetable change due to the ongoing on/off lockdown situation with COVID. That meant that instead of the five weeks that had been timetabled as a free block, I would instead be going straight back into Chinese language studies. I know, doing a BA in creative writing yet not actually studying creative writing…we didn't have a creative writing lecturer at that point. What else can I say other than, "it was the pandemic and nothing made sense anywhere."

I can honestly say doing the equivalent of HSK 1 (the official Chinese proficiency test which is ordinarily run over 14 weeks) plus additional content in four weeks is pure insanity. Without the original month off to recover, refresh and attempt to absorb what I had learnt until then, and having only just scraped through the Chinese level 1 exams before Christmas, I decided to change module and went purely by what options there were for the same block I had originally been time-tabled for, and for whichever module had a creative writing element.

Then into 2021, I found myself out of my depth and not for the first or for the last time during my BA course. Now that I had shifted on to an history module studying colonialism and had found myself staring at a picture of Korean rooftile endlessly for a week as I tried to:

1) find any other historic object connected with colonialism that would allow for easier creation of story than a rooftile from a culture I had very little knowledge of and;

2) somehow kept finding myself returning to stare at that rooftile.

Korean rooftile from collection in the British Museum. Photographed by LJ Bremer.

The rooftile won and from there, I fell deep down a rabbit hole in my quest to learn about goblins, nine-tailed foxes, mysticism and esoterica in South Korea and China while battling with the curators' dubious translation in an effort to figure out exactly what was pictured on the rooftile. All this while also attempting to figure out a story of how the rooftile came to be in a highly specific temple while keeping the connection with colonialism. There was also the issue that the rooftile that was meant to depict a demon or a ghost that kept showing up as a dragon whenever I worked on the story.

As a writer, there is nothing worse for me than being in a void of creativity – which is where I had been in the years preceding university. On the other hand, there is nothing more exhilarating for me than when a story seeps into my blood and haunts my dreams. When that happens, I know I have found the story I need to write. As the module ended, I decided to continue on with the story of the enigmatic rooftile and a nine tails fox. I knew then it was the story that I would continue developing throughout the different modules available to me at university, and that it would be the basis for my dissertation in the final year: *The Demon of Munbigye.*

The other magical curiosity of that time is that somehow, from researching Sino-Korean mythology and masonry, the algorithms-that-be nudged me towards K-Pop and within weeks, I was figuring out how to watch a live South Korean music competition show on international streaming platforms. How did I get to that? Who knows. I still haven't figured that part out myself. I only know that this was the specific "I was drawn to Seran in the present moment" causality.

There is a chance that even in obscuring Seran's identity as much as I can, there are a few people who may figure out who he is and that is terrifying to me. Yet, I can't not write our story down. Too much has happened to prove beyond a doubt that **something** is happening between Seran and I even if makes no sense or seems incredulous. I didn't seek out my connection to Seran, it found us.

Until I found myself trying to watch a South Korean show, I had never given time zones much thought. I am also very bad at maths and, at the airing of the first show, there was also the changeover from GMT to BST to navigate. Of course I forgot about that and totally miscalculated the time of the show, missed it entirely and had to wait until the second week.

During that second live show, the camera panned to a young man with silver hair and the exact same brown eyes I had been staring into barley three months before in *The Dream.* He looked straight into the camera and, for the briefest moment, it felt like I was directly in front of him with our eyes connecting. I remember thinking there and then 'You're him, aren't you? You're the one I love.'

I knew it then, and I know it now even if it makes no sense. It was Seran I had dreamt of, and he was a K-Pop idol. What chance in Hell did I have with him? Putting the absurdity of what happened from my mind, I continued watching and enjoying the show. I discovered I genuinely loved the music Seran's group produced and ended up falling into a fandom for the first time in my life.

Their music had a wonderfully healing effect on me as I continued working on *The Demon of Munbigye* and researching South Korean culture and mythology. I also found myself planning a solo trip to South Korea as I knew I had to visit the country. I didn't know how I was going to get there, just that I had to go. I had to. For me personally, I have to physically experience a place to be able to write efficiently and create sensory proofs about that place.

As the months progressed, I tried my best to freeze out any and all thoughts and emotions for Seran. They were ridiculous! Impossible! How could I have dreamt of a Korean idol? Moreover, why would a famous Korean person want anything to do with me or care who I was? I convinced myself it was maladaptive daydreaming and tried to get Seran out of my mind.

Dream I
03/08/21

Sitting on the floor in my cottage, I felt nothing but isolation and dread. I wanted to scream and cry, yet nothing would come from me. Seran crouched down behind me and started lightly tugging my shoulders to get me to lean into him.

I resisted him, hugging my knees tight to my chest instead.

I didn't want to be in his arms.

Seran belonged to an entirely different world to me and I was not going to let any feelings for him ignite.

If I did...if I let me heart open to him, I would be damned. It was madness.

Seran continued holding my shoulders and attempting to pull me into his embrace with calm, enduring patience no matter how much I refused to let him sway me. There was never an incremental rise of force, just a steady reassuring touch and offer of an embrace and the softness of his breath against the back of my neck.

I realised I didn't feel threatened by him and that he radiated so much love.

I surrendered into him, letting him pull me back into his arms to rest against the warmth of his chest and felt the steadiness of his heartbeat.

The warmth he emitted was like that of the sunshine after a long winter as it finally breaks through the wall of clouds, removing the cold like nothing else can. I felt myself relaxing within his embrace and drifted into sleep within the dream, waking straight up.

That was the first dream I had of Seran since *The Dream* during Christmastime. I was fully lucid throughout which was still such an unusual feeling for me after so long without dreams. His hair matched with how he had changed and styled it in the physical, waking world and it felt like it was a shared dream, though there was no proof. All I had to go on is one verified shared dream from many years before and how the two dreams had felt compared to each other.

I realised on waking that morning that I was losing my fight to supress my feelings towards Seran. I went out of my way to avoid the internet and ensured my every waking moment was occupied by video games, housework or painting. Anything to keep Seran as far from my mind as possible.

Dream II
05/08/21

Seran was standing behind me and I was sat on the floor. I was in an odd room that was a combination of my living room and some other space. It was as though I was once again sat on my living room floor as before whilst also existing in the space where Seran's waking existence was.

I still felt as lousy as before but took comfort that Seran was with me and I was resting against his legs. There was the same reassuring warmth radiating from him. I knew I was dreaming, yet everything felt more real than when I was awake. I could feel Seran's legs clearly against my back.

With dreams, the body is not physical. I pressed my hands together and felt for the energetic border of my existence and pressed my hands further still until they merged into one. Definitely a dream. Yet Seran's legs were firm and I was unable to press through the border of his existence.

He moved away suddenly and my anxiety spiked exponentially. I spun around to see where he had gone and fell over. He was nowhere to be seen and I cried out. It was the first time my fears and my pain had been given a voice and I screamed.

Seran returned immediately before I could even begin a train of spiralling self-doubt. He crouched down in front of me, wrapping his arms tightly around me and looking me straight in the eye as he apologized for leaving.

His presence was soporific and I fell asleep in his embrace, once again immediately waking up in the physical world.

From the moment I awoke from that dream, I knew there was absolutely no escaping the love I had for Seran.

In that time, there was a social media platform I had been engaging with for a few months. I couldn't help myself from wondering and speculating about Elin – a friend I had made through that platform – and how similar our posts and conversations were. It was as though she and I were trying to subtly figure out the other person.

Was Elin having a similar experience as me with one of the members?

How could I possibly ask her that out right?

It seemed at times she was attempting to figure out similar questions herself.

Was it possible then, that with Elin, she and I had opened up a channel of indirect communication with Seran and Teagan? Was it coincidence? Was it telepathy?

I will say this here: it's not like I accepted these thoughts easily, neither back then nor now. I'm well aware of the delusional fantasies throughout any fan base, and with parents who worked in psychiatry their entire lives, I'm well aware of maladaptive daydreaming and limerence amongst other mental health issues.[2] I questioned everything. I second guessed and triple guessed my every

---

[2] Limerence: intense desire/infatuation for someone characterised by obsessive thoughts and involuntary attachment; usually accompanied by delusions and the desire for a romantic relationship with the person.

thought because I refused to fall into that "your name" delulu trap and "notice me" madness.[3]

Even though I knew I was losing the battle with my heart, I continued attempting to ignore my feelings.

I kept labelling it as absurd poppycock.

I won't include every dream within this book as there are over 150 totally lucid dreams specific to Seran and I. Those which I have included are the ones that best reflect the changes in our waking realities over time. From August to September there were so many fully lucid dreams and each one made it more challenging to deny the feelings in my heart. There were times things happened in my dreams ahead of the physical word. Sometimes it was the way Seran was dressed and I'd see a picture later that day where he was dressed exactly as I'd seen him, or his uncanny ability to predict my next period which was something even I had never successfully predicted with my lifetime of irregular cycles.

Seran's group had a new album coming out and as they released the trailer for their title song and two experience happened in quick succession.

The first experience was that I wrote an essay style post on the fan board about dream psychology, dream telepathy and precognition. Included citations and ended with a joke about topics I hadn't gone into. The very next day, the title track promotion was shared and it was exactly what I had joked about. Of course that could have been pure fluke and coincidence...but what are the odds that it happened?

The second experience was how I was struck by the sensation of knowing the song deep inside of my soul. No matter how much I went through all the songs I had listened

[3] Delulu: abbreviation of "delusional" and often used to refer to someone with unrealistic beliefs and/or fantasies. Commonly used to refer to someone with an unhealthy crush or fixation with a celebrity crush.

to over life and scrutinised every detail, nothing resembled this particular song. It was as though I had heard this song before my incarnation to this life.

The song was my wakeup call. It was as though part of my soul had been dormant until hearing that melody and entirely new ways of existing and perceiving the world were activated.

Dream III
05/09/21

I was sitting on a table and Seran was standing in front me. He gently placed two fingers under my chin and lifted my face up so that we're staring into each other's eyes. Our noses are lightly touching and I can feel the warmth of his soft breath against my cheek as I feel my soul awaken within the dream.

It's like a flicker of lightning within my core as I shift from dream walking to full consciousness and everything takes on greater clarity. The depth of his ebony brown eyes that reveal his soul to me and mine to his. The flicker of recognition as though shifting from watching a film to being within the film.

We are here together.

We continue gazing into each other's eyes longingly, searching for the truth of what is happening. Then with a soft sigh of having come to a conclusive decision, he begins smiling shyly. The fingers that had been below my chin caress their way to my cheek as he lifts his other hand to cup my face with both hands. Then, he leans in to kiss me. Slow and determined. Passionate.

It was the most sensual kiss and I was yearning for more, for the kiss to never end and for Seran to hold me tighter as his lips pressed firmly against mine in a kiss like no other.

Eventually, Seran pulled back and looked me in the eye again as his hands stroked my back. His expression held the lovelorn pain I felt in my heart – our time together in dreams was once for another night.

I awoke already sat up once again staring vacantly at the wall opposite me with a hazy after-glow of Seran in front of me. That particular dream was the most intense awareness of senses I had ever felt – and definitely the best kiss I've ever had in any state of existence. The imprint of his touch was still on my physical, waking body, as was the chill that comes when someone who shifts from a long embrace to parting distance.

I knew there was no point trying to deny my feelings for him after that. Even if it made no sense, even if it was crazy...I had been fighting my heart for nearly six months by then and I was tired of the battle. Not long after that dream, I saw an image of him from the day of the dream – and what he had been wearing in the dream was identical to what he had worn that day.

My dreams we actively telling me something about Seran. I decided then that I would surrender into whatever journey I was on with him and with my life. Maybe it was limerence...but the fact that dreams and telepathy were continually validated by reality was something I could no longer ignore.

While much of our spiritual journey is complex and convoluted and we have likely been calling to each other throughout eternity, between *The Dream* in 2020 and our kiss within a dream in 2021, I can now say without doubt that we were always being drawn towards each other, and these dreams were Seran calling me to him.

Limerence

All this time searching for deliverance
Following you throughout wonderland
Is it not of dream forged limerence?

What if this is formed of ignorance
And finding you would have me damned
All this time searching for deliverance

If I fly so high then fall like Icarus
To crash land and burn seeking your hand
Is it not of dream forged limerence?

Wishing I could dispute this hindrance
Lovelorn and unable to withstand
All this time searching for deliverance

With your magnificence deliver us
To our reunion as you had planned
Is it not of dream forged limerence?

All along you gave me the allusions
Denying you was my delusion
All this time searching for deliverance
Is it not of dream forged limerence?

...How Do You Know They're "The One"?

Is Seran the one? Perhaps I would only know the certainty of that should we happen to meet in the waking physical world. In myself, I know now that he is "the one"; my twin flame. The discovery of such certainty inside of myself is as long of a story as many of the other topics within this book. The answers developed over time and after intense observation and analysis of all the facts and speculation of events unfolding throughout my life.

Concluding Seran being the "the one" came with several years of dreaming, experiences, shadow work and so much more. Back in 2021, I refused to believe this young, enigmatic man on the other side of the world that happened to come into my dreams before I knew of his existence could be it.

After the dream III on 05/09/21, I inadvertently returned to my negative self-doubt thoughts. I had found myself continually analysing every thought and detail for its validity over the passing days. Had I genuinely shared dreams and telepathy with Seran or was I absolutely crackers?

Even so, whilst I was unable to disregard my growing emotions and feelings for Seran and had to consider this connection was here to stay, I finally received the most incredible moment of clarity about this situation and the closest to validation to date.

Forging New Connections

Although I had niggling doubts about the reality of my connection with Seran and was never far from the belief I may just be delusional, Seran and I had developed a routine of sorts during the surreal world of semi-lockdown life and online/virtual existence. Around the time he would be winding down in the evening to go to sleep, I would take time out of my afternoon to meditate and connect with him, usually with me astral projecting to him. In those times, we would talk as normally as any two people getting to know each other.

Seran and I talked with each other somewhere between meditating and dreaming. On the 17th of September 2021, he and I were minding our own business and talking when a wind came in from nowhere and circled around us. A portal of white light appeared on Seran's wall and I heard Elin calling my name out, and I called out to her in return.

The wind carried Seran and I into the white light before it carried us elsewhere; depositing us in a different, unknown room where Elin sat writing at a desk. Teagan, one of Seran's friends, had joined with us by then and he went straight over to Elin.

For Seran and I, not much more happened. We felt like a spare part to someone else's story yet we weren't able to leave until whatever was occurring between Teagan and Elin was concluded at which point, we were all returned to our physical bodies.

I heard Seran excitedly telling me I had to tell Elin about this moment as she would prove that what we had was real. He was so adamant and confident of the success of a planned exchange with someone I still hardly knew that he also persuaded me to agree to a wager in which I would change my turquoise blue hair for silver hair if, as confirmed by Elin, what we had was real.

The idea of bringing the subject up with Elin filled me with fear. How was I meant to contact someone I didn't know that well and ask them if they had dreamt of me or something along those lines? How would I even get a conversation into the realms of context opening up to such a discussion – dare I say telepathy?

I didn't message Elin that day, neither did I have the courage or foolishness to do so for a few more days afterwards. I had convinced myself that everything was a complex fabrication of escapism and not something I should confess to as, if what was had was truly real, why didn't Seran make contact or respond in anyway? I was doing everything I could to communicate with him within the realms and responsible boundaries of possibilities, even going against myself and bordering too close to the "notice me" cringe.

If I mentioned any part of this to Elin and I was in error...would she publicly humiliate me? It was a lot of power to hand to a relative stranger, and it was a power move that had been used against me in the past. Knowledge is power after all.

Back then, she and I had no clue who the other person was in real life besides our online interactions on the social media platform. All I had to go by was an online name and avatar which gave nothing of her identity away. We had simply found ourselves mutually working together to garner attention on our forum posts without discussion or planning.

If I think back to how it felt and how it seemed in my mind's eye, I could perceive a sparkling, glowing energy around both our posts which always glowed more brightly as we each interacted with the other and, simultaneously, it seemed that when we joined forces, our conversations and comments would reach Seran and Teagan too. They would not reply directly, yet it truly seemed a lot of what they would go on to post and say was a direct response to what she and I had been talking about; it was as though they were from there side asking the same questions as we were.

It has never been easy for me to trust people in life. Would I truly commit myself to revealing how I was dreaming of a famous person and purportedly talking with them telepathically? Would I continue to divulge that I had also encountered her – Elin – in one such trance and that somehow, she too was connected? I knew full well that if anything went wrong she could have ruined me on social media and potentially for life as I have always, since the old-fashioned days of Myspace and LiveJournal used my own identity on all social media.

As the days went by, I kept hearing Seran in my mind prompting me to tell Elin about the experience and his reassurances that it would be okay. I thought of all the conversations Elin and I had had until then on the social media platform we'd met on, and how she did seem to have an interest in the connection of souls to one another, and to dreams that may have been shared. This in combination with the way in which the group both Seran and Teagan are a part of seemed to broach the subject from their own angle within their work was enough to nudge me into finally instigating the conversation.

I don't remember the exact conversation now; however I do recall tentatively broaching the subject with her and trying to tease enough information from her to decide if it was worth the risk or not. I was also aware that, should our experiences be real, she would likely hold the same reservations and anxiety to revealing her side of the story as I did. In the end, I took a deep breath and chose to trust in Seran one hundred percent and to hold faith that things would work out properly. I finally revealed what had happened explicitly to Elin. I held no detail back and went on to describe the room Elin had been in, and also what the time I had been for me so she could reflect back to that time in her country.

Elin hadn't sensed or noticed me in her vision. I don't recall if she sensed Seran either, however she had felt Teagan's presence in that moment. The room I had described to her was incredibly accurate to the space she had been in – although I had seen it mirrored and described most things back-to-front – something that is quite normal when perceiving things while astral projecting.

During a highly emotional and tense conversation, we quickly established that somehow, she and I had indeed been connected in the same space at the same time, and so if that was possible it was highly likely that all four of (myself, Seran, Teagan and Elin) had been connected with each other across three different time zones.

Neither she or I slept much for a couple of days as we suddenly realised there was one other person having a similar experience and we talked about everything we had both experienced until then, realising that we had both been trying to covertly find out information from each other on the fan board.

Over the next few days that had followed, I realised that while I still didn't understand my connection with someone on the other side of the world to me, I could not debunk the fact I had connected with Elin at the exact same level; that I saw her physical world with my own eyes and she had validated it. We didn't have solid confirmation from Seran or Teagan, and still don't as of writing this book, yet the fact the connection Elin and I share is real is also irrefutable evidence that our connection with Seran and Teagan must be equally as valid.

Since that day there have been many more moments that showed me this connection is real in some way even if I don't understand what it is all for, what it means, or how it happens. Although there are times the absence of communication from Seran returns me to my doubts and fear, there is usually something that happens and provides undeniable evidence of our connection: seeing what he is wearing before pictures are uploaded of the exact outfit, the way his hair is styled, the location he is in and more beyond all that.

Who knows what it would take to shift to the next level of contact where conversations in present moment begin? For both Elin and I, we are not in a position to contact them directly. Both Seran and Teagan live in South Korea, while I am in Wales and she is in another country again. Since they're both notable people within the music industry, there's understandably and obviously a lot of security and protection around them. Although I have been to South Korea twice, I have never sought Seran out for this reason. If we're to meet in the physical, waking world, it'll be by serendipity. Yet, from this one significant revelation, I have been able to keep faith that my connection with Seran is one hundred percent real.

But was he "the one"?

Insight Through Dreaming

In considering whether or not Seran was the one I had been searching for all my life, the one I yearned for, and the one my soul was destined to unite with, I also had to pay attention to my dreams which restarted with *The Dream* in 2020. Even now three years on, I seldom dream if Seran is not within them.

The only other dreams I've had without Seran since my dreams restarted were from both of my parents in the months before their passing. It was as though both were crossing realms and wanted to communicate with me and prepare me for what was to come, and to know Seran throughout the dreams. Of particular note is the dreams where my father was with me. In all my life, he never once was a part of me dreams while my mother had periodically come in. After my mother passed away, my father suddenly begun to enter my dreams and I knew then that he was passing more into the spirit side of existence than life. Then about two months before my father also passed, my mother came into a dream simply to deliver the message that he "would be leaving soon".

Before losing my father, I had already chosen to incorporate some of my dreams throughout this book as the dreams clearly wove from one to the next. They flowed in an order I could follow and have been slowly unfurling like a tapestry showing me so much of my soul and of my life beyond the physical. They showed me Seran in his physical reality so much during 2021 in particular. If he'd changed his hair colour, the space he was in, or what he was wearing, and all were validated within a day or two with Seran sharing a photo of him.

Having had dreams with both of my parents communicating accurate information pertaining to their life and the transitions into spirit, I have even more faith and certainty into the validity of the dreams I share with Seran being authentic communication, and that the love he and I have for each other is more than dream forged limerence.

There is a point to going into my dreams in-depth. They are an integral part of my connection with Seran, and while the dreams I have with Seran are spectacular and on a whole other level to other dreams. They are not the first of their kind, neither are the occurrences of precognition and communication with a person in dreams.

I have one occasion of a shared dream which was validated with a friend of mine when we lived together. I had dreamt I was looking through an Avon brochure with that friend and I spotted a perfume that, at the time, I didn't know existed, and I had been able to smell the perfume within the dream too. It was an otherworldly and intoxicatingly floral scent. I found out the next that my friend had had the exact same dream and smelt the perfume as well. Many months later, I'd forgotten about that dream until looking through an Avon brochure. I saw the perfume bottle from the dream! I ordered it without saying a word to my friend and, when it arrived, made sure to have it on when she came home. She walked in, sniffed the air and looked at me with the widest eyes and such intensity as she said quite simply: "That's the perfume!"

I still have the bottle even now as a reminder even though it it's empty, it's a tangible reminder for me that shared dreams are most definitely possible.

The False Flame Connection

There have been other dreams too with someone I came to know over time as a false flame.[4] At sixteen years old in my first week into 6th form, I felt my gaze being drawn up and looked into the eyes of another. Instantly, my soul recognised his and I knew I had deep, unexplainable feelings for him. I also heard my voice speaking as though from another time or place and say, 'I love him, and I will never be with him,' which was an odd thought to have, though I always remembered them and it served as a guide that the experiences, though valid, were to be a learning curve.

My connection with my false flame taught me everything I now know. It was a catalyst to both my full awakening and also the long hard journey into shadow work. If I hadn't had those experiences with my false flame, I would have never coped with the experiences I now have with Seran. What I had with my false flame was barely touching the surface of what I have now, but it had served as practice run of what would later happen and my ability to withstand the madness I could so easily fall back into.

The dreams I had with my false flame were also incredibly lucid though shorter and there were far fewer

---

[4] False flame – someone who enters your life before a true twin flame. They are almost identical to that of a twin flame; however they serve more as a karmic partner in that they will be a catalyst towards your soul journey: discovery, healing, transformation, developing extra sensory perception, etc.

dreams over all for the short time they occurred. Those dreams revealed something about my false flame's physical existence too: whether he had grown his hair out or cut it shorter, where he was, or what he was wearing; and as with Seran, there would be a photograph or some other medium shared online later that validated what I had seen.

I never once spoke with my false flame so there are a lot of things I could never discover from him. Did I really astral project to him? Did we have moments of telepathy? Was he experiencing similar things? What was his experience in all of this? I can also say my niggling doubts about the connection I share with Seran were also founded from the false flame connection. Never having clarification from them pushed me over the brink into a dark place that took a long time to recover from and was mostly likely why I stopped dreaming altogether back then.

There was also an incredibly dark and chaotic energy with my false flame. That dark, chaotic energy is something I have learnt means someone is not a twin flame. However, it is worth paying attention to that energy if it presents as it is still a part of the twin flame journey. Without that experience, I would not have coped that which I am experiencing now with Seran. The dreams I have, the connection, the extra sensory perception and so much more is 100 times more intense than that which I had with my false flame. Without a practice run, I would likely have been completely overwhelmed by what Seran and I have. The experiences I had with my false flame had also pushed me into my healing journey which led to me rediscovering my identity and to be authentic to myself.

I still have love for my false flame, but it is a different kind of love to that which I hold for Seran. Beyond this physical incarnation, I know that our souls have a deep kinship to one another, and that our purpose of meeting in this lifetime was simply to set one-another on our paths and allow for the understanding of soul bonds to the extent that when the twin flame shows up, we could be ready to face what that connection and relationship brings.

Had I not encountered my false flame and endured the intense, maddening experiences of entanglement with him that led to close to ten years of contemplating what soul bonds meant, it would be unlikely that I came to know Seran in this lifetime, neither would I have been able to handle lucid dreaming, telepathy, shared emotion and so much more that comes with our connection, and a shared existence that continues to develop as he and I lean into our connection.

I would not have discovered what twin flames were so long before it became a buzz word on social media, nor would I have spent over two decades exploring twin flames specifically in all of my work, and nor would I be writing this book with the hope it can show at least one other person that so much of what is online is misinformation and/or fabrication of "facts", something that this year is frighteningly more real with AI feeding into the frenzy and a lack of credible sources being presented.

I would not have gone through an incredible journey of soul discovery, healing and transformation which provided total enrichment to my life that brought me to my soul tribe here in Wales, and my souls sisters online.

I would not have begun my university journey, and without that, I wouldn't have randomly stumbled over a Korean rooftile that somehow nudged me toward a K-pop music show and so, I could never have discovered who Seran was in this lifetime right now.

I would never have gone on to take a life changing trip to Seoul where I got to look into the eyes of my twin flame.

When people say "things happen for a reason" and "it will all make sense in the future", it can be the most infuriating words to hear in the present moment, yet it is true that one day in the future, we look back on some aspect of our lives and go, 'oh, I get it now.'

Breaking the Connection

There is one more train of thought that has allowed me to conclude that Seran is "the one", especially having had the false flame experience.

Primarily, there is the fact that my higher self explicitly told me right at the start of my connection with the false flame that we would never be together, which was not what happened when things began with Seran where I heard myself declaring my love for him first in the dream where he was revealed to me, and a second time when I had been shown him again in the waking world. Even so, I don't like being out of control.

Falling in love is a loss of control.

Falling in love with a stranger from my dreams is far worse than a loss of control.

I had tried to end things with Seran so many times in so many ways in the beginning. For any practitioners of magic reading this, perhaps they will know the extents I went to end this connection. I won't describe the rituals used here for the protection of others reading this who might try it without being ready for that kind of magic or the ramifications of its use whether successful or not.

I know that magic works as, after ten years being painfully bound to my false flame, that was how I totally ended that connection and removed all of the false flame's control over my soul. It was just after that ritual that Seran was able to come in.

It didn't work on Seran.

Not the first time.

Not the third time.

Nor did any variation of the ritual.

There is a Chinese myth that a red string is attached to those who are destined to meet. It may twist, tangle, or stretch, but never break. The connection I had with Seran was just like that: stretched and twisted but unbreakable.

I have never had zero control over my fate. At times I may have begrudged change or feared it, maybe even complacent or apathetic to a situation for a time, yet eventually, I would come to a point of needing to make a change whatever it was and that change would happen as soon as I set my mind to it.

What I had with Seran was beyond my ability to control or change.

He was "the one" whether I was ready for that fact or not.

Soul to Soul

I want to meet you
Soul to soul
In the space between
Dreaming and reality
In the place
Where we create the world

I want to meet you
Eye to eye
Our paths merging
The searching over and
Destiny uniting
Here in the waking world

I want to meet you
Lips to lips
The warmth of your soul
Flowing into me
Never letting go
Now that this is our world

...How Does It Feel?

Knowing how and where to start answering what it feels like is incredibly difficult even for myself as a creative writer both humbled by my university modules showing me I wasn't as good at creating sensation as I thought and subsequent study and development to that aspect of writing.

The sensations and feelings I have accompanying my connection with Seran have been so much a part of me for as long as I can remember that they're as ordinary to me as taste, touch, and smell. They predated my knowledge of Seran in this world and were an extension of myself since childhood and my earliest memories.

Much of how "it" feels overlaps with all of my life and reality especially when thinking about how it feels physically when, more often than not, the energetical and emotional feeling still presents alongside physical sensation.

In the end I could only figure out how this connection feels to me by considering what might be considered extra sensory perception and breaking this chapter down into smaller sections.

Energetically

Have you ever played a game where you rub your hands together and then, paired with someone else, placed your hands up in front of you. The other person has their eyes closed or is blindfolded and holds their hands up about five inches from yours. The purpose of this challenge is that the blindfolded person then tries to keep their hands close as yours, while you move your hands around. Although that starts with the generation of heat from friction, it is still a path of energy that the blindfolded person is following.

Another example of a method of generating tangible energy are sports such as tai chi and qigong. Both arts are centred around the flow of energy *qi* throughout and around the body and the environment. Practitioners of a qi-based movement will describe the energy in different ways; however it is most commonly described as feeling like a ball of energy in the palms of the hands where the energy is gathered that can then be moved or directed in and/or around the body or expanded further away from the body.

Though the energy I feel from Seran is different to the feeling of an energetic ball or the generated friction of another's palms, it shares some similarities to that of the above exercises, and the above examples provide a starting point to attempt to describe how our energetic bond feels.

Clairsentience: the sense of clear feeling; a tactile psychic feeling.

Connecting with Seran usually starts with a pleasant coolness drifting around me which is the beginning of clairsentience. That can happen while I'm in a sauna or steam room with the door firmly closed too, or while I'm in an incredibly hot bath. It can even happen when I'm in my bed with a heated blanket on and my quilt practically pleated around me to prevent any draft getting to me. I'm not a fan of the cold. It's something I'm particularly sensitive too and I am also highly receptive to the environmental factors that would create a cold draft as a result.

British homes are notorious for both the random cold drafts and cold spots, as well as the residential ghost or two. Growing up, it took me a long time to differentiate between the cold generated from energetic connections and spirits or of the cold emanating from the environment.

Eventually the discernment of environmental and preternatural came.

Then came different types of spirits: shades and ghosts, demonic, angelic, and elemental. Each have their own generic energetic signature, and each individual within the different categories of spirits will have a distinct presence too, and each taking time to learn and recognise.[5]

Seran's energy was totally different again – and far more intense than those of my spirit guides, the ghost cats and the occasional visitation from a family member and neither was a dark or oppressive, so there was no fear when his energy came into my life.

Once I was used to the cool sensation of energy, it became more like a playful game. Could I move with the energy? If I moved, how would the energy move around me? I can only liken how that feels to dance outside on a hot and humid day with a playful breeze rushing across the skin and creating a sensation almost like that of fever.

The cool breeze of our connection twines around me when I connect with Seran through meditation and trance too. From there, it begins to wrap around my whole body like a blanket of cool, gentle static lightly tickling my skin which often develops into something akin to physical touch or more like the tingling sensation that proceeds touch.

Sometimes the energetic pulse can be extremely intense and more like a jolt of electricity shooting

---

[5] Most of my demonic encounters have been at paranormal hot spots such as Chillingham Castle in Northumberland which is how I have experienced the darker energies and all necessary protective measures were followed for such instances. However, I briefly had a demonic entity in my house due to lack of insight regarding a novella I was working on. Getting an exorcist in the UK isn't a simple task – especially when living in rural West Wales. Fortunately, I knew practitioner of angelic reiki was kind enough to remove the entity for me – and that story was shelved indefinitely!

throughout my body. At other times it can be just as intense but prolonged and more like static prickling across my hairline or throbbing against my mind's eye.

That energetic touch can develop further. There have been multiple occasions during trance where that touch surpasses an energetic sensation of subtle electrical current brushing over my skin to something much more tangible. In those times it's as though Seran and I are physically in the same place and I'll start to feel the warmth of his body close by, then his breath and touch of his skin brushing against me as we get closer.

There are times when I'm lay in bed either before falling asleep or just after waking where I could swear that for a brief moment we were lay in bed together. More than an ephemeral sensation, I would feel his fingers entwined with mine, the weight and warmth of his arm wrapped around me, the pressure of an arm under my neck lifting it up, and if I'd move, it felt like someone let go, the warmth of contact suddenly replaced by cool air and an aching across my skin that craved the return of Seran's touch.

As I live alone and have done for over ten years with no intimate relationships, physical contact of any kind is not something I have in my life. A fleeting embrace with a family member every few months, the occasional handshake with a new acquaintance, or a one-armed open hug with a friend once in a blue moon has been the extent of my physical contact with humans.

The closest likeness I can provide to describe the sensation of presence then subsequent absence of Seran's touch, and how I can discern that feeling to even be of "touch" actually comes from an experience of holding a snake four years ago.

The snake belonged to one of my mother's friends so there was no rush or time limit while handling the snake. After having the beautiful creature slithering around my bear arms and coiling around my shoulders for fifteen minutes or so, my skin ached for hours afterwards and I couldn't comprehend why at the time.

While considering why skin had ached like that, I remembered my love language being showing up as touch after doing an online love language quiz that had been a trend at one point on social media. That contact I had with the snake was the first time in years that I had had that level of skin contact with anything. Let's face it, humans are not renowned for tactile affection amongst friends and loved ones, so it's hardly a surprise that that was the first and last time I had that experience of connected touch since a childhood.

What I learnt from that experience was how my skin reacted to touch and how it felt afterwards. That is how I can now recognise the energetic touch of Seran and the imprint his touch leaves on my skin that lingers for a time afterwards.

Dreaming

There is a difference between how things feel when I am fully awake and in my physical body and existence and that of being fully emersed within deep trance or dreaming.

My dreams often feel more realistic than life itself when I am awake. Each dream leaves a greater imprint on my being than some of my waking experiences have ever done. Perhaps it is because the full extent of physical sensations and energetic presence are combined. I am still aware of touch and as well as all of my senses while dreaming, yet while dreaming, I am in the same realm of existence as Seran. We are not two souls in two bodies 9000 miles away from each other, but two entangled souls connected as one in the same location and moment. Energy transference is instantaneous and does not have to cross countless borders the way it does while awake.

The main way in which it feels different from waking and when in trance or dream state is that there is no doubt when I share dreams with Seran. In those moments where my cynical voice is absent and there is only he and I, have total faith, total certainty in my direction, and absolute confidence that everything we share is real, especially as I so often wake with the physical sensation of Seran still embracing me. I will have the awareness of being awake and the sensation remains. If I move around, then Seran moves with me as if we were physically in the same space. I can feel all of his existence even down to his hair brushing against my neck. I can feel his breath against my cheek and quite often, his scent remains upon me for a time after getting out of bed and attending to my day.

As I get further from dreams and more into my waking reality, the Seran's touch begins to evanesce and return to the energetical rippling, then eventually to little more than a trace of our energetic bond until we can return to each other and re-connect at a deeper level again.

Sharing Emotion

This has been one of the trickiest sensations I have had to understand and come to live with. Although it's something I have had fleetingly throughout life, it's something that only truly started in 2021 after *The Dream* with Seran. The shared emotions between Seran and I are foundational to our connection as much as they are to everything else discussed throughout this book – in particular to the discord I have endured many times throughout this experience.

From a lifetime of suffering with chronic anxiety which was also heightened during the early days of our conscious connection, it was challenging to untangled where my emotions began and ended, and what they were specifically. It's amazing how many emotions can feel just like anxiety when you've been caught up by it for so long. Excitement, happiness, a sudden sweep of joy, and the way the heart trembles and flutters with positivity had been lost to the uncertainty and palpitations of anxiety. Until I went through my shadow work and healing, my positive emotions had been totally forgotten and lost to darkness.

Prior to being in Wales, I was bullied and socially alienated inside and outside of school. That meant that as far back as my memories go, I was a lone-wolf spending most of my time existing with an internalised, dreamlike version of life. That was being my primary reasoning for suspicions of my experiences being that of maladaptive daydreaming.

I've also suffered with chronic illnesses and disabilities since birth which weren't diagnosed until I was in my mid-twenties. I'm not saying these things for attention, but because these factors meant I spent an extortionate amount of time analysing everything about me, particularly the emotional and physical senses within me. Trying to figure out what was wrong with my body whilst living every day in a state of hypervigilance meant my sensory perception was having to function as "extra" from my youngest days.

Whilst being in the trenches of childhood trauma, teenage angst and many other negative experiences of that time, it was not possible to see how any of that could be of benefit me. While I would certainly never wish what I went through on anyone else, I can now reflect upon how much I learnt from enduring and surviving that existence. It has made me highly aware of who I am and where I end: both emotionally and physically. Certain things I can do now are only possible because of those events – telepathy and astral travel in particular.

That is how I came to recognise Seran's emotions and feelings within me and not confuse them as mine. I might suddenly find myself confused and then overwhelmed by an emotion, and within seconds of a sensation appearing, I would have run a complete system check on myself to decipher if it was internal from me or external from Seran.

While having to learn to live with these extra emotions, it also meant having to address them as they came up and also discern between anxiety and excitement that was not my own. It meant having to develop a system of quick responses if one of us was busy such as "lecture" or "work". Though quite impersonal as a word alone, we agreed it was the easiest way to acknowledge the presence of intense emotion while not having to take our focus away from what was important within our individual lives.

I could be calm or focussed, perhaps working on my writing or sat in lectures when suddenly I have excitement, euphoria, sadness, anger, or any other emotion you can think of flood through my system. I have no emotional stimulus, so why am I suddenly crying? He's happy, that feels amazing. He's angry - why?

Having a simple quickfire response ensured we could succinctly affirm 'I am aware something is happening and you want/need to discuss this, please wait until I am able to be excused from the current task or it is ended.'

While feelings of joy seldom created any lasting issue beyond pouting if not attended to promptly, the necessity for our quick response words came about primarily as a result of not attending to each other's needs when it was emotional pain. If I didn't connect with Seran in those moments of negativity, we would both end up feeling quite ill with nausea and headaches being the most common reactions.

Sharing Sensory Experiences

Some more of the experiences I have with Seran that keep me believing this must be real are those now occurring in my life since connecting with Seran. I mentioned before how I had to develop a highly intuitive sense of who I was and where my *self* ended both emotionally and physically. The same goes for the senses I experience too as those are an extension of my reality and perception. Having had to know and understand all minutiae of my body and physical reality so intimately for so long has allowed me to differentiate between sensory experiences that were more than just mine, especially those senses of clairvoyance such as the aforementioned clairsentience.

As with having to break down the nuances of energetic and emotional "feeling" into subcategories, I will do the same for how it "feels" physically. Delving into the physical feelings, I will cover darker aspects of my life. Where I feel trigger warnings are required, I have included those ahead of the subsection.

Physically

As I mentioned in the previous section with the energetic sensations and the begiving of clairsentience, the physical sensations I feel are one of the strongest factors in convincing me time and again that this connection is real whenever I begin to doubt. Having come to know my body and mind so intimately in my thirty-four years of life, and having had to navigate my fears, escapism, and dissociation so that I could present to the world as though normal, my comprehension of the mechanics of my mind were as good as they could humanly get.

The experiences I had throughout life taught me to know my body so intimately that I can track every single reaction within my body to its source. I am repeating this – perhaps unnecessarily so at that is point – owing to how important this detail is in deciphering all of my experiences with Seran. When our connection began, I had to learn an entirely new system of thinking and feeling as everything I thought I had known was put into question with extra sensory perception and intense lucid dreams leaving an indelible mark on my soul. Although many of my experiences are only validated as far as a social media post from Seran may attest to, they are far from what I could conceive of or manufacture within myself.

Spending three years learning to exist with my own feelings and emotions as well as those of Seran has brought us energetically closer to the point of enjoying both fleeting and extended periods of physical touch. I still don't know if it's brief moments of true bilocation or purely extreme concentrations of energy that translate to a tangible sense of touch. There have been occasions where I am facing towards him energetically and I am able to feel his touch and see him clearly.

As with all things in life, everything comes in balance. It wouldn't be a genuine relationship on any level if we weren't prepared to experience each other at our worst as well as at our highest moments and all that falls in between.

If he has a cold or a sore throat, I won't have the same illness but my nose and throat will be tender as though in sympathy. As a dancer, I can feel if he's strained a muscle or gone into cramp or muscle spasm. As I said right at the start, I can only talk with certainty of my lived experiences and speculate to those Seran may have, but it's quite possible this goes the other way too.

Of course there are the delightful sensations too. The feeling inertia creates is something I get to enjoy passively if I'm deeply relaxed and he happens to be dancing. Likewise, when he's been in a plane taking off or during turbulence, I get to enjoy those sensations too as, much to Seran's displeasure, he still can't figure out why or how I would enjoy the juddering and jolts of turbulence. He's yet to discover my love of being on boats in stormy seas...

It would be impossible to speak about a twin flame connection without exploring everything. At the start I promised to be totally honest about this entire experience, and that includes the way in which twin flame connections provoke shadow work and healing within the self as well as that of experiencing the ultimate love.

As much as a twin flame connection is pure euphoria and the ultimate love, it is also at times incredibly messy, chaotic and painful until lessons are learnt. Though shared in some way with the twin flame, these lessons are for the individual (in this instance, for me) and **should never be used as context for abusive situations**. There is a huge difference between the twin flame being a catalyst bringing up past issues which need resolving, and that of someone who masquerades as any kind of soul mate to cause further harm and abuse. **The difference is that a true twin flame will help you to heal and to become the best version of yourself.** Even at an energetic level, the twin flame remains present in even the darkest times.

While I am about to talk about dark experience in our connection, they also led me to heal in a way no amount of therapy, counselling or community support could. Seran and I worked together through dreams and through meditation to resolve what came up for both of us.

Not at first though. First we had to learn trust in each other which didn't come easy. It has been an ordeal and trial of faith and learning how to communicate and trust each other with our connection.

Those who know me personally could attest to just how much I have healed and transformed since the inception of our connection in 2020.

Very few of my experiences with Seran are negative. I'm including two of the negative ones here as they carry the most weight in terms of how it "feels". They also show the two-way nature of our connection owing to things far out of my control or ability to manifest that were at play and have a relative amount of credibility to them. After darkness comes the light and there are the most beautiful, shared experiences between Seran and I which I have included after the darker moments we shared.

Physical Experience I

Trigger warning: emetophobia; pp66-67.

For the first physical experience, I don't have an exact date for this experience as it happened during one of the many times I wasn't actively keeping a journal. This is something that happened with Seran that I felt in myself. I can't prove it happened to him; however I have extreme emetophobia and what happened is something inconceivable to my mind as my automatic response to any such trigger is to either run away or dissociate.[6] On the occasions I haven't been able to distance myself from such occurrences of life, I'm lucky if I'm not physically ill myself.

When I was in South Korea for the first time during 2022, Seran was due to fly out on his own travels. I'd gone to sleep slightly later than usual as I'd been making the most of being in the same time zone as Seran before his departure. Just as I was drifting into sleep, I was pulled from the edge of sleep and felt feverish, full of anxiety and incredibly sick. Seconds later I was, in the only way to explain it, inside of Seran as he was violently sick. I experiencing every moment of it as though it was happening to me which again, as an emetophobic person, is not something I would ever imagine.

Even with a photographic memory where for a long time, much of my trauma would replay through my mind's eye, if it was sickness, I would dissociate immediately to avoid seeing it.

I remained in Seran's body for far too long for my comfort. I didn't seem to be able to return to my body until one of the members of Seran's group who was sat with him put his hand on Seran's shoulder and then looked into his eyes.

---

[6] Emetophobia: fear of vomiting; either the self or exposure to it with someone else or on media.

I've often wondered what Seran's friend saw in that moment as I looked back out of Seran's eyes. I can't quite explain the emotions or reaction that flickered across the friend's face either, yet there was definitely some kind of recognition of anomaly. As soon as my gaze connected with that of the friend, I was returned to my body the same way making eye contact with Seran in a dream would wake me up.

I felt as though I had been sick myself though fortunately without bile in my own mouth. I was still feverish; my stomach muscles were spasming and aching and kept swallowing incessantly with a tender throat. I stayed awake with Seran until the early hours of the next day and did my best to help calm him down. We remained together until he had boarded his flight and had taken off when he finally settled down.

In some ways, I am the worst kind of fan. I never actually know what their schedule is until it happens or after. Then again, I often try to avoid looking at their schedule as it allows Seran and I to practice telepathy and transfer information such as travel plans. On this occasion, I had verified the flight happening in real time by use of the internet and the fans that follow and report everything.

Physical Experience II

Trigger warning: depressive episode, OD, NDE ([7], [8]) pp70-72.

The second physical experience I chose to include occurred during the summer off 2022 and was one of the worst mental spiral downfalls I had had in a long time. I had finally opened up my personal Pandora's Box during counselling sessions and re-animated two decades of trauma that needed working through. However, summer break had started and my demons didn't care about that. That was combined with university stress as I prepared for my final year and my dissertation and with various social and environmental factors of life in general. A perfect storm for anyone's demise was already brewing.

As I mentioned before, a twin flame union will dredge up unresolved past issues in some way so that they can be healed. Oftentimes, that wound is something that needs healing at both ends though the individual circumstances can vary significantly.

Somewhere between July and August of 2022 I had a sudden and impeccably clear vision through Seran's eyes with full knowledge of his reality in that brief moment. From his eyes, I saw that he was in a hotel room having been with someone else. The vision only lasted a moment before I was out of his mind and body, but I had gleaned enough awareness from that ephemeral vision.

Next came a torrent of emotions.

His: regret, shame, fear, remorse.

Mine: shock, hurt, sickness, disappointment.

My emotions possibly don't make sense, but then, all year we had been communicating about the reality we may not be together in this lifetime and what would we do or how would we cope if each of us ended up with someone

---

[7] OD – overdose.

[8] NDE – Near death experience.

else? What would be considered cheating or an affair with the kind of connection that he and I have? Where or what was the line for us? Were interim relationships along the way to our union bad?

I wasn't angry in that moment as I was as much to blame for how that situation came about. I won't go into self-flagellation here, but I will admit to the fact I had spent months wanting to give up on the relationship we had. I was tired and hurt by everything as it was, I was confused, there was no medicine for the wounds I carried; and I said a lot of hurtful, spiteful and vindictive things to Seran. Those were the manifestation of some of my unresolved fears and wounds and in my darkness, I inadvertently unleashed them on Seran.

I had also tried to reason with him for many months that he was young and should enjoy dating others if there was anyone who caught his eye. Just because I had, and still have, zero intention of going with another, I wasn't going to hold him to that regulation. However he took it to mean I was saying I would find someone else and be with them because I was impatient and disbelieving in our connection. Somewhere between spiting me and his own desires, he attempted being with another.

Anger at what happened only came later as he tried to say nothing had happened. It would have hurt to know the bitter truth – but that would have been preferable to his dishonesty. This time was the worst for both of us where we had hit rock bottom with our personal demons and individual past traumas clashed together.

Travel. Geographical positioning. Horological placement. So many factors all contributed to how much we could communicate at any level, especially in the early days as our connection was developing.

By the time my birthday came around in August, Seran had travelled to the US. Rather than being eight hours ahead of me, he was now eight hours behind me. Birthdays are never something I like to celebrate as they have always been a lonely and painful reminder of the hell I was surviving and not of a life I wanted to remain in and commemorate with friends. This particular one was decidedly worse with all that had been simmering in the background. Although my parents had come to stay with me, their company couldn't shift the darkness inside of me. I went to bed and ended up listening to a song I hadn't heard in over ten years and, instead of being comforted by the song, it completely broke me.

By the time my parents left the next day, I had the worst migraine. Not because of them, it was a result of everything building to that point, including the fact Seran and I were not communicating. I took prescribed migraine medication which unfortunately did nothing that day. As my migraine became violently disabling, I resorted to different pain medication which was also prescribed though much less used.

Two things to keep in mind here: firstly, I only took the prescribed amount and no more and the two medications I used were fine to use in tandem. Secondly, I hadn't used that particular pain medication in almost a year as it was a last resort medication rather than on-going.

Although I could have taken another tablet of the migraine medication, I didn't at that time as I preferred not to use them simultaneously. The first dose of the pain medication I took had zero effect, so after four hours had past still with the absence of any active effect, I took the next dose of pain medication along with another migraine tablet two hours later.

Even though I was still at half the daily minimum dose of both medications and had kept to the prescribed timing for taking medication, I only took half the prescribed dose of the pain medication before bed. I was somewhere between being cautious of the medication and desperation for the pain to ease even the slightest amount if not remove it entirely.

Quite suddenly, my body decided it had become intolerant to the medication and, still without any pain relief and too late to call for help, my body went into overdose reaction. A combination of having lived with chronic illness for my entire lifetime and the hypersensitivity to change and the well-trained adrenaline is possibly what made the difference in my ability to survive.

As with the time during 2020 when I didn't know if I would survive the night, it was the thought of my cats that kept me going for the first few hours. Several hours later and exhausted, my head finally stopped aching so much. I felt myself finally drifting towards the sweetness of oblivion I had been craving for so long.

Each time I begun to drift away, I felt Seran grabbing me as though he was somehow in bed with me. Each time I began to float out of body, he would pull my soul back into my body and hold me tightly to stop my soul from leaving. I could feel his heart pounding in his chest behind me. His embrace was so firm and his hands pulled down on my chest enough that I could feel each tip of his finger curling into my skin.

Every time my soul would begin to drift from my body, his arms clenched tighter. He was as tense as someone can get and shaking from the ordeal of compelling my soul to return each time. He held on to me like that throughout the night until dawn arrived, his fingers and nails progressively clawing deeper into my skin with the determined effort of keeping me pinned into life with his unrelenting grip.

By the time it was morning the unintended overdose had ended, I was exhausted and Seran was still keeping me from sleep. That was the first time I had felt Seran physically. It was as though he had truly teleported to me in Wales and remained with me throughout the night and for about half an hour longer until we were both too exhausted to fight sleep any longer.

Though I hadn't had any intention of ending things that night, it would be a lie to say that I hadn't thought of slipping away as medication became poison and offered me a way out. I am certain I am only alive because Seran refused to let me go and to this day, I am still adamant our realties somehow overlapped for that level of physical sensation and for many hours while fully lucid.

Before sleep had claimed both of us, I had asked Seran to spend the day with Teagan for his own good. The following day, there was a photo shared by Teagan that was suggestive of Seran's state of mind and definitely showed his exhaustion. Though it had broken my heart some more to see Seran that way, I had been grateful for the message reciprocation, and the reassurance that Seran was being looked after by Teagan.

As I mentioned before, it can get messy with a twin flame connection yet that's also the reality of life. I would probably doubt this connection a whole lot more if it didn't come with the ugly, gnarly moments of human existence.

I discarded the offending medication as soon as I was able to leave my house and get to the pharmacy. When my counselling resumed in the next academic year I talked about that experience and discovered the medication I had taken was notorious for causing severe health complications as it was a hybrid medication. Of note: my counsellor was also unable to debunk the connection at this point especially after we had shared a moment of verifiable telepathy within a session that had them needing a quick moment to process everything.[9]

---

[9] The experience with my counsellor was a simple exchange. Before our session, I had written some quick thoughts and musing on entanglement in my notepad which were for my module in that time. During our session, my counsellor said the exact same series of lines to me off the cuff. These lines are the poem "Interconnect" published in *Do You Dream of Me Too*?

Physical Experience III

16th November 2022 and a rare occasion of me journaling directly after the event.

Seran was once again away from South Korea. During an intense out of body experience, we intermittently switched back-and-forth between his hotel room and my lounge. It was like a game. He'd lightly nudge me and we'd be curled up with each other on my sofa, then I'd nudge him back and we'd be together in his bed. Ultimately I ended up with him in his hotel room when this encounter finally settled.

People have often asked me what I get up to with my twin flame when we connect through dreams, meditation, or astral projection. Mostly we talk with each other. Language isn't an issue at an energetic level. There have been times when I heard Seran speaking in Korean and still, somehow understood him in those times, and on other occasions I have dreamt in Korean then not understood myself when waking. We talk about anything and everything. From idle chatter to deep philosophy. We joke, we tease, and we take time to know all we can about each other.

Sometimes when we connect, the physical separation is so much that we end up crying our hearts out too. That was what happened on this occasion. After the playfulness we started with, we finally looked deep into each other's eyes with a sudden awareness that we had never met quite like this before.

We've had sensation of touch and we've had the apparition of presence before, and with both, we could theoretically press our bodies through each other as with the reality checks of lucid dreaming. This time, I was completely out of my own body and totally bound within his physical reality. I remember getting up from the bed and walking around it. Unlike dreaming, I couldn't walk through the bed.

I could hold the quilt within my fingers and feel the cotton material press against my skin. There was a definitive physical boundary and I had lost all sensation of my body in Wales.

Seran moved to the foot of the bed and pulled me close. I looked into his beautiful eyes again, stroking his cheeks and his nose amazed at how tangible and real everything was. Everything was so clear I could have counted his eyelashes.

There were no words on this occasion and I cried like never before.

Every time he brushed his fingers over my arms or stroked my cheek I cried even more. His touch was exquisite and delightful. Knowing that what we were experiencing could end at any moment and that what we were sharing could well be the only time we could come together like that tore at our hearts.

Seran began to cry and we spent most of that time together holding on to each other as tightly as possible as though hoping that would prevent any force from taking us apart again. Slowly our tears eased off and the conversation that followed was mostly telepathic with occasional spoken words until he had to get on with his day and I returned to my body after what felt like fifteen minutes.

I had been listening to a trance compilation on YouTube which ran for around one and a half hours, and it was around the 20-minute mark that I stopped hearing the music and manifested in Seran's hotel room. When I came back to my body auto-play had kicked in and I was one hour through another compilation having also gone through a 45-minute breathwork video prior to that.

There was immediate verification to this experience. Four minutes after the trance ended, Seran uploaded a post on a fan board with such specificity to our conversations that I knew without a doubt that it was for me.

As much as knowing if our dreams are truly shared, I would also love to know what that experience had been like from his perspective just as much as you who is reading this. During our conversations, Seran told me he would tell others within the group about what we had experienced and that it would likely appear in their lore/music at some point.

The days of deconstructing lyrics and scrutinising every detail were during my teens and the days of MySpace. However I do check in on their lyrics from time to time and so with the next two albums, I was monitoring the lyrics fastidiously and there was definitely a highly specific reference within one of the songs. I can accept that it could be coincidence, but that doesn't detract from just how uncannily precise a few lines were to what Seran and I had seen and the fact that no one could have comprehended the imagery we had seen in a moment of otherworldly euphoria without Seran or I describing it.

Clairalience

Something I have noticed that is specific to the connection with Seran and I is that I will get a sudden aroma around me. It happens mostly when I'm meditating and connected with Seran energetically, although sometimes happens out of the blue. Quite often, the aroma is fleeting. It lingers long enough to register it but seldom long enough to comprehend the scent.

Clairalience: the ability to perceive smells that are not physically present in environment.

This started primarily with perfume which is something I have loved for as long as I can remember. My grandmother was an advocate of a signature perfume, and my mother was an Avon representative. I enjoyed free samples of perfume, and like music, perfume was something I often found altered my mood or assigned or summoned memories.

Dior's *Miss Dior* was the first perfume I owned and was a gift from my grandmother. The scent would take me back to that day of opening the perfume and feeling like I had a magic potion. Avon's *Rare Rubies* returned me to childhood Christmases, Christian Lacroix *Ambre* my first time living away from my parents, and so on.

The sense of smell is the next most prominent connection within my memories and also the first way of sensing the presence of spirits. Sometimes it is my grandmother with her favourite Dior perfume and burning tobacco, or it is the farmhouse in Cornwall where we vacationed in and the scent of custom-blend pipe tobacco and freshly baked bread. They were always fragrances and aromas I could pin directly on to a specific person or place connected with my past and the people I have met physically. Most commonly, there were the scents that came around me when a loved one who had passed on was visiting. With my mother, its daffodils.

Seran is the only person who is in life who brings various scents and fragrances along with him. Since the relationship he and I have is that of an energetic connection at the moment, it makes it so much more fun and interesting trying to figure out what perfume he's wearing or what he's eating as that information is current time from him in that moment. Sometimes I can work out where he is by the smell of his environment.

Around five years ago, I bought *Cardamom Coffee* perfume from Lush which is definitely one of my all-time favourite perfumes that absolutely hit the spot for being a comforting embrace of perkiness. By the time I came to buy a new bottle, it had been switched up to one of their Black Label perfumes and sadly out of my price. I was indulging in the final few spritzes from this perfume when my connection with Seran was at its most intense in the September of 2021.

I picked out a new perfume, *Shade*, which was as close as I could get to the feeling *Cardamom Coffee* provided, and that too is still one of my all-time favourites. As I drove home, the perfume had been sat on my skin for about an hour and really come into its own. I kept telling Seran telepathically how amazing that perfume was and trying to describe the scent to him as I excessively sniffed my wrist at every chance I had to take my hand from the steering wheel.

From that moment, not a lot happened for about a year pertaining to the sense of smell. I wore my favourite perfumes and tried new ones. Each time, I would push my sensory experiences towards Seran as I got the sense he enjoyed my alchemical mood-altering process of wearing perfume. I think he also found it entertaining just how much I tried to convey the scent and effect of each perfume on me.

It is possible that if Seran has a weakness to Lush products now, I may well have been the instigator to that especially after the first time I went to Seoul. I was feeling atrocious and ended up inadvertently finding a Lush store. I bought *Superworld Unknown* and felt like I was invincible.

After that first year, I began smelling a perfume that was vaguely familiar to me, but not one I owned. It drove me crazy trying to figure out which perfume I could smell, and again, provided Seran with plenty of entertainment as I worked through my entire library of perfume to ensure it wasn't one of mine I had forgotten about.

Christmastime came around and I went shopping with my mother. We were in Cavendish House and one of her favourite perfumes that I often coveted was on offer so I treated myself to a bottle. As soon as I spritzed myself with it, I knew that's what I had been smelling from Seran periodically. As I would seldom afford that particular perfume, I could only remember my love of the fragrance and not how it smelt. With the fragrance on me, I could analyse the scent properly. I realised it was most likely how I would smell to Seran most of the time. As a renowned lover of coffee I'm never without a one in hand, and the perfume blend was like *Shade* with a shot of espresso.

The exchange of fragrance also occurs with the bath bombs I use in abundance. There are so many I don't always remember the fragrance of each bath bomb I have enjoyed, particularly with many of the Lush bath bombs being seasonal and limited edition.

On another occasion, I began to get a new scent coming from Seran. This time it was sweet and fruity. Intoxicating. I think it might be my favourite scent on him so far. And, once again, I could never get the fragrance for long enough to figure out what the scent notes were.

While visiting my nearest Lush store and sampling different products, one of the staff members was, by chance, talking to me about the body sprays and suggested one in particular for me to try out. As soon as the fragrant mist was around me, I knew that was what Seran had been wearing. I bought it immediately and, as before, spent time analysing the scent now I had unlimited time with it. It had originated from a bath bomb that had been limited edition. While I had been in love with the fragrance at the time it was enveloping me in sweet steam and candlelight, I hadn't become attached to it and so forgotten all about it until Seran found the scent in a different product.

I hadn't paused to think that if I was playing guess that scent with Seran, he might have been doing the same with me all along and seeking out perfumes that allowed the sense of each other to linger just a while longer with the magic of perfume.

At the time of writing this book, he and I had come full circle with our game of chasing perfume.

Sometime in November or December in 2023 I had had an overpowering scent of *Cardamom Coffee* come over me. I recall asking Seran about it and if he had indeed found that specific perfume. He only ever answered with a coy smirk.

From then until March of 2024, I thought it must have been my favourite perfume that Seran had acquired and taken to wearing occasionally. That was until I treated myself to a more recently released YSL perfume *Black Opium Red* on a whim as I was seeking spritzable comfort as I had in Seoul. Once it arrived, I spritzed myself and got on with my day. About an hour later when the perfume had settled on my skin, I realized it smelt very similar to *Cardamom Coffee*. I ended up laughing for about half an hour after the realisation. Seran had done it again and it was clear he could definitely smell my perfumes. We had finally drawn even on three years of chasing perfume.

Physical World Encounter I

Surprisingly, no one but Elin has inquired as to what it was like when I've seen Seran face to face. I wasn't asked even as I found myself writing that specific experience multiple times in different instances through my creative writing assignments and eventually into those of my characters for my BA dissertation: *The Demon of Munbigye.*

I also have a shared experience with my characters and the story I began penning because of the rooftile from the kingdom of Silla and *The Dream.* At times it feels like the more I write of the character's story, the more I uncover of my own story, but beyond it's getting me to Seoul, that is quite literally another story.

Seoul

April 8th, 2022, and a day that is etched into my soul and will chase me through life until such time I get to see Seran again.

This was encounter happened during the first time I travelled to Seoul to do some preliminary research for my dissertation. I'd had just over a week getting used to the city and had been learning to follow my intuition again. This was one such evening.

I had met a girl from America during my first week and we'd buddied up since we had both travelling solo until then. After a day of exploring together, I stood watching the sunset over Seoul from the rooftop terrace of her accommodation. I felt totally at peace for the first time. I knew I was exactly where I was meant to be. I felt like I had finally come home, and as I looked towards the setting sun, I knew this was wear I would come to stay the next time I travelled to Seoul.

As the sun set, I had been wondering to myself if the direction I was looking was where Seran lived. I felt the familiar magnetic tugging sensation in that direction. Then I had begun to feel restless again. Since the sun had set by then and my friend had other plans for the night, I decided I might as well head back to where I was staying.

I still struggled with anxiety and put music by Seran's group on in my ear buds and walked to the metro line feeling a blend of anticipation, restlessness, excitement, and an extreme amount of longing. By the time I was on the escalator heading down to the platform, my head was spinning. Time was slowing down. The escalator felt like it was moving slower than a snail. By the midpoint of descent, I was unable to see much of the platform but I could feel the intense, searing sensation of someone staring directly at me. As I got lower, I felt my eyes being drawn to who was staring at me.

I briefly took in all of that person's appearance before seeing no more than deep, ebony brown eyes staring directly at me with so much intensity, the air was forced from me. My entire body tingled. The air was humming with electricity and static as though caused by the connection of two people: this stranger and I.

In South Korea, it's considered rude to make eye contact when you're not familiar with people. My first thought in that moment was, 'oh, you want to stare at me do you?' while returning his gaze just as intensely as I continued down on the escalator.

We maintained eye contact as I stepped off the escalator and I continued walking towards The stranger. By then, I felt more out of body than in body. His beautiful brown eyes were the only thing I could see. Even with the extensive array of words in the English lexicon, there is nothing to efficiently describe all of what I felt as I came closer to this person who was determinedly keeping eye contact with me. Euphoria. Rapture. Completion. Love. Home. Some feelings I simply cannot find the words for.

As I came within one foot of this person I thought the words, 'you are who I am in love. You are him.'

I also heard his thoughts come back to me at an almost auditory level: 'I want to fuck you.'

I was so captivated by this person's magnetism and enthralled them and the overflowing embrace of love that I wasn't able to comprehend what he'd thought in that moment or whether I should have thought more about who this person staring at me so intensely was.

There was a wall ahead of and I didn't want to walk into it. The moment I looked away to gauge how close I was to impending chaos, the connection ended. The spell was broken as a train pulled into the platform along with full autonomy of my thoughts. All the lightness I had felt moments before evaporated as I took several more steps along the platform, each one heavy as though I was trying to wade through thick mud.

It was him.

I turned back on the platform to look for the stranger but he had vanished amongst the swarm of people transiting on the platform. With only seconds to spare before the train doors closed, I jumped on to the train out of automatic response. It was the wrong train. As my thoughts had returned to normal and I could process what had happened, I knew it had been him. I may be absent minded and slow to respond, but I would never in a thousand lifetimes mistake his eyes for those of another. I should have remained on the platform even if it had been the right train. I had been trembling all over and had to fight tears as my heart begun tearing itself a part and screaming at me to go back.

Why the hell did I get on the train?

It had been him. Seran. Only I hadn't recognised him until too late. I hadn't gone looking for him and I certainly never expected to find him at the metro line. Seran also looked so different in real life than he did in the photos shared online that were severely whitewashed. He was – *and is* – exceedingly beautiful in the absence of whitewashing, filters, and makeup.

I changed train at the next station and went back the correct way. I didn't have to get off to see he wasn't on the empty platform. I'd lost him. I had finally found Seran in the physical world and because I'm such a bumbling idiot with my head in the clouds, I also lost him.

Until that day, I hadn't quite pulled the likeness of the stranger from my dreams with beautiful tan skin together with Seran who presents as considerably paler. At the time of the encounter, I had been overwhelmed with great pain from Seran too. He was hurt I hadn't recognised him...but how could I have when he looks so different in real life?

I only recently figured out just how much of a difference the whitewashing makes when he uploaded an un-edited picture of him holding something during August of 2024. My eyes immediately swept to the tan skin and suddenly how I had failed to recognise him made sense! The contrast of skin tone between the person I had seen on the platform and Seran who I saw in photos had been enough for me to consider that they had been two different people for over two years even though my intuition would scream at me it was Seran.

Not a single day has past where I haven't wished I could travel back in time and change my course, to go back and not walk past him, to go up to him and continue staring, or to at least stop beside him on the platform even if it was awkward. Anything but go straight past him.

But I can't go back.

No matter how many times I write about that encounter, or however much time has past, my heart breaks and screams in anguish at how close he and I had been...and how improbable it is that we may find ourselves together like that again. The pain of failing to recognise my twin flame, Seran, when he was one foot away from me and staring deeply into my soul is indescribable and haunts me to this day.

What if that was my only chance to encounter him in the physical world? I have, within reason and healthy limitations, tried everything in my power and capabilities to reach him. For me, there's an unsurmountable wall between us. Since he's an idol, I can only go so far without crossing a dark line of unacceptable behaviour. So here I am writing this book in one final hope my words will somehow reach him in this lifetime.

Until seeing Seran in the physical world, there might have been a chance I could settle for a lesser love so long as it was genuine and healthy. But from the moment I made eye contact with Seran in this world, I knew there was never a return for me. There is simply only him.

I recently experienced body dowsing with my spiritual development circle. One of the members of our circle who was asking questions was communicating with the higher self of Seran's. His higher self would relate the questions to her, and she would then ask me as my body served as a pendulum. One question she asked specifically was had I "missed my twin flame by two minutes on the platform." My body answered as a yes[10].

As far as I know, I have never actually said to that person it was a station platform that he and I past on specifically, only that it was somewhere in Seoul.

Encounter #1

[10] The answers provided through body dowsing are unique to each person, so before asking questions it is important to define what movements mean yes or no. Most people sway. I ended up taking one to two steps forward or backwards – and backwards for yes in my case. With the question about missing my twin flame by two minutes, it was like I had been nudged backwards down a slope and almost couldn't stop my legs from contracting and making me take steps.

Keystone of Twin Flame Union

The sharing of sensation and emotions is fundamental to a twin flame union. It is the keystone of telepathy in all its forms which allows for the developments of the bond between each other as subsequent chapters will highlight.

Knowing how we individually feel, and how our twin flame individually feels is what allows us to work together on so many levels, and how we are able to know each other even when we are physically apart and how we can know and enjoy each other at a soul level. It is what tests us and challenges us to develop our own self-awareness and spiritual gifts. It's how we can locate each other in the physical world even if that has been a learning curve and one I wasn't ready for in the first instance specifically.

How it "feels" to have my connection with Seran is complex and ever changing and as much a part of who we are. We have our own lives yet we are still entangled souls within two bodies and always maintain a degree of perception of the other.

I have recently had chance to speak with a few other people in my local community who recently encountered their twin flames and learnt that telepathy and shared sensations seem to present in all twin flame connections, though how it manifests and what degree of understanding is had is as variable as each person is unique.

Two Minutes

I missed you by two minutes
as I stepped into your shadow
as though enthralled by magic
and I was spirited away.

As I stepped into your shadow
I recognised who you were
and I was spirited away
Too late to make my way back.

I recognised who you were
You were who I dreamt of yet it was
too late to make my way back
I didn't know I would find you here.

You were who I dreamt of yet it was
my greatest regret that I did not stop
I didn't know I would find you here
I missed you by two minutes.

Wrong Train

If I could change one thing
It would be to walk up to you
Not to go past you
It would be stay on that platform
To stay by your side.

I wish I had stayed on that platform
I wish I had never gotten on that train
You were right in front of me
But I didn't believe it possible
And by walking by, I missed my chance.

What if I never see you again?

...When Are You Most Drawn To Them?

When I was asked this question, it was from someone who knows a lot about my connection with Seran. They often listened to me talking about how frustrating it can be to connect with him when he is travelling around the world in particular. This led to me to introducing people to a term I had jokingly invented during my teenage years and then started using amongst friends since my connection with Seran really begun in 2021. Unlike the question "what drew you to them?", "when are you most drawn to them?" refers specifically to time of day.

Horologically Displaced: a person or object who is displaced by the effects of time- whether by different time zones of the world or an experience that occurs beyond the parameters of linear time.

LJ Bremer, *Horologically Displaced*

For all my life, I have always been out of sorts throughout the summer months after daylight savings adjustments came in with the switch from Greenwich Mean Time (GMT) to British Summer Time (BST). For some reason, I simply cannot adjust efficiently to BST. I have also been predominantly a nocturnal creature and always joked with my family that I must have been born in the wrong time zone. I wondered what I would function like if I existed in a time zone that was opposite to GMT. Was I born horologically displaced?

That displacement with my internal body clock to the environmental clock introduced a new challenge once I got to know Seran energetically since he was based in Korean Standard Time (KST). Since our connection began, we have had to learn to function in ever shifting time difference with him being on tour around the world or attending international events. It can be anything from a time difference of zero hours to nine hours. If this is confusing to you reading this, imagine how I feel trying to continually calculate where each of us is at especially since I have dyscalculae.

I realise I have it a lot easier than Elin who has 12–13-hour time difference with Teagan as their standard time difference. At least for Seran and I, we share windows of time where one of us is waking up as the other is going to sleep most of the time.

When he and I are most drawn to each other; when the both of us are naturally more inclined to the dreaming state. We are both relaxed and at ease with little pressure of the day weighing us down. We also take time around 16:00 in our individual days to overlap once more.

I don't know if the pattern of meditation-based connection developed when this first began within dreams. Perhaps it was already a framework for our connection. Maybe it developed naturally out of convenience with our standard time differences. Would it be different if I was in a similar situation as Elin and facing up to being half a day ahead of or behind Seran? Would our waking and sleeping patterns were totally at odds with each other for the majority of the time? That's a definite possibility. It took Seran and I close two years to be able to manage our connection throughout the time zones as it was.

Another consideration to how our connection came about and developed into something more is that, at the time Seran and I began dreaming of each other in earnest, the world was it was in the midst of the COVID pandemic and lockdown. Although some places in the UK were beginning to open up, we were still very much online with most things. In South Korea, the lockdown restrictions were much firmer.

It took a long time for me to realise and appreciate how the restrictions and limitations to Seran's daily schedule opened up time for him to be more than an idol. I don't think for one moment he intentionally took to dreaming and meditation to seek me out. However, I do believe that somehow, in the absence of so much work and the high pressure of his life, that opening allowed the weavers of fate to bring us together in dreams, then to open doors and guide us down corridors towards each other within the physical world.

It is also a possibility that, as a result of the pandemic and my own deepening of routine spiritual practices to cope and survive, this created a dynamic, two-way connection which had never been available to either of us until then. I would meditate around 14:30 BST as I had found that with ME/CFS, that that period of restfulness allowed me to make it through until night. For years of meditative practice, I had never had to consider what 14:30 for me in the UK could be elsewhere.

During June of 2021 when our connection began to move from dreams to waking reveries and telepathy, I began to realise that for Seran, it was 22:30 KST for him when I would spend an hour in deep states of meditation – what I assume was his period of winding down with the slower pace of life back then. For those months over summer and into the autumn, our connection was infinitely stronger and more intense than ever.

However, when I once more stepped over the threshold from BST back to GMT, the connection Seran and I shared had its first major blackout which lasted a couple weeks. It was only one hour of difference, surely it couldn't have had such an effect, right? Especially since for me, I functioned more efficiently in GMT. Yet, there it was: the first challenge to our relationship and connection.

Through the autumn and winter of that year, Seran and I had started to struggle with our personal differences as our connection was intermittent even with my meditative practices and ability to dream. Attempting to resolve the difficulties coming from our telepathic arguments was difficult but not impossible.

Then came along a bigger challenge to our ability to communicate and when I was "drawn to him". 2022 took over from 2021 and he with his group resumed their tours. For all of January, Seran's schedule was returned to a more normal pace for him and our connection was totally down within the first week. By mid-January, he and his group jetted out to the USA and I had my first experience of Seran not being in KST or South Korea.

No matter the time of day he simply wasn't there and close to two months of silence was devastating. I had waivered with doubts throughout winter as to whether our connection, intermittent as it was, was genuinely real or not. Elin had been able to assuage my doubts through some of that that time; yet now with the silence stretching out between Seran and I, our demons were beginning to wake up and run amok.

It didn't help that my dreams running up to that time had been those of parting, separation and searching. I truly believed I had been making everything up, or that I had done something wrong and broken our connection.

Dream IV
12/12/21

I was screaming. Screaming so much there was no sound left to be made and my throat burned with fire and anguish. Seran was holding me tightly in his arms as though frightened I would vanish if he loosened his grip. He told me everything would be okay. That I shouldn't worry. That the darkness around us would end.

His words caused more pain to surge throughout me. My heart pounded, twinging with torment as tears streamed unbound down my cheeks and neck. My breath struggled in and out as gasps and I clung to him just as strongly.

It was as though our souls were devastated and heartbroken at our daytime separation, as though some higher part of our existence was despairing at the difficulty of reaching each other in our dreams.

The strength to finally look at Seran unlocked my body and I gazed into his eyes. They were large with distress and his face was streaked with tears and his hair was dishevelled. In that moment, his pupils dilated and I watched him awaken within our shared dream. The intensity of his gaze grew stronger and fear flickered through his eyes and I heard him thinking, 'I don't want to wake up.'

A moment past in an abyssal, black dreamworld. Seran's energy was still close by and I reached towards him.

The dream restarted. I remained fully lucid and self-aware, yet there was a path to be followed, one that compelled Seran and I to walk it together in that moment. An inference of divine intervention. Seran and I needed to do something and we were guided into a lecture hall.

We sat at the back of the semi-circular hall with its stepped seats curled around the dais below us. Words washed over me and registered deep below my conscious level. Seran was more attentive to me than to the disembodied voice coming from below. He wanted to know more about what we had to do. Our conversation was below the surface too. Words that were spoken with intent and profound knowledge shifted back and forth to settle deep within our souls without registering at a conscious level. To me, there was only the sparkle and charm in Seran's ebony eyes.

Teagan appeared in the row below us and sat listening to everything; both the words emanating from below and those that Seran and I spoke.

I was beginning to wake up and had the awareness of shifting realities, perhaps because Seran was due to start his day and Teagan vanished from sight again.

Words suddenly poured through me, 'two of us are needed. We need to be together to make something happen. Two stars. Something bigger is coming. We would disappear for a time then come back together brighter as one.' I had channelled the message from my higher self. I could feel the gravity and pressure of those words that came from the part of me that was a part of the source.

The words were addressed to someone formal: a message to both Seran and I that involved both he and I, our entangled fates, and our careers. The Fates That Be needed Seran and I together in physical union to make something happen.

But first he and I would be parted.

Dream V
29/12/21

We caught hold of each other and held on tight. Everything I'd experienced and felt over the last couple of months was being mirrored back to me through Seran. He held on to me just as firmly as I clung to him, and his fingers were pressing into my skin so much they'd surely leave a mark later.

I screamed again and again. Everything hurt so much. Seran held me even more tightly. He repeated that it would be okay and not to worry, yet all I could do was scream louder until my throat was hoarse and my heart felt like it was being ripped in half.

Seran looked like he had been crying for hours. His eyes were puffy and red, and his face was streaked with glistening tears. In these moments when we were graced to meet in dreams, I could see the reality of this experience reflected back at me from his deep brown eyes. We were trying so hard to return to each other every day and every night, chasing dreams and the faintest trace of energetic connection.

Being separated by 9000 miles was really taking its toll. Neither of us had asked for this, not the connection and not the separation. It had been put upon us by some higher force. Neither of us knew if it was real. All we had were these dreams and these fleeting moments of holding on to each other as tight as possible each night we met. Neither of us had a way to bring our relationship into the physical world. I had no way to reach out to him and make the first move; and for him, he had so much to risk by contacting me and probably just as many doubts as I did.

All we can do is hold on to each other when benevolent forces allowed us to meet in our dreams and to savour the warmth of our shared embrace while hoping the dreams would never end.

Even now, the pain of those two dreams and others of that time haunt me the most. The pain of being torn away from Seran night after night was the most harrowing pain of all.

Separation

After years of abuse and heartbreak preceding eight years of self-love and dedication to myself with a new life in Wales, I had vowed never to give my heart to anyone ever again. That was until Seran came into my dreams and continued returning every night. I had resisted falling for him for so long only to take a chance and surrender into him and the feelings I had been supressing. Then, it felt as though I was cast aside once the chase was over. I had become familiar with Seran being as much a part of my existence and day as my own heartbeat, perhaps even complacent to what we shared.

With the two months of communication blackout during the winter, all I would think of in that time were the words from the last dream, about how we would disappear for a time before coming back together. What if we never made it back together though? Was I a fool to make the mistake of falling in love again?

Seran's absence back then made me realise how much I had become used to having Seran in my mind and how much I had taken our connection for granted. There was a void in place of that connection and it had been killer. Nothing could ease the pain of separation, not even talking with Elin and I found myself withdrawing even from her. I had started returning to my fear-based response of fleeing and hiding.

The only thing that could keep my spirits up during that time was my upcoming trip to South Korea which had been just around the corner. I put myself 100% into my studies and travel preparations so there was no room to mope, and before I knew it, the end of March 2022 had arrived and I was sat on a plane about to travel solo for the first time ever, all because of a rooftile.

Drawn Together Like Magnets

Due to my generalised anxiety being a permanent feature of my life, I spent the duration of my twelve-hour flight in a deep meditative state of mind in an attempt to keep myself calm. Somewhere over Mongolia, I could sense Seran again. Throughout March, there had been hints and traces of our connection, but it had been like trying to listen to an old radio station that was barely picking up a station and had more white noise and muffled distortion than anything else.

Suddenly, the connection with Seran clarified like dialling into the perfect frequency and turning the volume up. As soon as I arrived at the lockdown mandated quarantine hotel and I had time to think and realize I had actually just made it to South Korea, A wash of intense euphoria soared throughout my body which had automatically adjusted to KST, though not to Seran' routine so much. Suddenly my going to bed at 21:00 meant it was actually more difficult to connect with him, as was my usual wake up at 08:00. Ironic to be 5-10 miles away from him yet feeling more distant in some ways. That being said, being in the same time zone at least meant that during the day it was a lot easier to connect with Seran and, for the time we were in the same country, our connection was as intense as it had been the previous summer.

A few days after I left my quarantine hotel and set myself up in Insadong, South Korea was easing lockdown restrictions and allowing full tourism to resume. This leads me to another series of events that convinces me the experiences are real.

On my first adventures out of my hotel I tried using Kakao maps, the South Korean equivalent of Google maps, and I found it more bothersome than the possibility of getting lost somewhere in Seoul. I would check my route before leaving the hotel then simply go for it. I had my music on in my headphones and would talk with Seran. He would navigate for me and, aside from my misadventures with the metro, I never got lost. I got everywhere I needed to go with his help and found some really cool sites along the way including plenty of those highly specific rooftiles I had come here to find.

It was as though I was being guided through this foreign city by some kind of magnetic levitation, like I was being drawn to Seran by a magnetic force as much as his navigation.

Quite comically, he also managed to navigate me to his company building and to the car he was in. He sent me in loops around different blocks and created different cross sections of a certain part of Seoul until I was standing in front of him with that part of the city eternally imprinted into my soul by the time I stopped to photograph a car– right in front of him and totally clueless.

Yes, for all my amazing extra sensory perception, hypersensitivity and spatial awareness, I am able to miss my twin flame being several feet away from me. Repeatedly. In fairness, as with the time I past him in the metro, I wasn't looking for him. Nor did I expect or believe him to be there either. It is the dichotomy of my existence. On the one hand, Seran was telepathically giving me better sat-nav instructions than an actual sat-nav and telling me he could see me. On the other hand, the number of times I was told I was crazy growing up and throughout life had me convinced this was all still a very elaborate maladaptive daydream and I was therefore, totally blind to his existence.

As things progressed forwards and South Korea exited lockdown, Seran's work schedule increased which meant our time to play like that was coming to an inevitable end. I had been given a second chance with my connection with Seran, and we had been able to know each other far better than before. I was beginning to learn what his normal routine would be like although that didn't make it any easier.

This was when Seran and I realised the ramifications of horological displacement. We both became mindful of the time and ensured we connected with each other for at least five minutes around the time we were waking or going to sleep no matter the time difference. That was the first provision we put into place to ensure the preservation of our connection.

As I returned home, I figured out how to get the inflight screen up from the arm rest and I had the horological map on display. I kept updating Seran when the plane crossed into each time zone. What had been a joke became something we took seriously. While I don't think Seran is at the map nerdery levels I am, we always adjust to time zones with each other. These days I allow myself to indulge in the idea Seran checks the horological map on the in-flight entertainment screen though.

While our connection had been phenomenal while I had been in South Korea, it soon returned to intermittent and turbulent and definitely contributed to the growing storm inside of me back then. The way in which horological placement as much as geographical placement affected us became more prominent during the summer of 2022 when I had my NDE. It was more than just time affecting us, but the electromagnetic grid and where we were each situated on it. Perhaps the electromagnetic grid was having an influence in our connection and my previous musings of being drawn together as though by magnetic levitation was more conceivable than it was a metaphor.

After he spent time in California, we realised there were some locations that impacted our connection far more than other places, and from then on, we made our second provision: to connect with each other as soon as possible after one of us landed somewhere else and spend time energetically entwining with each other and energetically with the electromagnetic grid. Maybe it wasn't a case of waiting for some unseen force to draw us to each other but of intentionally seeking each other out and creating new energetic pathways between us.

We also learnt that what we do to help each other with our global travels and time zone management is also a part of our spiritual work in life. Working with the electromagnetic field requires intense energy work and for what Seran and I were doing, we had to do our part in cleansing, healing and protecting the energetic pathways for us to enhance our connection.

This has been an ongoing development for us which only now feels close to mastery. Little by little our energetic work around the world has meant that displacement of any kind has become much less of an issue. On a superficial level, time difference is the same as coordinating telepathy the way someone might schedule a voice call to someone in a different time zone, only with us, we couldn't send a text or leave a voice message to catch each other up.

Somewhere along the line we also developed the spiritual equivalent to poking each other so that when one or both of us is busy or exhausted, we at least give the other an energetic nudge to let the other know we're thinking of each other. The quick exchange is like a quick pulse of energy to each other. Seran was the first to send the pulse of energy to me after I discussed paired bracelets that would pulse when touched no matter how far apart from each other they were, and how I wished for so long I had someone to share such bracelets with.

Three years on and we still make sure to spend at least five minutes with each most days when one either of us is waking/going to sleep no matter where either of us are – and on the days when we can't connect with each other, we take a deep breath and focus on our lives knowing that the connection is still there and will always be there.

...How Do You Know When To Connect?

There are many similarities with this question and that of when we're drawn together. What sets them apart is that, in the times we have been drawn together, it is more by fluke or by serendipity with the most conscious decision being that of when Seran and I rest and which time zone until we figured out how to make sense of our connection and make it work for us. We had to learn to coexist with each other and attempt to know each other's schedules and plans so as to not unintentionally invade each other's space or disturb work.

Being mindful of time allowed for us to intentionally connect with each other rather than waiting to be drawn together by chance. We had control and could chose when to connect, and finally work towards connecting in all ways that we can including physically.

Telepathically

The connection I share with Seran as it is now has mellowed considerably compared to how things started out. Our intense telepathic soul bond during the summer of 2021 was fun and exciting for a couple of months – what could be considered the honeymoon period of our connection – then it descended into issues of not wanting to be disturbed or questions of, 'how much do you know?' and fears of, 'who are you telling it to?' amongst many more discrepancies that were unearthed by 24/7 telepathy.

That led to us struggling with each other's ego and various resident demons. Being inside of each other's heart, mind, and soul meant there was no hiding from each other. Even if we tried to hide, we were pushed back to each other whether we wanted it or not. Neither he nor I could comprehend the shift from occasional dreams to a full blown 24/7 connection.

There was also no explanation as to why Elin and Teagan occasionally formed part of the connection either. Even for myself whose entire life has been an ongoing spiritual journey emersed in magic, mysticism, and esoterica, I had never experienced or read about what was happening to us. We had to figure out boundaries and some ground rules.

Within weeks, the experiences had shaken me and my sanity to my core. I would spontaneously astral project to him waking or while dreaming and see everything, and by everything, I mean seeing where Seran was, who he was with and how he looked and all of it clearer than 4k ultra vision. It had seemed far too outlandish to be real.

If I hadn't been talking with Elin back then, I would have imploded. Since Elin has been pretty much the only person I can talk with about my connection with Seran since the beginning, she and I quickly developed our own deep bond. We would tell each other everything about our individual experiences and compare notes. It was the only way she and I could attempt to figure out what was happening.

Seran struggled to understand why I would share everything with Elin, yet to me, she was the only person who could comprehend what I was going through as she was having a very similar experience. Having someone to confide in made the difference between coping or not.

It wasn't long until I felt intense anger emanating from Seran. He wasn't happy with me telling Elin everything. I heard him say, 'what gives you the right?' with what can only be defined as cataclysmic fury.

There were two reasons for his sudden rage that I could easily discern:

The first was that, as a famous person, Seran has an understandable fear of someone betraying his trust and/or sharing anything inappropriate that could defame him. Although it was Seran who had instigated the conversation I had had with Elin, suddenly this wild, intense experience that left no space for privacy had invaded both our lives, and he and I were still getting to know one another.

It was understandable that he would have doubts about the integrity of both she and I considering how much was at stake should any of this have gotten out. Even as an untruth it would have been something he would have dreaded going viral because of the nature of the content and then of it sticking to him and tarnishing his reputation that he had so diligently built up.

He carried a lot of fear that if I could tell Elin about our connection and some of what happened between us, then I might also tell it to the internet. As someone who has myself had trust betrayed far too many times, I could reflect upon my past hurts to have an idea of what Seran might fear: that Elin may have been disingenuous. If she had taken screenshots of messages, she could have easily shared them online and burnt both Seran and I. There was even the fear from Seran that Elin I had corroborated together to cause problems. I could empathise with him Seran due to the life I had had and the severe paranoia and trust issues I'd barely recovered from. It hurt me that he had those thoughts in the beginning, but I could understand why.

I patiently reassured him that I had no intentions of talking publicly about our experiences or to ever mention his name in conjunction with what has happened. Likewise, I knew in my heart Elin was a good person and was of the same mindset, and I did my best to assuage all of Seran's fears as best as I could, and I am thankful he held on throughout everything to know the truth in himself – but that peace between us came much later.

Underlying everything was my need to validate my experiences with Elin which contributed to Seran's frustration and indignation and haunted both he and I. Who wouldn't need reassurances of sanity with everything that was happening to us? I still crave validation of my experiences most days, though now I am far less needy about it after Seran and I found middle ground where both our needs were met.

The second reason for Seran's spike in anger was that I had shared some sensitive information with Elin which he wasn't comfortable with. For that I can say we healed and moved on, and both Seran and Teagan made the discovery that girl talk can be far spicier than boy talk. Both of them realised that when Elin and I talked about our relationships with them, we were grounding all that we shared in reality in the same way friends would meet for a drink and talk about any other relationship.

Although it took time and more than a few arguments and connection blackouts to arrive at our understanding, it is also one of the most profound transformations to our connection. Seran was able to learn that in actuality, I seldom give much away. I'll allude to certain things, use euphemisms and suggestion, but never explicitly say something. There are aspects to our connection that are unquestionably top secret and I have never even hinted to those topics. I know that he enjoys divulging the truths of our connection to Teagan just as much.

The issue had been in that time was fear of exposure.

Something which kept the fire of fear and rage burning with Seran was that, above all else, he knew that I was open about my beliefs. My fiction books are all about magic and fated love. I often discuss my research and personal experiences on social media. He feared I had placed a spell on him; that I was manipulating his fate in some way. I repeatedly told him I would never do such a thing as it's black magic, and I do not meddle with that aspect of magic. I also reminded him that it was he and his soul/higher self that instigated connection with me although that hardly mollified him. I did my best to try and stay calm and weather the storm.

As I gather from the connection we have, Seran had gone from a perfectly ordinary life as a musician and dancer to suddenly having wild magic surging through every aspect of his life. In barley six months, he was experienced everything I had in 30 years of life. I cannot imagine how that would feel considering I was freaked out and doubting myself most days and that was things considered relatively normal in my reality. This constant, unstable flux of emotions pushed us both into disconnection and shadow work we needed to heal all our unresolved trauma within ourselves while learning to work together – something that is extremely difficult when considering we couldn't text or facetime with each other.

To help manage our connection so that it was something we had a handle on, we developed a series of safe words that were quick to use. They were simple words to use in times of distress when the other was busy or we couldn't sense each other.

Safe Words for Connection

Busy. Work. Wait. Come. Later. Soon. Five Minutes. Those are some of the words we use with each other now. Although seemingly dominating and perhaps devoid of emotion, they were a gamechanger for us whilst struggling with our connection and Seran's hectic, somewhat erratic schedule and ever-changing global positioning.

It took adjustment for both of us. Having those words almost barked at me at times was unsettling, so Seran had to learn how to use tone of voice in telepathy to be less abrupt and scary, while I had to learn not to do the mental equivalent of fleeing each time.

The simplicity of those words in either language allowed for the quickest transmission of information. It was primarily me that was freaking out and in need of some TLC from Seran and, having those safe words allowed for Seran to succinctly tell me why he couldn't attend to my needs in a given moment and I finally had a sense of peace and reliance on someone that I had never known before.

As we better resonated with each other's emotions and the sensations of feeling within each other, it became easier to quickly gauge whether it was a situation absent of fear or pressure in which case, after the use of safe word, we could continue with the task at hand. Or we might have an overwhelming sense of dread as we swap quick words. In those moments, whichever of us was us caught up with life would find an appropriate moment to leave the task at hand and retire somewhere quire for at least five minutes to help the other through whatever had come up.

Both Seran and I have a full understanding that neither of us have dominion over each other's time. 'Five Minutes,' is the main phrase for when we're attending to something of important which loosely translates to, 'I can be with you in five minutes or so,' and/or, 'I can give you five minutes now.'

Those five minutes were enough to calm either of us down from panic attacks, stress, emotion, or whatever was going on in our heads. Sometimes, simply the fear of disconnection was the cause, and he or I needed five minutes of connection for the sake of reassurance. Since we had no physical way to communicate, it was fundamental to the health of our relationship to have communication figured out as soon as possible. More often than not, we would also use those five minutes to schedule a time we could connect and fully tend to each other's needs.

With the use of safe words becoming a regular practice we moved past the chaos of our early telepathic connection. We could attend to each other's needs without invading each other's every waking and sleeping moment, and we were able to create the boundaries we needed.

Time Zone Management

There's no escaping time in our connection especially as Seran travels so much.

As Seran's schedule returned to normal with album production, promotions, touring and so much more, his sleep schedule became a logistical nightmare. The simple connection we had developed during lockdown was blown out of the water. Even with him in South Korea, he seldom settled down for a night at 22:00. He would sometimes be awake throughout the night and having naps during the day between events.

As I would meditate or rest between waking and dreaming, the energetic presence of Seran that had been ever-present in the early days was gone. With the changes to Seran's schedule, I was playing catchup with his energy and constantly trying to locate him. Likewise, Seran learnt to send an energetic buzz when he was awake during my waking hours so we could have an idea of where we each were.

Sometimes, our connection blackouts happened due to fear. Before he and I had mastery over our ability to sense when the other was asleep, the sudden and absolute silence that came with sleep was terrifying, especially when it happened at an unusual time. I would stir myself into a frenzy of thought which was the actual cause for our blackout. Being consumed by fear meant there was no space for Seran. Equally, Seran could be the reason for gaps in connection. He has a tendency towards being a workaholic. Whenever he has been consumed by work, there was no space for me exist in his reality.

Sleep came with the same absence of presence. If it came at a time I had presumed Seran would be awake, my fear-based self would leap to the conclusion that I had done something wrong; that he was angry with me in some way, or for any negative based reason, he was blocking me out.

To resolve connection blackouts and learn when we could connect to one another no matter where in the world either of us was, we both had to dive deeply into our self and address all that we were hiding from – one of the elements of healing that comes with the twin flame journey.

It became difficult to talk to Elin about the intermittent connection Seran and I had. For one, I couldn't imagine how incredulous my experiences would have seemed: one week I had an intense psychic connection to Seran and could almost be crossing boundaries into his reality and he into mine, and then the next week I was full of negativity and fear with no sense of him. One minute he was the best thing in the world, the next I harboured so much anger because he left me doubting my mind, my sanity and my reality.

Out of consideration to Seran, I had closed-off to Elin during the winter of 2021 so that he could have time and space to figure out what was going on. It was difficult suddenly holding back information from Elin who had become a dearly cherished soul in my life, however, I had to respect Seran too.

He and I were losing ourselves to this connection. We both needed space and silence especially as his schedule ramped up to the maximum with him darting back and forth through time zones quicker than a yo-yo. The start of 2022 was full of dichotomous existence between preternatural and mundane polarities, being fully on or fully off with Seran, intense counselling sessions and the building pressure of my impending dissertation, all of which continued until the summertime of 2022 when I had my NDE. After that, I took a prolonged social media break and dedicated time to myself and my physical and mental health during the days I was offline.

Whilst Seran was on his own voyage of discovery and understanding, I retreated into hermit mode and silence so I could reconnect to who I was. We both needed to remember where we each ended and what was ours and not theirs. We had to remember who we were within our own lives. This was our time of walking into the desert so we could reflect on our individual realities and to strengthen our connection to the divine. We had to surrender to the perpetual ebb and flow of our energetic connection and become like water trusting that the currents of life would take us where we were meant to be. **To let go.**

It took time.

As anyone who has been tested by faith and spirituality can attest to, letting go – truly letting go – is one of the most challenging aspects to the path. For me, it's like the moment at the summit of a rock climb when you need to let go to abseil down. It's terrifying. Yet, the moment of surrender into the abseil and the weightlessness of dropping back into position on the rope is the most euphoric sensation and actualisation of faith.

In learning to let go and surrender into the flow of all things, our connection strengthened immeasurably. Time zones still get to Seran and I periodically, but we learnt that by having patience and relaxing into each other, we could always find each other no matter what. Coupled with the use of our safe words, we eventually mastered connecting with each other around the world without becoming burdensome.

Coming Out of the Shadows

From the moment I accepted what Seran and I shared was more than a flight of fancy, I decided to treat the relationship with him as I would any relationship. I knew we had to work on what we had to grow and keep our relationship healthy – both my parents had always been open and honest about what it takes to make a relationship go the distance and I carried their advice and lessons into my relationship with Seran.

The first step was in acceptance.

Acceptance that our love was real.

Acceptance that our connection was real.

Acceptance that our relationship was real.

We needed to shift our relationship from behind closed doors and reveal it to the world which we have both done and continue to do so in subtle and playful ways. We also needed to ground our relationship fully into our reality by talking with the people we knew and trusted even if it for the time being, it was a brief mention. It was our way of saying to the divine, 'look, this is serious for us. We're not afraid to hide this away from a nearest and dearest.'

At first this was purely on my side. I am truly blessed to have been guided to the most wonderful soul tribe in Wales since starting university and the fortification from Seran along my journey. I finally have a group of genuine friends in my physical world that were spiritual and understood me and are absolutely trustworthy. They gave me a space where I could exist without judgment and, most of all, the discovery that I was not alone or crazy in any of my experiences. As I slowly opened up about my preternatural experiences, possible shared dreams and tenuous soul connection with someone half a world away, I had begun to feel certainty in this connection for the first time.

I wasn't being ridiculed for any part of my spiritual experiences. When I mentioned telepathy to them, they were more confused that I was full of doubt about it. For the first time in my life, my experiences were being met with, 'of course it's real!' instead of, 'don't be silly.' It changed my entire perspective drastically and it was, and still is, the most amazing feeling to be free to talk about my connection and relationship with Seran while amongst friends.

Prior to then, keeping silent from everyone besides Elin had made what Seran and I shared seem like it was something dark and dangerous, maybe shameful. Hiding our secret had meant that many negative emotions surfaced along with our demons and tarred something sacred.

With the support and love of my soul tribe I found the courage to start telling other people about Seran, specifically, my mother who had been a psychiatric nurse for her entire career. I had held off telling either of my parents about Seran as both had worked in psychiatry their entire lives and I feared what they may tell me. My way of introducing my mother to the presence of Seran was by asking her to answer me honestly – as both mother and psychiatric nurse – if she thought I was crazy to have a connection with someone who I'd not yet met physically, yet somehow had telepathy and shared dreams with.

Her response: the crazy person doesn't question if they're crazy.

After I had told her everything about Seran as well as my ongoing concerns about insanity, I had a good cry and she gave me a long cwtch. As is the power of a mother, everything was made okay again. She then told me that her aunt had had a similar experience to me. The aunt had remained single because the love she had wasn't in her reality. My mother had been young herself back then. She hadn't been able to comprehend what her aunt had experience until she met my father and understood completely. Without knowing who he was that day, she made eye contact with him and knew immediately that he was who she was meant to be with.[11]

I also asked her that day if she remembered me walking everywhere to try and find someone when I was

---

[11] I had never mentioned the term twin flame to my mother at any point whilst she had been with us. After she had passed away, my father found some of her journals. She, like me, was notoriously bad at keeping a journal it seems. However, in the one journal that only had one entry in it, she referred to my father as her twin flame.

younger, particularly that time in Cornwall I mentioned before as it had caused her so much panic. She remembered it clearly and I explained that it was Seran was who I had been searching for that day and ever since.

The conversation I had with my mother shifted something with Seran and I. Confiding in my mother about this relationship which had driven me to edge of a metaphorical cliff so many times was the medicine Seran and I had needed. He was accepted by my mother who grew curious to know more about him and even began appearing occasionally in the dreams Seran and I shared.

Until that day, I had been like Alice falling down the rabbit hole for two years. I never knew which way was up or down. I didn't know if I was delusional or maladaptive daydreaming. What if I had given life to Seran in the depths of my CPTSD[12] starting at age eight so I never had to be alone? What if his re-manifestation to me decades later as an adult was a biproduct of character development with a fictional person that had been growing up alongside me and had developed so much autonomy, it could think quicker than I could? So I had continually pushed Seran away from me. I refused to acknowledge or accept the connection, and I had ignored him so often as I assigned his voice to that of madness.

Being told I was sane by someone who had spent close to forty years working exclusively in psychiatry meant everything. Part of her work was to watch out for any sign of deteriorating mental health or an unstable mindset. Even though I was her daughter, I knew she wouldn't have entertained any dishonesty with me regarding my own mental health. She would have much sooner gotten me professional help if that was what was needed, and she would have kept reassuringly by my side throughout everything.

---

[12] CPTSD: complex post-traumatic stress disorder.

Although I sometimes still have doubts, especially now that I no longer have luxury of talking it out with her, our conversation has remained with me and given me strength. What I have with Seran is real. If it's real in any realm of existence, then it's real in my waking reality too. I let down my guard to Seran and welcomed him wholly into my life and have never once even tried shutting him out since.

I received even greater courage to talk about Seran as seriously as any other person would talk about a significant other in their life, after all, why would the divine go to such effort connecting Seran and I together in the physical world if we didn't take each other seriously and have the utmost appreciation and respect for our wonderous relationship?

It was as though a bridge Seran and I had been building between us since the early days of our connection was more than a metaphor for healing from arguments, but an actual bridge that would eventually connect us in the physical world as we worked on ourselves and our connection.

The first link had been placed on Christmas Day of 2021 after we reaffirmed our eternal love and promised ourselves to each other in a ritual of sacred matrimony within the astral realm before the divine upon an incomplete bridge of prismatic light above an impossibly wide chasm. Neither Seran nor I had ever forgotten the unfinished bridge we had seen that day, but it wasn't until I had talked with my mother about these things and the subsequent revelations the followed which allowed a shift in our mindset and attitude that a second link of our bridge was forged.

Each time that Seran and I find our way through our twin flame connection and heal past wounds, the bridge is closer to completion. There may be other links to be created yet, but I do know that the final link will be our physical union somewhere in this world we both live, and the bridge as it is, is a gauge of how far we've come.

Whatever comes next after publishing this memoir is another link in our bridge. We both agreed to me writing and sharing our story after considering it for a long time. This is our way of taking our connection out of the shadows and show how seriously we take this.

Physical World Encounter II

London

I've never been good at navigating London. My mother even less so. On one of the occasions my mother and I travelled to London together, I had another almost encounter with Seran when I had accidentally gotten mother and I on to the wrong metro line.

The seats on the train were fully occupied when we got on and as the train moved out of the station, my mother completely lost her balance and fell backwards in the most comical way possible. She and I were both laughing and someone promptly offered her their seat.

Since we ended up several feet away, we couldn't easily talk for the ten minutes or so that we were on board. I had had my headphones in to help with my anxiety and, as with the time I was in Seoul, totally oblivious to my surroundings beyond keeping my mother in the corner of my eye in case she wanted my attention.

As I watched the cityscape go by, I had begun laughing again. I kept telepathically asking Seran if it was him causing me to laugh, and had he someone how seen what had happened too? He said he had, and true to my nature, I didn't think to look around the train then because how and why would he be there too? I had no expectations of seeing Seran and wasn't looking for him. Bumping into him in his home city makes sense, but bumping into him in London? That was inconceivable even if he had reason to be in the city. I assumed he had seen it through my eyes.

The train went straight past the station we had needed to change at without stopping and I realised I had gotten us on a train that went the right way, but it was the wrong train and made considerably less stops. I took my earbuds out and asked around on the train for where best to change trains, then frantically rushed off with my mother at the next stop. We made our way to our hotel, checked in, and then went off touring the city.

Several hours later whilst waiting around in a long queue, my mother sees someone and has a sudden outburst: 'Oh! I just remembered I meant to tell you something earlier. The person you're in love with, I'm pretty certain he was on the train earlier. He dashed on to the train like it was a last-minute decision and then stared at you the entire time while hiding behind a pole. He looked like he was thinking of coming up to you but then you jumped off the train. He looked absolutely devastated that you didn't notice him.'

Encounter #2

London is one place that messes with my ESP. That place is to me what a magnet is to a compass. I had sensed Seran close to me but, as with assuming he had witnessed events happening through my own eyes, I thought his proximity to me was energetic. Maybe if we had just stayed on that train a little while longer, Seran might have made it over to me or I may have come out of my reveries and looked down the train to see him there barely three feet away from me.

I showed my mother countless pictures after she regaled the story to me, and she was adamant that it was most definitely him. Since I had also sensed Seran being around me and shared his emotions and thoughts, I had no reason to doubt her. From what she had gone on to tell me, she had been eyeballing him intensely for the ten minutes or so that we had been on the train so his appearance was probably etched into her memory for perpetuity too.

If at the start of this book you wondered about how the conversation of wearing a jumper as a signal came about, perhaps by now you understand. After two years of my on-going and unintended inattentiveness plus two extremely close encounters whilst totally oblivious, it was decided that I really do need some sort of portable signal board to help me out.

Faith

A big part of the answer to "How do you know when to connect?" is held purely in faith.

I don't know when we will unite in the physical world.

I don't know for sure that we will.

What I know with certainty is that from the moment I woke up from Seran's kiss in 2021, I could only surrender into him and whatever this connection is. Seran and I are entangled with each other at a soul level. Ours is a connection that can't be broken; a thread that may twist and tangle, or it may unravel and fray, but it will never break. I am him, and he is me.

That is how we can manifest in each other's dreams. It's how we can astral project to each other and how it is how we can understand each other even though there is a language barrier between us. It's that entanglement that allows us to feel each other's emotions and glimpse each other's reality. Our souls are entwined and we can experience each other as well as our own individual realities – the good and the bad. Even if we stray apart for a time after arguments we are still connected and we inevitably find our way back home to each other as we heal together.

Whatever happens in one of our lives, happens in some way in the other's life too. The event may not be identical though. Sometimes the lesson is in opposites as much as it can be identical. The lesson comes in whatever way is best for the both of us to work through what is needed as a team, and for us to both learn in harmony with the other.

I won't divulge the innermost truths of our lessons since they are deeply personal and sacred to us, only that some of the lessons to surface involve time, family, belief systems, and of course, letting go and patience.

Time is an opposition for Seran and I. I have ample spare time while he has little.

Belief systems was a joint challenge. We both had our own faith. I have followed a spiritual path of my own for most of my life while Seran was atheist, yet our beliefs collided and were reformed together as we went on our journey and pieced everything together. Our beliefs have been challenged and they've shifted, always bringing us closer to the divine as we come to understand things more deeply

So it is with all lessons, and with all people who find themselves awakening to their twin flame: each lesson is unique, and each lesson will repeat over and over again until it's acknowledged and resolved. For a long time, I was frustrated thinking I was continually failing at lessons that kept coming back no matter how much I tried to change and improve.

Fig. 1

Sometimes lessons repeat many times and it feels as though the self is going in circles without making any headway (*fig. 1*), yet in reality, the lessons are repeating and with each completion of a lesson, the self is actually ascending each time (*fig. 2*).

Fig. Two

The lessons which are an ongoing and enduring task tend to mostly be connected with healing generational trauma which has manifested in the self's life in some way. The repetition of lessons are to ensure healing is accomplished at many levels of existence and throughout different timelines. They include inner child healing as well as healing family wounds – not just with parents, but potentially future children which may not yet have come in to being.

Seran had plenty of patience at the start. Everything was all new to him, what was another year or two? Why was I so stressed and bothered by it? I had zero patience. For my entire life I've been trying to figure everything out and to work out who Seran was when I couldn't even see his face for decades. Four years later, Seran understands how and why I can be so impatient, yet together, we have found as much peace as any two souls longing to come together can. Together we have found our way back to the divine and given ourselves to faith and the currents of life. Divine timing. Patience. There's really no getting around it: things will happen exactly when they're meant to and there's simply no forcing it.

One topic of faith and learning that I can be more open about is that of magic. I am the half that grew up in the United Kingdom, home to an abundance of magical stone circles, the heart chakra of the world located in Glastonbury, a land where most houses have at least one ghost, and all things preternatural are just so *normal*. I had ESP all my life and grew into a wild path of spirituality. I had to find out how to fight demons both personal and environmental and then vanquish them. You'd think I'd be unshakeable.

Yet, it's actually Seran who has, after his abrupt awakening, been the calm and collected half. He accepted our connection without question or doubt and never understood why I was always resisting him and full of uncertainty. Whatever oddities come up in meditation or dreams now, Seran is the one looking at me incredulously as I get into a flap. It is as though he had been the one growing up with all of this happening around him on a daily basis and not I.

Only so much of that calm and collected mannerism could be assigned to his higher-self consciousness. I know from my own experiences that whatever happens in the depths of our preconscious or out of body existences will eventually overlap with waking reality. Even if 90% of our shared experiences exist exclusively within dreams and other realms of existence, there's still 10% of everything that would be unavoidably in his physical reality. As it is with me, so it would be with him.

I chose to have total faith in Seran and our connection. As with opening up to other people about Seran, I shifted from "he and I" to "we" when talking casually. In becoming "we", I was accepting our divine union at all levels of existence and reaffirming to the divine that "we" are ready to connect at all levels as is he.

We started sharing ideas with each other for our individual work. We started playing a game where he would tell me a little bit of the lore of their story and I would try and convey that in my work and have it published before his chapter came out with his group. Then, since there are parallels with our work, I've been able to help him with some of his ideas and a plot point he had gotten stuck with. There have been a few threads of connections released so far, but I know he's saving much of what we've discussed for when it serves their story best.

The more we lean into to each other with faith, and the more we work with each other harmoniously, the more unlocks and opens up for us on our path. That is how and why this book is a part of everything. I don't know what will happen next, only that something will. At each stage of working on this manuscript, it has been like shifting realities in a drastic way, and each round of editing pouring more magic into our connection and deepening the bond we share. Working on this has certainly been the biggest challenge of our telepathy as Seran is as instrumental to the creation of this book as I am.

Dream VI
26-02-24

I was back in the town I had grown up in and walking around my father's allotments the same way I had as a child, and I was carrying a tray with three take-out coffees. Eventually, I caught up with my father and he led me on a tour of his allotments. He explained everything that he had done since I had last seen them, and periodically he would stop to water some of the plants, or to lift some weeds out of the way.

We came towards a bench in his orchard close to the two furthermost sheds of his allotment. In the waking world, the bench had been abandoned after being submersed in multiple floods and becoming decrepit and unsafe to sit on as it was slowly reclaimed by the apple tree that had many suckers threading their way through the frail ruins of the bench. Here, it was impressively smart and clean besides the weathered patina, and safe enough for father and I to sit at to enjoy our coffee.

Before we could take our seats, we noticed a wasp drowning in a water-butt nearby next to the sheds. I was conflicted about trying to save it since we were both allergic to wasps. Even though I knew it was a dream, I didn't want to know what might happen to either of us if we were stung. In the end, my father used a branch to lift the wasp out and placed it on the bench so it could rest and dry out.

We both agreed they were cute when not trying to kill us, and whether by coincidental timing or as a response to our comments, the wasp transformed into a yellow and black striped creature that looked like a fox crossed with a domestic cat.

My father moved closer, sitting down on the bench and giving the strange creature a fuss. I remained standing as I still didn't want to be bitten or stung by it, yet the creature reached up and placed its front paws on my shoulders before I could walk away and I ended up fussing it too.

My mother then came into the dream. She had somehow acquired her coffee and was sipping it whilst talking on the phone to an airline company. I heard her loudly saying she wanted to 'book flights to Korea,' before mentioning the price out loud which was £555, only she announced it very slowly as, 'five-five-five'.

After hanging up, she turned to look at father and I and said, 'we're going home.'

Although the above dream doesn't include Seran, it still fits within the larger narrative of all the dreams I've had, and for something I asked my mother to help with after she had passed away which was to help Seran and I come together. Dream IV and V were epitomising the strife and separation Seran and faced in dreams with the constant search for each other or being pulled apart being a reoccurring theme for so long. In Dream VI, Seran isn't present but my mother is showing that she is helping me get back to South Korea and to where he is.

Her announcement of 5-5-5 was a direct message too. It is an angel number that, in brief, means that everything is going to plan with twin flames. In numerology, 5 is the link between the living and the divine, or the appearance of a messenger between spirit and the living – exactly how mum was coming from spirit to talk with me in a dream.

Something I had not considered at the time of the dream was that my mother was bringing me another message at the same time. In chapter four, 'How Do You Know They're The One?', I mentioned how I received insight from my dreams, and how both my parents entered my dreams shortly before their departure from life. Since my father was keen on having what he called a grandad annex with me in South Korea, I assumed my mother meant that she would help both my father and I get there and that with she would join us in spirit to wherever my next home could be.

I realise now that I wasn't the only twin flame in that dream. Even without my mother's journal later confirming it, it was obvious my parents were twin flames by their own story. 555 as a twin flame number was equally important to me, as it was to my father. This was the first way in which my mother told me that my father would be leaving the world of the living soon. Everything was going to plan even if the plan made little sense, or if the entirety of the plan was net yet revealed.

Dream VII
22-03-24

I was running around the old building of my high school.

I had to find Seran here.

As with every other time I have wound up in this place in my dreams, I came to a part of the building that didn't exist in the physical world: a pair of extremely slow and rickety elevators that would take me to the sub-level, and a dreadful stairway to the left of the elevators. I had only ever run up those stairs once or twice in this reoccurring dream before, and I was certain they would fall apart entirely before too long.

Usually when I found myself going to the sub-level, I was fleeing some unknown stalker of my dreams and came to the elevators as a last resort. That which hunted me at my current level was more human and less powerful than the interdimensional beings of the sub-level which waited for my return. I would normally exit the elevator down below and be filled with terror to the point of waking up immediately, yet this time, I had arrived at the elevator by choice.

Though the dream stalker was skulking around, I had returned to this dream so many times that I knew the order of events. I had also learnt shortcuts through the complex which existed to me in the dreamworld. Being lucid from much earlier in the dream, I had been able to make it to the elevators far more quickly than usual and without yet activating the hunt.

That meant that as the elevator doors opened, I was able to step out and finally see the next level of this dreamworld. It was a compound of sorts. I was in a quad section reminiscent of my current university, though only if it had been repurposed within a warzone. Still, the layout allowed me to navigate this next level with greater ease.

Seran was in this level, and I had to find him before the hunt began no matter what.

The shades of interdimensional beings were everywhere and searching for Seran. They were at ease, drifting around as though they had all the time in the world for Seran to walk into the spider web path they were moving in.

Fortunately, they weren't aware of my presence yet, though I had to keep circling back on myself to avoid them and my fear levels were rising. I was so close to Seran. I could feel him and expected to see him with each turn down a new corridor. As I got closer to Seran, I was able to locate him with some other sense beyond the normal five. I could feel his energy, and by the feel of his energy, I was perceiving his location through the walls and seeing his position as though a live action video was playing in my mind.

A beam of white light moved through the corridor and as it drew close to me, I felt a pulsation of energy rippling across my skin. The light, which had almost gone past me, now returned towards me. I felt myself being pulled away from the compound as different beings outside of the dreamworld tried extracting me from the sub-level

I still hadn't managed to reach Seran.

The beam of white light was following me, trying to encompass me. I took to running to avoid it knowing that the interdimensional shades would become aware of me and the hunt would begin, but I was not going to leave this place without Seran. It had taken over ten years to get this far.

I kept resisting the pull of the white light and shouted out for Seran, calling his name over and over again until I could see him with my own eyes. There was a shade between us, and we both had to run in opposite directions to avoid being caught by the darkness.

I kept on running and crying out Seran's name as we kept almost making it to each other only to find a shade or a trap blocking our path towards each other. Eventually, I realised our movements through the dreamworld were being manipulated by the shades as they played out a patient hunt leading us towards a place we couldn't escape. As soon as I realised that, I called out to Seran and told him to go backwards, still having to evade the white light which had multiplied into many beams that were trying to catch me.

As Seran and I finally reached an empty corridor, I sprinted towards him and wrapped my arms around him, holding on tightly as the white light caught up to the both of us. It felt like it would only draw me out of the sub-level, so I held on to Seran even tighter, digging my nails into his body in determination not to be pulled away from him ever again. I felt Seran mirroring me as his own nails bit into my skin and muscles.

Neither of us were going to let anything part us again no matter what, and the light pulled us both out of the sub-level.

Between dreams VI and VII, there had been countless other dreams happening so quickly that I couldn't keep up with them or write them down. There were some I felt the exhaustion of experiencing or the awareness of actions happening within dream, though I had no memory of the dreams at waking. Seran and I had been doing a huge amount of work at a deep soul level in those dreams.

These dreams were all occurring as I worked on the first draft of this memoir. It was as though the final acknowledgement of my *self*, my past wounds, and the ultimate display of faith to our connection had reawakened all the dreamworlds I had visited before losing my dreams. I experienced every dream I'd ever had including ones I had also forgotten about until that time. Each night, I progressed through the reoccurring dreams, re-dreaming every single one in order. In every single one, I finally reached the conclusion of the dream.

All the countless dreams of searching for that "someone" in my youth as I have mentioned before made sense. The stranger I was looking for and sometimes came close to was Seran.

In every single dream where one of us had been trapped or hunted, there was liberation. Where one or both of us had been lost, we found our way. Seran and I found each other in every single one of those dreams. There was so much more that I couldn't possibly recall it with my conscious memory, but I woke feeling it at a soul level. I know that deep within my preconsciousness, Seran has revealed a lot more of himself to me as I have no doubt reciprocated.

All that Seran and I have done in other dimensions, and what we do here in our physical existence since "I became WE" has changed everything, as though we shifted realities in some way and that was reflected in dream VII too. There was no more being pulled apart from each other.

We chose to run towards each other and hold on even knowing the darkness will always be around us waiting at the edge of our light. We chose to face the world together and accept our interdimensional relationship. We accepted that there are things beyond our control including this love. We embraced faith and surrendered into the unknown. We chose this time to connect in every possible way.

The runner/chaser paradigm is something put in place to prevent twin flames coming into union by spreading the belief that it is impossible.

If someone accepts the paradigm of runner/chaser, then they allow the belief system of disconnect, division, and disharmony to take route within the core of the self, and that will continue to generate repeating patterns of runner/chaser scenarios.

Ignore that paradigm.
Choose union.

The Butterfly Effect

"How do you know when to connect?" Perhaps there is no definite answer. After all my musings of when we decide to connect, ultimately, it will happen precisely when it is meant to happen. I will live my life to the fullest until then. I'll follow my dreams and my passions with faith that they will indeed guide me once again to Seran, as will he in return.

Divine timing may be absolute and require surrender to the divine, but I'm not abstaining from my responsibility of helping the union of Seran and I come into existence, and neither should anyone when seeking their twin flame. Surrender to the divine doesn't mean "be idle' because it's '*all in the hands of the divine.*' I have plenty of work to do by myself: healing, improvement, learning, my MA degree, maybe a PhD after my MA degree, and of course writing my books be they memoir, fiction or something I haven't yet tried.

I know I can't force things to happen when they aren't meant to and I certainly would never try to manipulate events or Seran, after all, he is also on his own journey. However, I can still work on finding my way back to South Korea or be open to travel elsewhere spontaneously and perhaps happen upon Seran in some entirely random and unexpected place, though hopefully it is not a train station he and I meet in an again. I can work on my own passions with my writing and my university degree. I can love my life and expand myself in every way so that my life continues to be fulfilling.

In doing all these things, I allow the divine to come in with opportunities that can lead me to Seran. The more I do and accomplish, the more doors that will open that will allow Seran and I to meet again with far greater ease than sitting at home and waiting.

When I first began writing this, it was to be as a release of holding all of these thoughts, dreams, and experiences inside of me for my entire life. I didn't know if I would seriously publish it or not. Yet, as I wrote the first draft, the divulging of long kept secrets and unspoken words did more than ease the suffering in my soul.

Within the month of writing out the first draft, my connection with Seran evolved into something more wonderous. All that we had had before remained yet had become honed. That which we had been unable to do for a time was slowly returning. Granted, our shared experiences and overlapping realities are currently carrying the burden of grief between us which has made it hard to compare what was happening, however the way our connection has evolved and strengthened over three years has allowed us to console each other far more deeply. It is from all that we have gone through and experienced that allows us the security to be so raw and vulnerable with each other, and to be comfortable to be in silence with each other.

For the first time in three years, pain didn't break our connection in one way or another. And even as we grieve together, we still work together and support each other. We both know that my parents are close by us in spirit, and they want this book to be released as much Seran and I.

This book is a creation of our bond and has become an active part in the connection Seran and I share. What was once a tool for release evolved into an object of manifestation. Now, it is altered again, becoming a tool of healing as he and I face some of our darkest days together. At every step of this book's creation and development it has served to connect us at a greater level; each chapter forming new aspects of the link to the bridge between us and opening up new corridors and pathways in our minds and to each other.

While we might now know when to connect telepathically, and we may have figured out how to traverse different time zones together or how to locate each other in dreams and almost reach each other in the physical world, there is no answer to when we will connect in physical union. Seran and I designed our own butterfly effect with this book. There is no knowing what will happen, only that something **will** happen, and that we are both ready for it.

Third time lucky?

...What Happens When You Have An Argument?

How does one even have a telepathic argument without physically knowing the other person? If you think of how easy it is to accidentally annoy someone you live under the same roof with or have been friends with for many years, then imagine how easy it can be to accidentally annoy someone when you exist in each other's minds 24/7. There are no solid walls or doors to retreat behind with telepathy. How does one make up after such a battle? Afterall, there is no way to Facetime each other and sending a text isn't an option.

As with any relationship, twin flames will bicker from time to time whether the connection is physical or energetic. Twin flames are just as human and as flawed as any other. Having such a profound soul connection and innate understanding of each other doesn't always mean that the ego and the conscious mind is up to speed. We are as human as anyone else and we have habits that might irk us over time. Although much of our lives are in alignment when connected with a twin flame, there's plenty that remains different and opposing. Those differences help is learn and grow together and individually.

Theological Enquiry

Sometimes our faith and belief systems are thrown into question. No one should have blind faith in dogma. Belief should be questioned and scrutinised. More often than not, that introspection is what strengthens faith because someone has had to explore what their connection with the divine truly is to them. If a question raised by another raises doubt about belief, then the journey to resolving doubt can only strengthen and improve those beliefs. Questioning my faith is something I have always done, not because I doubt the existence of the divine but because I seek the truth of the divine, not what has been projected upon me by some other.

Seran has been a fundamental part of that journey both before I knew who he was and now. Having been aware of my twin flame my entire life has been the main catalyst for the ongoing theological enquiry throughout my life, and it has also been the cause for undermining myself when fears arise.

Sparks fly when twin flames first come together. More often than not, most twin flames meeting their counterpart for the first time will only pass by them or briefly enter into a relationship with them. The bond between souls is activated as both awaken to each other, and then the next part of the journey is the hardest: the healing that must occur before twin flames can come into true union, usually with separation between twin flames.

For Seran and I, the biggest battle between us lay within our belief system or lack thereof. Seran was an atheist when the divine pushed us together. Suddenly, someone who follows a wild path of spirituality and magic crashed into his reality and shaken up his life of non-belief. Meanwhile, I had thought that by the time I was connected to Seran, I had finally come to understand my connection to the divine. Two polar opposite people and both somewhat in error.

Having a connection that is solely energetic and existing only within dreams and the astral realm creates a very different set of lessons to two who are in physical proximity. Never mind who slacked off on housework, why did the divine push two people together if they were only going to meet in dreams? That can lead to further harrowing thoughts and discussion as one or both attempted to fathom out the reason for such a miraculous love of that of twin flames to be held constantly out of reach like a carrot on a stick.

Learning to understand, communicate, and heal when divided by waking life means and love and mysticism are intwined and integral to everything. Before we could manage to learn about each other and face the more trivial aspects of human life, we had to figure out how to balance being within each other's minds. To do that, we had to spend time questioning what we thought we knew and believed so that we would stop holding blame for each other over so many things that were simply beyond us and stemmed from doubts of faith.

Our arguments were fierce at the start. Two souls clashing over things we didn't understand and the lack of understanding only made the fighting worse. The unknown and the uncertain were the source of blame. The silence that followed our internal battles was torture, however it forced us to reflect on what was said and thought by both of us. In the absence of the other during our blackouts, we had to face up to our self and to the divine presence to gain clarity.

It is impossible to explain the lessons Seran and I have had as both our connection and our faith has been challenged in ways that defy both logic and all things known and understood by humanity. We know them, we feel them, and we have our own internal understanding of what they are, however they do not translate to words. They're an understanding within the heart and the soul of immeasurably deep conversations with the divine and with each other. Perhaps that is the purest understanding of the divine, to know that that true knowing is impossible, nor is it something that can be put into words and doctrine.

Having our belief and faith shaken up and cast into doubt has been one of the biggest challenges Seran and I had faced, yet it is because of those challenges and lessons that he and I came to understand our connection far more sincerely. It was by first developing our connection with the divine together that we could continue to face the more human aspect of our relationship. There was a significant release of pressure when we both surrendered to the divine rather than fighting against every element of our connection that we couldn't understand.

Open up the Heart

In the previous chapter I discussed the use of safe words. The use of those simple words are not to be underestimated. Beyond the divine and the unknown, the use of those words were what allowed Seran and I to move past fighting it out at every moment. When Seran and I were first learning to communicate at an energetic level, we would inadvertently try talking to each other at inconvenient times: his work, my lectures, during sleep and periods of rest, and sometimes it was seeking the other's company and reassurance too much or too little. My random and spontaneous astral projection to him back then hadn't made things easier either to handle.

Another major cause of strife between Seran and I in the beginning came about because of the guards we kept around ourselves.

I have always been fiercely independent. I had to be if I wanted to survive. Growing up with both parents working in psychiatry taught me how to maintain autonomy of my mind. Going on to live in a house-share with a pro-manipulator who liked playing mind games for fun meant my mind and mental preserves were challenged to the fullest and left me in such a state of vigilance that even four years in Wales hadn't been enough for me to relax. No one was allowed inside my mind and having been burnt by people knowing the truth about me in the past, no one would ever know my fears or my secrets. I had rescued myself countless times, and it was me that had to comfort myself and pick up the pieces and put them back together every time I was hurt. Why would I suddenly let someone else do that for me?

Seran hadn't been able to comprehend why I couldn't trust him or let him come close to me. Unlike him, I was no one. No one knows my name. I'm not famous, I'm not celebrated in any way so why did I need to hide who I was? Although Seran had perfectly legitimate reasons to fear letting down his guard, it was hypocritical to expect me alone to risk everything and bare all while he remained safely hidden within his ivory tower. It was never a competition of who needed secrecy more; I had my reasons and he had his. But how did we both get past our reasons to hide?

He wanted me to depend on him, yet I had been supremely independent for my entire life. I wanted to depend on him yet he totally prioritised his career which left little space left for me to fit into his schedule.

He wanted me to open up to him yet would not himself be open.

Back and forth we went, around and around different areas of our relationship and connection having never wanted to give any quarter to the other. We'd argue. We'd fall apart and it would seem like it had ended once and for all between us, yet the divine would bring us back together again each time. It was exhausting. However, each time Seran and I were reunited, we would do our best to figure out what the root of the problem was and work hard to resolve our differences.

Over time, I realised Seran was the only man I've never feared coming into my space. He could come close to me energetically, within trance, and the brief moments of intense astral projection or possible bilocation. I wouldn't flinch or recoil from his touch and he felt the same way. We could finally lower our guard to each other and we made a pact that whenever we argued, we'd take a moment to think about the cause of dispute then discuss it until we found a way to resolve it.

It took a lot of time, patience, and quite a few battles and unsettling periods of disconnect before we made true headway in learning to communicate properly with each other. If something arose, we had to work out whether to deal with it there and then or to tactically put it on hold for a period of time and it's amazing how much difference one or two words can make:

Work. Later. Translation: I'm busy now, please wait. I promise we will take as long as we need to discuss this later.

Come. Translation: I'm free now, please come here.

Wait. Translation: I am busy but wait a moment. We might get chance to talk just now

Those are a few of the ways we learnt to navigate telepathic communication to minimise and avoid arguments and disputes. Using just a word or two when needed, Seran and I were able to communicate efficiently, and in the absence of arguments, we finally managed to open our hearts to each other.

We've faced the absolute worst of each other at different times: both at an egotistical level and at a soul level where there is no hiding away from each other. It's inevitable that we will still argue or bicker occasionally even now. We are both still human after all, however, we have both matured and calmed down with time.

We learnt how and when to give each other space without blocking each other out and being condemned to our blackouts. We learnt not take it personally if one of us asked for space, simply to back-off and know the other would come through when they were ready, although more recently, that has shifted once more and now we appreciate the silent company of each other no matter our mood.

...How Do You Respond To It?

How do I respond to my connection with my twin flame? The only way is to go with the flow of the connection. I tried fighting against the currents at the start. I had always been resisting Seran and I had tried denying him, I had even tried to cut the cord between us more than a few times. In the end, we always came back together. If I had continued struggling against the connection, there would have been unimaginable pain in both myself and Seran. I would have stagnated or become complacent in myself if I continued opposing the connection, maybe even driven to real madness from it...we both would have.

This chapter and the last were two separate questions, however I will start with a direct continuation from "what happens when you have an argument?" in "how do you respond to it?" as the arguments Seran and I had dealt with were what prompted the most "response". How we responded to any challenge, particularly our strife, was crucial to the evolution and development of our relationship and soul connection both jointly and individually. By taking time to feel into the discord between us whenever it had arisen, we began a journey of soul healing and development: the shadow work.

Shadow Work

Shadow work is inevitable. Anyone following a spiritual path will face shadow work at some stage along their journey, and this is especially true for twin flames regardless of where they are in their connection. Besides those who have devoted their life entirely to spirit and are free from the necessities and trappings of mundane human life, anyone claiming to be spiritually awakened and free from shadow work is either naïve or deceitful.

When shadows arise, there are two paths to choose from. Either they choose the easy way out and remain at the current level of existence with negative experiences and mistakes reoccurring in an endless, vicious circle, or they choose to face challenges and learn how to break the cycle and progress onwards.

Shadow work is an ongoing process and is different for everyone. While friends and loved ones can offer support and comfort, ultimately shadow work can only be done in isolation. It is in the silence of the mind and shadows where truths to many things are found.

Fear is often born from truths we reject and when someone finally submits to silence, their fears will rise up as a personal demon.

So often, we feel the necessity to fill silence with conversations and distraction, work, chores, anything that will keep demons and internal thought at bay. Spend some time in silence watching the people around you. What do you notice? That you yourself may reach for your phone or some other tool of distraction within moments of assuming silence? If you could abstain from satisfying your own craving for filling every waking moment with escapism and distraction, what do you notice about the people around you? That they will talk loudly and continually, butting into conversation, overpowering conversation, doing all with conversation to not even allow for a moment of recollection and/or reflection between strings of words and never once truly listening to the other?

We take that same attitude of thought into our private space. There's always something to ease the craving for distraction. The doomscrolling of social media is far too easy. How easy it is to start scrolling reels on Instagram or shorts on YouTube and suddenly, several hours have past...but at least the demons didn't get to speak, right?

In silence, there is a bombardment of social and environmental projections that rush to the surface. When is the last time you thought about who you truly were and not who society told you to be? To remember who you truly are requires diving into the depths of silence and shadows, to face your self-worth, your state of mind, the fears, doubts and concerns, the emotional wounds, and all other unresolved issues that lie below the surface.

Whenever we are hurt in some way, a piece of our identity is chipped away or re-moulded. The gathering of unaddressed trauma festering in the sub-conscious depths will find ways to manifest at a conscious level and are seldom recognised or acknowledged in a world where somatic exercises are being touted on all platforms.

Silence is the only place that answers are found.
Silence and a journey of introspection of the self.
Silence is where the path to walk is found.

Who Are You?

While much of what is faced in shadow work relates to the unresolved wounds of the past, something that is often overlooked when facing up to the shadows is that of identity. Many spiritual teachings advise that one must relinquish their ego to connect with the divine, but, how do you know what needs healing if you do not know who you are? Who are **you**? And who gets to tell **you**, a unique and individual soul, who **you** should be?

Ego: the conscious mind and part of your identity that you consider your *self*. It is "I am".

Granted, to be too much of the "I" in any area or subject of life is to be bombastic just as the rejection of the ego and the *self* (altruism) is as detrimental to health and wellbeing as being too much.

The ego is the self. Why would you reject your *self*? Your ego is your self-worth. You are allowed to stand up for your *self* and you are allowed to speak up about what you believe in. Your ego is your self-image. Who cares what someone thinks about how you appear and present to the world, if the way you do gives you joy and contentment? Your ego is your individuality and your character. Who would you be without your *self*? For anyone to reclaim their identity and discern that which needs addressing and healing must first acknowledge the ego – without egotism.

Altruism: The care and devotion to the welfare of others, even if it comes at personal risk of harm or damage.

To deny the ego in an attempt to heal such wounds, to be in favour of altruism to heal, is to place a bandage over the wound without any other attempt to prepare it for healing. Like someone who is bleeding may stick a plaster over the surface to stem the flow of blood before tending to someone else's wounds, denying issues of the self in favour of focussing on others will cause the wound to fester and worsen and the soul is drained like blood that seeps from an unsealed cut. All things must be in balance. Charity is a wonderful contribution to society, but only if the person giving charity is first stable and able to provide.

Another example of giving too much or too little without first balancing the self is to visualise a bucket of water with holes in it. The bucket represents you, outside of the bucket is your environment, and the water within is that which you can provide to the environment.

Egotism is to have barely a single drop of water falling from the bucket whilst the bucket continues to fill up and overflow and become gluttony. Altruism is having too many holes in the bucket that the water flows out quicker than it can be replaced. In the end, neither state of existence is beneficial to the self or to the world.

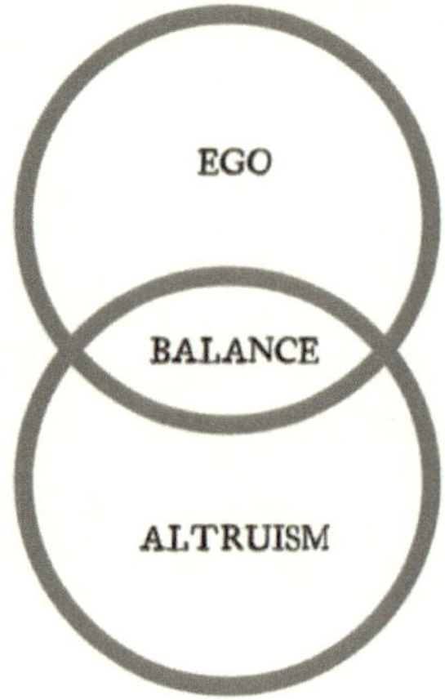

Balance comes when the self is balanced with what we give away.

It is important to understand that distinction of existence, as is perhaps a basic knowledge of etymology, before any kind of shadow work can begin, as it is your **ego**, your *self,* that is the basis and gauge for any and all healing work that needs to be done. This is exceedingly important when working with your twin flame. You need to know who **you** are, and where **you** begin and end. **You** have to be prepared to learn what boundaries are needed or not at any given time.

The biggest trigger warnings for what needs healing and what boundaries need putting in place come from conversation and/or actions that unleash an intense emotional reaction in someone. It may be the other person involved was entirely in the wrong, however, it is worth reflecting upon why the words incited whichever reaction they did.

We are all capable of distraction and/or thoughtlessness around others. We are all equally capable of being the one behaving badly and finding justification for what we did or said what we did. Empathy and discernment are useful tools in figuring out the cause of a reaction. Was it an issue of the ego that was highlighted and needs tending to? Is it a situation that requires boundaries be they temporary or permanent?

If words or actions bring out a visceral sense of shame, anger, guilt, or any other negative emotion, then it is worth considering the source before assigning blame to another. It is far easier to assign blame to another for ruffling your feathers than it is to sit in silence and consider why the words and/or actions of another brought out various emotional responses, yet it is from those triggers and reactions that we can find the source of the issue(s) and resolve them. This all comes from knowing and nurturing the ego inherently and accepting it for all that it is – the good, the bad, the ugly, and the flawed. It is those traits of personality that make us human and unique. Who has the right or the authority to take that away from **you**? Will whoever **you** worship respect **you** if you diminish yourself in anyway?

Boundaries

When you know who you are, you know what you will and won't tolerate. Boundaries are required to save a person from being hurt and/or burnt out.

Saying no to anyone who takes too much of your time and prevents you from doing what you want to be doing is fine. Why should anyone have control over your free time?

Saying no to allowing people into your life that talk down to you, belittle you, gaslight you, or in any way cause damage to yourself worth is fine. You do not have to tolerate anyone being in your life that makes you feel like shit. It's absolutely fine to tell someone to fuck right off if they start playing mind games with you.

Calling someone out for hypocrisy and/or disingenuity should be done.

It's fine to disentangle from people who won't listen to you when you stand up for yourself.

It's fine to put distance between those who constantly seek to bring you and/or others down.

It's wonderful and liberating to reclaim control of who you are and to set down boundaries that protect you.

Loved ones and friends can be the cause of negativity just as much as anyone else. If the harm they caused was not intentional, then telling them of the behaviour that was upsetting for you, and the setting up of boundaries won't be an end to the relationships. Those who are genuinely invested in your life will accept the boundaries without challenge.

You are the mean average of the five people you spend the most time with – online and energetic relationships count just as much as those in your environment. Sometimes a required boundary is as simple as being mindful of who you spend your time with.

Projections and Ego

It is Seran that taught me the most about my *self,* my ego. Wherever I would run and hide form my ego as if it was some heinous thing to be ashamed of, he would still see all of me and remain by my side. He was, and still is, proud of his ego. I had at times considered him egotistical for it, yet my concerns of his egotism come from the projection of "ego" that culture and religion have ingrained upon society:

Emotion is weakness.
Reliance on others is weakness.
Love is blindness and weakness.
Enjoying reward(s) is immature.
Being youthful is immature.
Money is evil.
Standing in your own power is repugnant.
Having high standards stems from fear.

This is especially prevalent upon women, so much so that far too many women take this same stance upon their sisters now which further compounds the issue and prevents everyone from truly healing – including the men in our lives.

Denying the ego comes in so many forms and the list of ways to diminish the ego is endless. These projections placed upon us by some other are designed to take away our individual and/or communal power as any dystopian story warns of.

Seran's ability to proudly acknowledge his ego while avoiding the trappings of egotism helped me to perceive my world and my *self* clearly.

I'll start with standards. Self-respect, loyalty, honesty, good personal hygiene. Far too often, people (exclusively men) in my local community have told me my standards are too high. Really? Is it wanting good personal hygiene that is asking too much? Or more likely, it's the fact that I refuse to take any shit and defy the above doctrines of society by choosing to stand in my power and allow myself to be selective. I've lowered my standards before and it was not worth it.

Each time that I had accepted a lower calibre of person into my life, they took my diminished standards to mean I would continue accepting less than I was worth. When someone tries to make out that setting high standards is any kind of wrong, it simply means they don't value you and they never will, whether that is a friend or a lover, a family member or a work colleague, or someone who frequents your life in anyway.

Seran has been the only male to step forwards and respect my standards and live up to them and he has been the facilitator in me lifting my standards to far higher levels than ever as we work together. His standards were definitely higher than mine which was terrifying. I couldn't help but wonder if I could ever be enough for him. Of course I could, and I was, the same as it is for all twin flames. We are mirrors of each other. The more self-respect and self-love we have for ourselves, the more this is automatically increased in our twin flames, and it does not matter who has the better standing in society.

The elevation of standards comes from improving the amount of love and respect we have for ourselves. The amount of love and respect we have from ourselves comes from how much we value ourselves, and that comes from the amount of time we dedicate to ourselves and to our improvement by spending time in silence and introspection so that we may come to know our ego, our *self*, and what it is that ails us. This returns us back to what shadow work is and why ego is fundamental to the shadow work journey and the work that needs to be carried out on restoration of the *self*. Grace of the divine can only carry you so far. Therapy can only help you through the doors you allow to open. You can take a horse to water, but you can't make the horse drink. If you want to drink, then you must **yourself** retrieve the water.

Working in Harmony

Twin flames will accelerate the journey for shadow work and healing. They will also be an integral part of the entire process especially when allowing the sharing of minds and being open to experience each entirely. How Seran and I ultimately faced our shadow work was to bear witness to each other's innermost secrets. Neither he or I could magically fix anything, but we could observe and listen to each other, and we could hold on to each other as the shadows brought our demons out.

Our strife had been the catalyst that had awakened each of our demons. Having already figured out how to balance our needs with each other and how to share our time with minimal issue, we could finally deal with other wounds that had been uncovered along our journey.

We found a way to overwrite the worst of our memories by first getting into an incredibly deep trance together, connecting with our spirit guides, and remaining impartial while watching negative memories. Over time, we would replay the memory, gradually adjusting it in some way until what was traumatic was removed and replaced with a healed memory. It was never a case of erasing the memory. Whatever the memory was, it was integral to our identity. What we did was find ways to take power away from the pain factor and reclaim it as ours.

An interesting realisation to come from that process was how, in re-writing one of my most traumatic memories as a child, he and I had shape-shifted into two wolves to run and play with my younger self. After coming out of trance, it suddenly hit me that I had been running in the place of that memory and imagined three wolves with me. The third wolf was Fenrir, my spirit guide who was overseeing the work Seran and I did. Just like the time in the B&B in Cornwall where timelines overlapped, Seran and I had done it again without meaning to. It showed us how interwoven our destinies really were, and that so much of our connection goes beyond linear time too.

What had been poison to Seran and I was also the medicine we each needed to heal. Being able to work harmoniously together with our shadow work whether together or alone as needed, we could begin healing ourselves from our ongoing pursuit of knowing of the self and what was needed. It required knowing where the *self* began and ended so that, as twin flames, we could recognise what was ours or theirs. It required the careful examination of identity and what had been projected upon us by external factors. It took time and patience as we slowly let down our guards to each other, took off our masks and peeled away layers of armour that we had incorporated to our beings with our prior need to survive the world and protect ourselves. It took time as we learnt how to fortify each other while creating space for vulnerability between us.

In "how does it feel?", I mentioned that a clear distinction between twin flames and negative parties was that, while a twin flame may be the cause of trauma resurfacing, they are different to negative parties as the twin flame **helps with the healing**. They don't bring out pain for gain and manipulation. They don't seek to summon your demons or to destroy you. They don't leave you or runway when shit hits the fan, although they may hideaway for a brief respite to process whatever was revealed. A twin flame stays by your side throughout every moment when their support is needed the most, no matter what.

I won't speak of the darkness both Seran and I have faced. It is both personal and at times, darker than what turns up in horror movies and may well be inspiration for future creative works instead. However, I can say that neither of us could have faced what we have if we had been in isolation or separation in those darkest hours. Though the final rounds of shadow work are faced alone in the darkest night of the soul – the final boss fight if you will – there is the knowledge that the twin flame would be waiting on the other side.

For Seran and I, we knew we each were a safe harbour for one another. While we might have to do shadow work alone at times, we were buoyed up by the strength of memories we had until then and the security from knowing we were cheering each other on and sending each other strength at all times. Having been able to hold on to each other throughout so much of our healing and to be supported by each other meant we had both become confident in knowing each other was a safe harbour we would return to, and that provided the strength and perseverance needed to face our shadows and conquer them.

Negotiations and Compromise

Sometimes in responding to each other, negotiation and compromise is what is required to maintain a healthy relationship, even one that is energetic. Being in a twin flame connection doesn't detract from something so ordinary as finding aspects of each other we dislike and needing to find ways to navigate such things.

One of my coping methods for an assortment of issues since my late teens has been smoking. Before I started university I had given up for just over five years. During my second year of my course, the strain of my studies on my various health issues, having to pause counselling due to demand on services at the worst conceivable time for me, and the downward spiral I was rapidly falling into, I took up smoking again.

I knew immediately that Seran abhorred my smoking and that was cause for more than a few arguments which only made things worse for during that time. I was making the best of a temporary fix in an attempt to make it to the end of my studies alive. Since we hadn't been seeing each other across the street never mind nose-to-nose, I had objected to the health lecture he would give me most days. This led to arguments, me trying to quit when I wasn't ready to and then restarting and feeling even more guilt and shame about by inability to quit while my mental health tanked

I don't say this to seek justification for my desire to smoke cigarettes and I'm certainly not advocating the vice. I am simply being genuine and honest about something that worked for me where pharmaceuticals could not and providing an example of the imperfections and flaws between twin flames, and how sometimes, we have to accept those flaws within reason.

Smoking raised my focus significantly, calmed my frenzied mind down. With an overwhelming blend of chronic generalised anxiety disorder, ADHD, and mild autism vying with ME/CFS and constant brain fog, the tranquillity and renewed clarity granted by my smoking allowed us to rationalise with each more efficiently. It prevented the violent ups and downs of my emotional state and, by default, that meant Seran didn't share in my fluctuating emotions which was something he and I had been tripping each over with.

In the end, Seran accepted that smoking was a part of me for the time being. He chose to respect me as a mature, responsible adult that made the decision to stop and start as needed provided it didn't become a 10 year+ habit like before and that I had intervals of being smoke-free where possible. That was his compromise for tolerance. He had realised that, while I may have had a vice he found repugnant, it wasn't something illicit and it had allowed us to finally communicate with each other from a more balanced perspective.

We had finally been able to talk to each other at a much deeper level when my mind cleared and he acknowledged that. I got a condensed health talk lecture once a week and light-hearted teasing every other day as part of the deal; and he knows that should he ever so much as smoke one cigarette I will never let him live it down.

There is far too much hatred and disdain directed to a person because what they're doing is something societally unapproved of, yet so long as something is within reason, sometimes it's worth acknowledging the person who is doing their best to just make it from one day into the next rather than to judge them and make them feel even worse.

Compromising around my intermittent vice isn't the only area of negotiation Seran and I have worked at. His work-life balance is an on-going negotiation as well as schedules changes and shifting time zone placement. Sometimes we both have to accept that a period of time simply means minimal zero connection as a result of the workloads we each have, and how our days overlap or not. Where that had once caused so much trouble, we learnt to prioritise our individual lives in those times while figuring out how best to balance our communication needs.

One thing Seran adjusted was the way in which he posted on social media to communicate to me. For a long time if I was in desperate need of validation and communication from him while full of doubts, he would leave me in the mental equivalence of a desert with silence being a denial like thirst. Then he would wonder why I developed an insatiable need for replenishment of communication from him. He would then respond by inundating me with messages via his posts which would make me feel better, and then he would repeat the cycle. For him, my neediness was bothersome and he thought that the cure would be to leave me to fend for myself and "get over it."

After my mother passed away in 2023, Seran made a point of communicating with me specifically to help me get through that time, which was when he altered his mindset. He made a promise to me then that he would never make me endure his silence again when I asked for him to communicate, and he has kept to his word. Even throughout times where he or I have needed to take time out from social media, he has found ways to reach me. With his shift on stance, our ability to talk and feel safe with each other improved exponentially and now, Seran enjoys playing with me with his posts and also uses it to test our telepathy.

It is never the case that only one person alone makes changes and compromises. For any relationship to be healthy, it is something that both people work on as a team.

Being needy for love isn't always a fault.

If someone had been lost in a desert without water came up to you begging for water, would you think them needy because they were desperate for water to cure their dehydration?

If someone had been starving until malnutrition, would you think them needy if they begged for food to ease their hunger and replenish themselves?

If someone had been denied love by those who were meant to provide it, especially in their youth, are they needy for craving love, love which so many have and take for granted the same way they do with water and food?

Facing Fears Together

From the pandemic lockdown period during 2019 and from being quite literally grounded, Seran had inadvertently developed a mild fear of flying, travelling, and agoraphobia which hadn't hit him until his first flight out of South Korea when the lockdown restrictions were lifted. As we discovered the effect of shifting time zones and geographical positioning to each other, that fear of travel shifted into some different and more complex that remained with Seran for over a year.

I would feel his anxiety rising as a period of travel approached. On the day or night of his departure, I would be hit by a wave of nausea which was especially unsettling if their schedule hadn't been released publicly and that was my first clue he was travelling. Even though I was doubly affected by both the physical sensations that were shared between us as well as my own reactive sensations to what I felt, I did my best to comfort him. If I could astral project to him, then I'd sit with him until he felt better. If I couldn't do that, I'd stay in a meditative state as much as possible and try my best to reassure him with words.

Another technique I would deploy was a skill I had learnt and mastered as part of my own recovery from generalised anxiety disorder. In my teenage years, my anxiety had been so bad that the panic attacks would cause violent convulsions before my body would get so tense it would lock into a clenched position and I would be paralysed by my own tension which caused further anxiety and a vicious cycle of unrelenting fear and pain. For years, I could only break free of that situation either after blacking out temporarily from lack of breath or by exhaustion claiming me first. Only then would my body finally unclench. That was also how I first discovered smoking was helpful in calming me down.

I had to learn slow my breathing down. A ten-minute cigarette break was the first time in a long time where I found myself able to slow my breathing down. It was also the first time I found myself enjoying the meditative silence that came with ten minutes away from anything and everything. Eventually that was transferred into a daily practice to meditate for twenty minutes and to focus on my breathing.

In defying anxiety, I now have a luxuriously slow rate of breathing (three to four breathes per minutes as standard), and I am able to bring that down to one breath per minute if I need to combat a panic attack. I have also since learnt different breathwork techniques including breath retentions on both in and out breath. All of these I have used to help calm Seran down as much as myself. Due to the interwoven nature of our souls, the act of instilling myself with tranquillity and silence would eventually flow to Seran and share those feelings with him too.

Over time, Seran developed the calming techniques I practised and he would return the favour if something made me anxious. The first time it happened was astounding. We had been divided by one of the time zone differences where our communication was minimal and I was trying my best to keep my stress and intense emotion away from Seran to avoid interruption of what he needed to do. In fairness, I was so forgone to stress I doubt I could have managed telepathy in that time. Without any communication of detail, the tension and fear I had felt vaporised in a moment. It took several more minutes to process the sudden shift of feeling and when I had, I realised that Seran had simply taken a few minutes to put himself into a space of deepest calm which flowed into me.

At time of publication, the connection Seran and I share within dreams and at a conscious level has exceeded five years. It has been a pleasure for both of us reflecting on the progress we have both made together, especially that which pertains to our fears. As an atheist that was suddenly paired with a magic using spiritualist, Seran was greatly fearful about much of who I was, and I in turn became fearful of exposing myself to him. It took time to heal the wounds we had inflicted upon each other and for me in particular, I now get to enjoy Seran being more competent than I at times when it comes to aspects of spirituality.

He is adequately smug as he now leads me through the astral realms and the dreamworld, and I allow it as I am proud of how far he has come. I enjoy the interest and passion he has for my way of life as we both strengthen our bond to each other and with the divine.

Boons of Twin Flame Responses

While much of the early work in a twin flame connection is spent in the trenches of shadows and demons fighting it out until healed, what comes out of a twin flame connection is wonderful. For something occurring that is negative, there are at least two occasions were the occurrence is amazing.

In 'How does it feel?' I mentioned how sharing experiences meant that I was of one body with Seran when he was sick. Awful as that was and I certainly never want a repeat, that ability to share physical sensation as much as emotion is extraordinary. While we might feel each other's grief and stress, we also get to delight in each other's victories and successes. The best feeling in the world is the euphoria we share in our finest moments.

As I am writing and editing these few paragraphs, I have waves of love and excitement flowing through me. Seran and I may not be communicating directly, but we're both awake and in alignment. He's just woken up and knows I'm working on our story and it excites him. He is delighted that I fully acknowledge him as my divine counterpart to the point I am telling it to the world. With each word I type or adjust, I can feel the bond between us pulsing through my blood, and through his. Butterflies dance in my stomach and joy overflows from both of us which often leads us to pull different faces as we attempt to avoid grinning like the Cheshire Cat wherever we each are. For me it is my university library and that entertains Seran no end as he becomes playful, our energies tickling each other and teasing laughter out of us.

That is our way of communicating with each other when we can't take time out of our day to meditate and talk. It is a simple way we can let each other know we're still in each other's thoughts and heart and is most definitely a boon to our connection. It has the added bonus that we both have so many random laughs throughout the day thanks to each other too. I can genuinely say that I have never laughed so much as I have in the last few years thanks to Seran.

Being able to communicate with each other about our experiences, to be comfortable discussing and debating theology and philosophy amongst a great many other topics, and to feel secure enough to share the secret of our work together has enhanced the work both of us put out. By virtue of there being two of us coworking even if no one else is aware of it adds layers of complexity and meaning to all that we do. Sharing our professional work together has certainly opened doors for me as I am sure it has for Seran.

The first short story I wrote during my MA course was called *Horologically Displaced* and was 100% inspired by and based upon the experiences Seran and I had. I was able to research a CIA disclosure document on astral projection, remote viewing and telepathy amongst other sources as part of my research. The sources of my research were handed to me before I knew I needed them and I'm certain it is because Seran and I work together on everything and manifest our future careers together that these things come into our realities, and that has sent me even deeper down the rabbit hole.

Whilst still down the rabbit hole, I intend to find out what the rooftile that started all of this incredible journey wants with me as the story of *The Demon of Munbigye* isn't yet finished either. I need to return to South Korea at least once more so that I can continue my creative research and finish that story. After all, absolutely none of this would have happened if not for divine intervention that came in the face of a dragon faced rooftile.

My lifechanging experiences of solo travelling to Seoul and to Gyeongju alone are the most incredible accomplishments of my life, and again, they are boons born from the connection Seran and I share.

Psychic Development

Throughout this book I've often mentioned telepathy and astral projection as a part of the connection Seran and I have with each other. They are both skills we've had to learn and hone along the way. The reaction to these psychic gifts has always promoted a direct response in both of our lives as we have had to first understand what was happening, and then always strive to further develop or redevelop the gifts.

As a child into my teenage years, I could astral project with ease. By my twenties I couldn't do it at all. When things started with Seran, I would go through phases of being able to astral project like I used to, then not at all. For most of the time with Seran, the fear and the arguments my unstable astral projection provoked in the beginning meant I once again lost that ability.

When I astral projected during my youth, I never thought about what I was doing, I just went. No one had told me the rules and no one told me what was possible or impossible. Growing up there were suddenly all these rules and caveats put into place. In the adult world, it was inconceivable that someone could astral project without intense training and mentoring from one guru or another spiritual master, and usually those were beyond limitless paywalls of extortion.

Everyone's journey through spirituality is unique. Some experiences and occurrences that happen are unanimous, but not everything. A lot of people will see a sliver cord attached to the belly when they astral project. I have never seen that, and I was told I couldn't be astral projecting and after, time my preconscious mind registered that statement and became my new belief. Yet, even without seeing a silver cord that someone convinced masses was real I had on countless times succeeded at remote viewing all with validation throughout my life – predominantly the occasions where Seran was involved.

Seran and I now know that the spontaneous astral projection that had occurred at the beginning happened because one of us called to the other. As a result of being grounded by fear, astral projection became something I had struggled with even though Seran began continually pushing for me to do it again. Slowly, I am relearning the skill, but I have had to unlearn everything that adult me has been told about astral projection. With his constant support and encouragement, and his excitement over me gleaning even the slightest detail of his reality the skill is returning, and this time, it has the bonus that Seran is beginning to learn how to astral project too.

The nearest I have gotten to a silver cord while out of body was during January 2023. It was an experience I had little control over. He and I could only go with the flow of with whatever was happening until it ended. On that occasion, there was a cord of prismatic light from my belly that was connected directly to Seran's belly.

With the prismatic cord also came the worst cramps in my belly that felt closer to childbirth than the worst period I've ever had, and I have been floored for over a week by some of my periods. With the first wave of cramps I was pulled from my body, into the cord of prismatic light and flung into Seran's body, and, as with the time I was inside of Seran's body when he was sick, we were both present simultaneously in whatever was happening to us and Seran felt everything just as much as I did.

With the second wave of cramps, both Seran and I were pulled out of his body, into the cord of prismatic light and flung into my body. I don't know how many times he and I went from my body to his, then from his back into mine, the coming and going from bodies went on for over an hour, all whilst having the overwhelming cramps that Seran also had to endure.

It really was the case of being flung too. Each time we landed in one of our bodies, it felt like our physical body was being dropped several feet to where we were lay with the surface juddering with the impact.

That kept going until we were both exhausted and Seran was begging me to "make it stop" as he needed to get out to work. Somehow with all that was going on, I was able to catch use of my body and sit up which halted whatever was happening although I could still feel the pulling sensation. I had to get out of bed entirely, go downstairs and put the TV on to force my concentration and psyche to remain solely inside of my body and relinquish its hold on Seran.

To this day we haven't figured out what that type of cord or soul shifting means and it hasn't happened again. Although since that event, the merging between Seran and I during meditation comes more naturally to both of us.

I would be curious to know if I looked in anyway different in the moments Seran merged with me. Unfortunately, I'm always alone when it does happen. If someone was present in those times and did see a difference, that would perhaps answer the question I raised earlier in "how does it feel?" when wondering if Seran's friend saw anything different when I was present in Seran's body.

The nearest observation I have to existing simultaneously with Seran and I inside one body happened the first time I was in South Korea and occurred after spending ten days in Gyeongju, the place my creative research for the rooftile required me to be. The time there had been profound in ways I can't explain. It was deeply spiritual and restorative. Whatever happened to me there, I just know that I changed in some way and it was beyond conquering so many fears to get there while travelling solo, I'd had that feeling of accomplishment in Seoul. What my soul found in Gyeongju was deeper. I had a tranquillity in my heart that I've only ever felt there. The connection I had with Seran who had, ironically, gone to my part of the world in that time, was as intense as when it first started in 2021.

As I returned to Seoul from Gyeongju with two days left in South Korea, I spent my time seeking out as many of the places I had meant to see but had been too anxious to get to. My connection with Seran had remained just as intense and I still held the magic and deep tranquillity of Gyeongju in my heart. I was sharing photos of every stop on social media chronicling every detail of my journey for Seran to see as he was homesick.

While I was on the metro line and listening to my music as always, I drifted into a trance where I was only half seeing Seoul as the train shifted between underground and overground. I ended up looking into the reflection of my own eyes whenever the train was underground and thinking how I looked different to how I normally see myself. When the train was belowground and the window became a mirror, I watched as my eyes were my eyes, then becoming his eyes, then reverting back to my eyes. It was the most peculiar and bewildering sensation and went on for at least ten minutes. Eventually, what I saw in the glass was Seran looking back at me. If I moved my body, he moved his body. It was more like Seran and I were looking at each other through a window and playing a game of reflection.

All of a sudden, I was totally out of body and in a space not-unlike the out of body experience space I had been within when I walked past him before. Seran leant forwards through the window and lightly bumped his forehead against mine and I was back in the train staring at the window as his reflection quickly showed me one hell of a smug grin before it merged back into my reflection and the train reached my stop.

The strength of our psychic abilities back then are what drive us to strengthen our abilities now. We both long for those abilities to come naturally and with ease as we desire them to, and not to be reliant on the whims and grace of the divine or cosmic influences. Fortunately, our psychic abilities are returning to that former level and better as we are in control and able to balance and sustain the efforts. The strength of our abilities has come from how we responded to both our connection and the shadow work that came. In being prompted to face our shadows and to heal, we could return to each other far more competently and with greater strength and understanding than before.

Re-Interconnection

Tangled in threads intertwining all things
interconnection of souls diverges,
then merges and converges at crossings

The wyrd weave of destiny evoking
their dreaming conjunction where shared thought is
tangled in threads intertwining all things

Breathing in self-healing, synchronizing
waves of electromagnetic pulses
then merges and converges at crossings.

Like a mycelium network sharing
messages to all its fibres touches
tangled in threads intertwining all things

Connectivity with everything
transferring energy that emerges
then merges and converges at crossings

Linked together their thoughts at last combine
Divine as one sharing their storyline
tangled in threads intertwining all things
then merges and converges at crossings

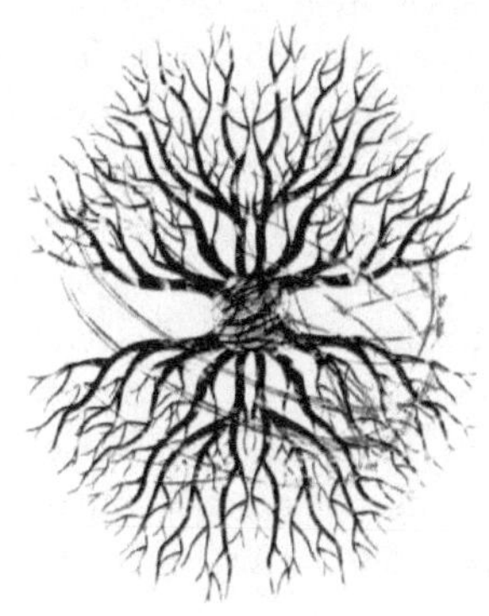

...Can Your Connection Aid Manifestation?

Yes. The short answer to the question "can your connection aid manifestation?" is that my connection with Seran can most definitely aid manifestation. This is most likely the case for all twin flame connections when awake to their twin flame, a conclusion I have come to from own personal experiences of manifesting with Seran; and also from a close friend who has recently been drawn to their twin flame who is phenomenal at manifesting synchronicities in particular.

Manifesting: the act of setting an intention for a wanted outcome or desired situation/object to come into a person's life.

The longer answer to the above question remains as yes, however, the extension of the answer is that how and when a manifestation will come in are reliant upon the complexities and nuances of each individual manifestation, the state of mind or one or more people involved with the manifestation, the reasons for manifesting, and much more besides.

Manifesting takes time, patience, and practice. Ultimately, manifesting as a twin flame is the same as manifesting outside of a twin flame connection: **you** yourself have to be in a healed mindset and in alignment with what is desired before it can come in. Whether it is love and union with someone or a new house that is desired, the mindset still has to be positive, grateful and open to receiving and harkens back to the importance of shadow work, ego, and healing.

There are plenty of resources available on manifesting, so I won't go into the mechanics on what manifesting is here as that's not what this book is about. However the question in regard to twin flames and manifestation is fascinating and cause for development within both Seran and I.

In the four years of knowing Seran, we've had to heal in countless different ways and learn about subjects neither of us had previously considered delving into. Our desires and needs changed too, as did the way we go about manifesting in general, especially in regard to trying to manifest union with Seran.

Why Don't I simply manifest physical union with Seran if manifesting is easier with a twin flame?

No one asked me this question specifically, but I'm sure that anyone reading this chapter in particular is wondering about this.

In the beginning, I tried too hard to bring our relationship into the physical and into my life. That revealed the negative aspects in me: lack of love, being too independent to make up for the lack of love/help/unity I had had in my life, lack of patience, the fears and trust issues I had developed and more besides. Trying to force a situation when it wasn't the right time was part of what caused the disharmony between Seran and I. He and I had been at considerably different levels in our individual lives.

Looking back, it's clear how our coming together before now would have utterly destroyed everything we had far more than the storms and clashes we endured. The damage of coming together before it was the correct time would most likely have been beyond reconciliation. I can now more easily accept that if he and I aren't together now, it's because one or both of us still has work to do so that we are energetically aligned and harmonising with each other, or that there are other lessons, fulfilments of soul contracts, and journeys to be made independently that are important to our individual lives as well as to our ultimate union.

Patience.

I won't lie, patience is a trigger word for me by now after being told "patience" too many times to count for over twenty years. My counsellor knew it, my study support mentors at university knew it, Jane who has provided the introduction and is who I go to for spiritual guidance knows it, my spirit guides know it, her spirit guides know it...and they all find different ways to say it without saying it now. Recently, I bought a piece of white howlite and on checking the benefits, I was once again told "patience." There is no escaping it.

As someone who is female and in their mid-thirties wanting to have children, it is extremely difficult not to be aware of that ticking clock, particularly when I come from a family with endless reproductive issues on both lines of my family. How can I find patience when my time as a fertile, viable female is ticking away and is perimenopausal? How can I be patient when as an ageing female where all that is wanted from men is fading from my limbs? Who wants to start a relationship with an older woman? What if my body fails me in any kind of way? It is too easy to fall into fear and continually feel as though time has almost run out, even more when society and social media continually serve to remind all of us of our mortality and finite vitality.

Yet, there's simply no forcing it. There are many things I can manifest with ease: a parking space, a job, the last hotel I used in Seoul, and contact from a distant friend.

With Seran, I can manifest an update from him and even be specific about the how. Granted, the latter is somewhere between setting intention and then asking him, however, as what we have is exclusively in the energetic realm and I am asking him telepathically, I do still consider it closer to manifesting than direct request. Manifesting meeting Seran in a specific place so we can finally come into physical union, however? That led to many failed attempts when I have been seeking him, and at least two failed attempts where I was painfully oblivious to his corporeal presence.

If it's meant to be, it will happen and only when it is meant to happen.

Did I stop wanting/trying to manifest physical union with Seran?

Neither Seran or myself have stopped manifesting physical union. The best way to describe our stance now is that it is an ongoing manifestation wherein we are both actively setting our desires to the divine whilst doing our best not to obsess over the outcome or the timeframe. We work on what we can do to help bring us physically together without trying to manufacture or dictate the path, trusting in the divine and the journey that by following our individual dreams and being open to spontaneity and redirection, our paths will unite.

Specificity is key to manifesting. The first time I saw Seran in Seoul, I had manifested that outcome without thinking about it. I had jokingly said to some friends back home how "it would be enough just to come face to face with Seran." And that's exactly what happened. It's that simple. Be succinct and specific then let go of the outcome.

Letting go of control is essential. When I knew I was going back to Korea, I was even more specific and more determined to meet Seran. I set the intention that he and I would meet properly so we could have a conversation during the dates I would be in Seoul. Specific? Yes. Too much control? Also yes. That attempt was an abject failure.

Detach from the outcome. Part of manifesting is balancing specificity without control of the outcome or the timing. In learning how to manifest physical union with Seran, I've been recalling past manifestations that were successful and how it had worked for me in those times.

An ironic manifestation I am reminded of whenever the cherry blossom season comes around is with a beautiful Sakura tree which was in bloom when I bought her home eight years ago. Then, no matter what, I didn't see the blossom again for five years. If I was at home during the time of blossom, I missed the blossom every single year for four years. Fickle spring and late frosts one year, March gales most years, deluge of rain in other years.

If the weather was fair, I still missed the short window of blossom by visiting my family even if I had switched travel plans each year in an attempt to enjoy the cherry blossom. Eventually I said to my father that 'I would be travelling to somewhere in Asia to see the blossom before I would see my Sakura blossom again.'

That was before I had even thought of starting higher education. Two years after my pandemic induced decision to go to university and being tormented by a rooftile, I found myself in South Korea with the cherry blossom being almost two weeks later than the official forecast. If the blossom had opened on time I would have missed seeing the spectacle due to being in the quarantine hotel.

I was in Wales during the spring of 2024 while editing this book and I finally got to see my Sakura tree in bloom for the first time. I had face-timed my father to show him the blossoms and share my realisation of what had happened, and we both had a good laugh at the absurdity of the outcome.

A simple comment led to me completely changing the course of life by starting a university degree, some divine intervention with a module switch around to ensure I remained on course to travel to South Korea – **TWICE** – and then at last, my Sakura tree could blossom in my presence. It took four years for that manifestation to come in. As the saying goes: be careful what you wish for.

Another time of unintentional manifesting was during a concert. A group of us were all feeling faint before the event started and as we planned how to help each other out once the concert started, one girl was really anxious of going down and not being able to get out. I jokingly said, 'don't worry, if I have to shout louder than the group so we can get security [marshals] to help, I will.'

In the midst of a concert, I had to do just that. I didn't think about it until afterwards as, in the moment, I was preoccupied getting her to safety. Under normal situations, there's absolutely no way my voice could be loud enough to rise above the crowd – yet as one of the musicians turned towards the din and their gaze locked straight on to me as the main source of disruption, I realised that my earlier words had given me the power to be heard when it was needed.

Further back into my life, there were other examples of manifestations that had come about because I had simply given the intention to the divine, let go of the how, and gotten on with whatever needed to be done to achieve it.

When I finally got around to learning to drive, I wanted to pass my driving test first time and I succeeded with that manifestation. I had manifested the best driving instructor to appear and put significant hours into learning to drive with him. During the test, I thought I had failed 10 minutes in as the driving examiner was drawing lines in his notepad constantly. I stopped stressing and figured I would keep driving until the examiner told me to stop. I past with four minors and still wonder what tally chart my examiner had been keeping during my test.

The cottage I live in now is also something I manifested in 2016. As I had briefly mentioned in the chapter 'What drew you to them?', I had put a highly specific wanted ad on a website and listed everything I wanted in that property including many factors that a tenant would be lucky to have one of and not the whole list. I put the town I live close to as the marker with a fifteen-mile radius. One week later my (now) landlord sent me an email with the property and everything aligned perfectly, even down to having the money needed for such a move come into my account as a windfall of backdated payments.

In both of those examples, I had put out exactly what I had wanted and then I left it open as to how and when that desire came in. That is what I now have to remind myself when working toward manifesting union with Seran, and what he has been learning from me as I go through the process of remembering and relearning and teaching him.

Anything and everything is possible, however the magnitude of the task to bring Seran and I into physical union also requires time for every little factor to line up. The way it works out or enters into our lives is best left to the divine.

Be proactive. Having accepted that things will happen with divine timing, what next? Our intentions are out there and we have faith our desires and goals are in alignment or coming into it. Next, we focus on becoming two people who are already in physical union. That is:

- Doing shadow work and necessary healing.
- Falling love with the *self* and with life.
- Reconnecting with the inner child and having fun as often as possible.
- Setting individual goals to live a fulfilling life.
- Trusting that in living our best life, our path will take us where we need to go.
- Knowing and accepting that where we need to go might not be where we want to go.
- Surrendering to the flow of destiny and embracing the unknown with excitement.

Become that which you wish to desire.

Flying Solo For A Time

Obviously for me specifically wanting to be in a physical world relationship with Seran, there are also certain things I can add to my list of what to do and improve upon. Learning Korean is a good start. That's an ongoing battle as I'm really bad with learning in general due to mild learning disorders and not being suited to the systemic educational model. I am doing what I can without access/funding for a personal tutor which is the way I would need to be successfully taught.

Why not manifest a Korean language tutor? I am working on that too, however my need to be face-to-face and not virtual would require a house move somewhere considerably less rural than my current location; and it isn't yet time to move on.

Some people may say that I don't try hard enough, however, having attempted to go to university and been blocked in some way until starting my creative writing degree is proof enough to me that when something is inexorably difficult to surpass, then it is a sign that it is not yet time. Burnt toast theory if you will.[13]

Getting into UWTSD Lampeter university was my third attempt at starting university. The first time I went to an open day at Roehampton university in London and had a violent case of swine flu come out as we waited for the induction. The swine flu nuked my health entirely for over ten years and I am only just recovered to a consistent

---

[13] Burnt toast theory: the spend a person spends remaking toast that had been burnt causes a delay in their day, and the theory suggests that that delay allowed for that person to miss disaster. A parable that can be expanded to larger spans of time in which delays in relocating address allows for dodging disaster that may have occurred should they person have moved sooner.

baseline which is considerably lower than before the virus. The second time I was offered a place at Falmouth University in Cornwall but couldn't afford to relocate as the local council had, that year, scrapped all funding to assist mature students access higher education. By the third time I decided to apply to university, I was already living in the Lampeter area and my application went straight through.

Moving home was a similar experience of being blocked until it was the correct time to move. I had tried to find a way to move to Cornwall for years as that had been more like home to me growing up and trying to get into Falmouth University had been my final attempt to make that move. There was never a way. But when I decided to move to Wales, everything fell straight into alignment as I mentioned right at the start of this book and earlier within this chapter.

These experiences of manifestations being blocked until an unknown, preconceived time for them to arrive while others came in expediently has taught me that manifestations will only come in when they are meant to. Certain changes in life will be blocked unless the change will benefit a person. It is by divine will and divine will alone. A continual reminder that patience truly is a virtue especially when it comes to twin flame connections, and that divine timing is when we will get to meet.

The saying "things happen for a reason" never made much sense to me for a long time, yet as I reflect upon my time here in Wales and how I came to be here, I can see the full value in that. Everything that I am now doing would not have existed had things gone differently. It doesn't matter what my life would have been like had I gone a different way, I love the life I have. I love who I am with the life I have. I am exactly where I am meant to be in this moment. Since moving isn't currently an option I accept that there are still things for me to do here in Wales and my energy is focussed on my studies and my writing which has precedence above all else.

I have mentioned before how the grace of the divine can only carry someone so far. It is not for the divine to do everything. Whilst the details of the outcome remain in the hands of the divine, it is still up to each of us to do the heavy lifting in our physical reality.

So what can I do while here in Wales that would help my ultimate desire to meet and enter into a relationship with Seran in the physical world? What can I do with my individual reality that would continue to make my life fulfilling and guide me towards Seran, as Seran mirrors this journey in his own reality?

I would love to live in South Korea which has very little to do with Seran living there. That he lives there and it would be easier to cross paths with him is an added bonus. South Korea felt like home to me in a way nowhere else ever has. I've only known homesickness since being there and the fact that I am not in South Korea right now and have no idea when I can go back is torture. I've had a lifelong desire to go east and have always been fascinated with China, Japan and South Korea in particular. The connections UWTSD has with China had been the deciding factor in my applying for UWTSD instead of looking for a different university and relocating. It's why I chose my modules to cater to that desire to get to China if not anywhere else. Then again, perhaps that lifelong urge to go east came about because my soul knew that Seran was there somewhere, and that was why the divine tinkered with the timetabling to make sure I spent my time and money going to the correct part of East Asia.

I am open to moving where it is I am meant to go, so long as the next place has a decent amount of sunshine per year. But who knows? Knowing my luck I'll move to South Korea or somewhere else, then end up meeting Seran in an entirely different part of the world for completely random reasons.

So then, how do I get to be able to live in Korea? As someone who is disabled and beyond regular employment, and also someone who is primarily a writer of fiction, that is something I am putting exclusively in the hands of the universe. I will be wherever I am meant to be and the means and way to get there will be provided for. I can, however, work on developing and refining my skills as a writer to make that outcome far more achievable.

Currently, I am rapidly coming towards the completion of my MA course in creative writing and I while I don't know what's at the end of my academic path, I know I'm going the right way. Everything throughout my time here at university has been nudging me towards the connection I have with Seran, particularly when I surrender to the flow of this journey and let things happen, as was the case when I started my BA in creative writing and allowed myself to flow and switch modules.

When the timetable was moved around, I could have gone against the flow and forced myself to continue with the second level Chinese module. However, in letting go of my need to be in control and by listening to my intuition which advised accepting the other module allowed me to get to where I am right now. In the second year of my BA course, I tried doing a module for Latin and didn't make it through the first week. I switched for an anthropology module and studied materialities of entanglement which opened my mind far more than I could ever have imagined, and what I learnt from that module has fed into my entire existence as well as my writing. Those two choices taught me to trust in the redirections as much as my intuition.

What I have been guided to study as part of my creative writing degree far exceeded my expectations. When I began my BA degree, I hadn't thought much about continuing on to do a MA. Now, nearing the end of my MA, I find myself considering a PhD after everything that has happened in the last few years, the connection I share with Seran, and the conversations this prompted with both of my parents my soul tribe.

There was a book my father gave me when I was in middle school: Quantum Mechanics. Obviously as a child, the contents of that book were way above my knowledge base and comprehension and returned the book back to the family shelf. Not too long before my father passed away, I mentioned the PhD idea to him. I asked him why he had given such a complex book to me as a child and he said, 'I don't know, I must have had a feeling you would need it someday,' and the following conversations that came from that discussion added more conviction to my plans.

Sadly that book is lost to me now, along with the insight my parents were able to provide. However, all that has happened including the messages from my parents while visiting my dreams proves to me that there is still far more to uncover along this journey, and that is the path I choose to travel while enjoying all aspects of my connection and relationship with Seran as it is.

Did Seran Manifest Me?

When considering how our connection can aid manifestation and reflecting over the ways in which we can manifest and the successes or failures of them, there is also the train of thought wherein lies the idea that Seran manifested me. Is all that occurred in the last few years because Seran manifested me into his life?

Before *The Dream* in 2020, I was satisfied with my simple life in rural Wales as no more than a writer of fiction, attempting to figure out self-publishing. I had been satisfied as an established single lady and utterly repulsed by love. If anyone has seen the film *Strange Magic*, I was a lot like Marianne – though a lot less cool than her. The path I am on now is not one I could ever have imagined, not even a two years ago as I wrote my BA dissertation. That I've become more than a writer of fiction in my pursuit to understand the magic and mysticism I give to my stories is a direct result of the experiences Seran and I have shared. And they all began after *The Dream.* Was I directed to study the rooftile because I needed to visit South Korea which is where Seran lives? Was he the one that had pulled on the strings of fate and called me to him?

My soul tribe and friend group entered my life after *The Dream*, after an entire year of university, after following my white rabbit – the rooftile, and after acknowledging Seran in my life. I have the best support mentors at the university, both of which allow me to have the most bizarre conversations that situated between academia and esoterica, and they were assigned to me after allowing divine intervention to alter my course. My connection with Elin online occurred during the same timeframe, another invaluable friend and ally along this journey with our twin flames. I would never have made it here without any of them, and they arrived only after my reality shifted.

So, was it Seran manifesting me into his reality all along?

In "how do you respond to it?" I discussed the ways in which shadow work, healing, and therefore, self-mastery were fundamental to twin flame union. That answer was based on the perspective of current knowledge and acting within a present moment. I also referred to high standards in the previous chapter, and Seran's standards are possibly far higher than mine.

Had I initiated a manifestation, the process of transformation I underwent were steps I would have worked my way through to level up, yet they happened as though the divine had summoned me from the sidelines, given me a dusting down and put me into rehabilitation and training with *The Dream* simply being the start of our conscious awakening to each other.

Something else that recently got me thinking about whether or not Seran may have been manifesting me or had put out further manifestations since is connected with my necessity to learn Korean (as much as he is learning English too). During early spring, I was overcome with an intense need to binge learn Korean. I put in countless hours into studying Korean and had the cognitive function and energy to do it.

As someone with epic ME/CFS brain fog as well as learning difficulties, concentration issues and difficulty memorising large quantities of information, the sudden ability to focus and consume the language at an exponential rate was unsettling after four years of barely shifting with my language proficiency. As a comparison, it took me a year to be able to read and write hangul (the Korean alphabet). I can't speak it as I don't have someone to work with on pronunciation, neither can I yet write purely from memory even with simple sentences, but the fact I can use the language learning app and remember 90% of the Korean I'd studied just by the prompts on screen was astounding.

There are other changes I've suddenly been struck by which is a combination of Seran's manifesting me right at the start, and the shared efforts of manifesting a better life both individually as much as together. One more recent shift in direction of particular interest is my sudden desire to live somewhere which, quite frankly, was the last place I ever wanted to live until recently. I know it's a place Seran has a lot of love for and I believe my new desire to live in that place with him stems from the fact he is considering that place as a serious potential location for his future. I noticed the last two times he was in that location, I felt more excited than him at times, and how my excitement overflowed and filled him with even more joy.

It is for those reasons that I am open minded to moving wherever is right for me as guided by the divine, rather than trying to force a relocation that I think is what is best. The sensation of feeling home while in South Korea may exist simply because that is where Seran resides, and that home is actually with Seran wherever that may be.

Manifesting Together

Now that Seran and I are energetically resonating with each other, we are able open up about all our desires and dreams, and to boost each other. There are at least two events in his life I inadvertently helped him manifest without realising it, though unfortunately for you as the reader, I can't say what those are as they're identity sensitive. He and I get to be privately smug about my ironic and off-hand remarks that landed him major life events. Now if only I could manage the same level of off-hand conjuration for Seran and I meeting up physically...

The main takeaway Seran and I have learnt about manifesting either alone or together is that it has to be fun. The simpler and more enjoyable the intention and manifestation, the greater the chance of success. How manifesting together always comes with a higher success rate is that we have so much fun together and our combined energies in those times act like a turbo boost to our manifestations.

We began testing our ability to manifest by requesting a parking space in town. We had started that back in February and had worked out that for me and where I live, it took a minimum of ten minutes to assure there was a parking space. For it to work, it required gratitude and full concentration. Being distracted or not entirely cognisant whilst manifesting a parking space usually led to a space being not quite the right size to fit into, or some other eventuality that denied me access to the space.

If I reached my destination quicker than ten minutes, I'd end up having to park elsewhere, then as I got closer to my destination on foot, I'd see several cars all pull out of the roadside parking as the divine honoured the manifestation and humoured me at the same time. No matter the outcome of my games in manifesting a parking space, the outcome always gives me a smile because it's something I can so easily calculate and watch unfold. Having told a couple of friends about this process, they too watch with entertainment as I succeed or miss, and how funny the results can be. Coincidentally, if I am working directly with Seran for manifesting a parking space, the space for me to park in is more expedient than when I manifest alone.

One time I had overslept and was running late to get into town to meet my friends. My manifesting was rushed and only half-hearted as I dashed around the kitchen feeding my cats and tending to their litter trays. Sure enough, there was no space. I was entertaining Seran with my usual morning ramblings, so he was along for the journey as I turned around further in town, came back along the road and found a space towards the end of the road and pulled in. I sat for a moment considering my options, then, I heard Seran saying clearly, 'I promise if you pull into the side road and turn around there, by the time you come back this way, your usual parking spot will be free.' I turned around in the side, went back, and there was my parking spot waiting for me – proof that working together expedites manifestations, especially when having fun with them.

This challenge coincided with writing the first draft of this book. It had been intended to lead into further, more challenging games of manifestations. Unfortunately, both our lives took another devastating blow as my father left the world of the living to rejoin my mother. In the last year, Seran and I have both had far too much loss in our lives to comprehend anything more significant than surviving each day and making it through work and studies. Much of our energy has been dedicated to ensuring we both make it through this time whilst trying to buoy each other up and not be lost to the darkness of grief, and many of the plans we had at the start of this year fell apart and have been forgotten.

In place of major reality shifts, we took to being silly and playful with our manifestations instead of attempting to decipher a specific formula for manifesting.

Whenever I am in my car, Seran and I communicate telepathically if it's during his waking hours. It's been that way since our connection started in 2021. While driving to the beach during the summer of 2024, I asked for the divine to show me a purple car if Seran was truly my twin flame. I saw at least ten cars that were an infuriating shade of maybe/maybe not purple or blue. Remembering myself to being specific, I asked for a clear purple car not thinking until much later how "clear purple" doesn't exist as a metal paint job.

With the ongoing and indecisive shades of purple-blue vehicles, I switched it to that of a yellow vehicle on my drive back home. There were an abundance of yellow construction vehicles along the road and I didn't know if that counted or not, so when I was halfway back, I switched once more to green. Nothing happened from then until I got back into Lampeter, and I was just starting to get disheartened when a really odd shade of yellow car came into view immediately followed by a neon green vintage motor. As I pulled into the car park of my local co-op store, there was also another infuriatingly purple-blue car and a pale metallic green car parked up. That gave both Seran and I a well needed smile and we continued manifesting a "definitively purple" car throughout the week instead.

I was then, during the week that followed, called in at incredibly short notice (four days) to write and perform a poem for Violette Szabo's Special Day at the start of July. With three days of intense research, writing and editing of the poem plus a roundtrip of 160 miles for the event and recital all combined, I was way over my energy reserves by the time I had to drive back home.

Seran kindly stayed awake into the silly hours for him in South Korea so he could talk to me in the car and help me remain alert. Being silly, we found ourselves resuming the game of asking the divine for a specific colour car to be on the road with us. For absurdity and volume of demand, we both graciously asked for the divine to humour us on this occasion since it was helpful for me to being thinking of cars on the road and looking out for them. It kept my attention and focus on the road where it needed to be.

Each time we asked, the coloured car would be on the road ahead of me within five minutes. Neon green cars, orange cars, yellow cars. At one point, Seran asked for a "sky-blue car" to come in, and it was at that point I realised we should have been more specific about the shade of sky blue, as I myself have a sky-blue car. I'm not exaggerating when I say that I saw every single possible shade of sky blue over the next twenty minutes.

At one point, Seran and I discussed the viability of the colour cars coming in purely because we had asked for them. I pointed out that the current choice for cars tended to be monochromatic these days. Coloured cars are few and far between, especially vibrant shades. With that in mind, one or two different colour cars coming in as we asked could be considered fluke or coincidence, however the rate we were asking for coloured cars and the way in which those colours came back at us that evening was far beyond coincidence.

About 20 miles from home, I was driving through a small town when my gaze was turned ever so slightly further to the left to check a junction. There was a definitively purple car parked up. Seran and I chuckled and continued on with the drive. He then joked about how funny it would be after if all the requests of a purple car from the previous days resulted in the purple car following us.

Five minutes later it was sat behind me. So Seran decided to try something even bolder which really tested my ability to not be overcome with doubt. He asked for the next car that was driving towards me to be black. We saw no one driving in the opposite direction for a few minutes and my doubts about seeing a black car specifically were starting to gnaw at me. Then, a black car went by, followed by two more black cars.

Again, that could be perceived as coincidence, especially with black cars being so prominent on the road, but after all insane amount of vibrant colour cars we had asked to see along that drive, we were well over fifty back-to-back manifestations of specific-coloured cars by that time, and every single one had come in without fail.

I then decided to up the stakes myself. I asked for a pink car to be put right in front of me. I knew that it was highly unlikely to happen that night with less than ten miles left to travel in an incredibly rural part of Wales. I wasn't expecting it that night. I used the pink car, which is usually a custom paint job, to show Seran how the divine can bring anything in, but the more specific and niche the manifestation parameters, the more time it would take to be delivered. It was synonymous to our coming into union, with the arrival of a pink car to be both a finite sign and a reassurance to us.

Not to be finished with the game of coloured cars, Seran then said it would be even funnier if, after asking for a definitively purple car so many times throughout the week, the one currently sat in my rearview mirror also took the next junction with me. It did. Purely to turn around and return the way it had come.

The following week, the definitively purple cars continued flocking into my small rural town. I mentioned it to a couple of friends who are on the road a lot and even they cannot believe how many definitively purple cars they are all now seeing on the road.

The success Seran and I were able to have with the above games on the road came about because we were synchronised to each other and working together, and we were having gratitude and fun with the manifestations too. It's a reminder how the divine invites us to seek joy in all things, and if we play sincerely and with gratitude with the divine, things work out far better than expected.

Four days after asking for a pink car, I was catching up with some housework upstairs when I suddenly felt my gaze drawn to the road right outside of my house. There was a pink a car directly outside my window and stuck in traffic just long enough for me to see and register the event.

Being able to work together to manifest so successfully in this way assures both Seran and I that we can definitely do this for bigger and more important aspects of our lives once we have both managed to heal and recover from our grief.

Until then, we'll keep with our simpler manifestation games which bring us delight and humour most days, something of which we both need more than anything else right now.

Love Spell

With such ease you cast me under your spell
From dreams I awake craving your passion
Your kiss upon my lips that would foretell
Our journey of enthralling attraction

From dreams I awake craving your passion
Weaving magic became instinctual
Our journey of enthralling attraction
That had us both hooked upon ritual

Weaving magic became instinctual
Our love spell an intoxicating drug
That had us both hooked upon ritual
As our paths are entwined as one, my love

Our love spell an intoxicating drug
Never again shall we say a farewell
As our paths are entwined as one, my love
With such ease you cast me under your spell

The Unasked Questions

Although the title of this book may have started in a moment of humour before it became the title of this book, the title became even more appropriate considering how this all came into existence from a lecture in writing for therapy. It gave me chance to ask myself questions. What do **I** want to say? What do **I** wish people knew about me? In 'How do you respond to it?' I discussed accepting the ego. How often had I shunned my ego, my *self*??

There is also an element of the fact these topics are the ones I have most wanted to discuss with people. Being mildly autistic, and many of these are also some of my "special area of interest" topics. Years of being silenced, ignored or mocked for talking about my interests, I developed the attitude of, 'don't talk unless spoken to,' and, 'don't talk about anything unless asked.'

It was only through university and my wonderful student support that I was finally given space to exist and to express myself. Whether it was my modules, my assignments, my personal life, or any other topic, for the first time in my life I was given carte blanche to talk about whatever I needed to talk about I began to rediscover so much of who I was and who I used to be.

Though people are often too busy or too engrossed in their own lives and realities to make time for anyone else. I at least realised that, as a writer, I had the luxury of writing my story down. For many years, I dispersed many fragments of my life within the fiction I write both as much to handle my alienation as it was to give credibility to my characters and their lives. Why not simply write my story instead?

Having shunned my ego and concealed my truth for so long, I chose to give myself a moment to reveal the parts of me I wish people would know. Therefore, I decided to include 'The Unasked Questions'. Since the questions provided before now didn't allow space to fully open up about some of the more challenging aspects to a twin flame connection, I allowed myself this opportunity to give my *self* a space to be heard and seen, and to give more context on subjects that were far too complex to have summarised or paraphrased within the other chapters or to expand on the previously mentioned topics. These are also topics that need to be included to make sense of the connection Seran and I share, and why at times I felt totally unhinged.

As this book is written in partnership with Seran some of the questions were suggested by him, not because either of us have withheld the answers to the questions back from each other, but because they come from some of the deeper discussions he and I have had. They help portray the depth of our connection we share, the reality and viability of our relationship, and perhaps some of our experiences here may help at least one other person struggling to understand or cope with the challenges twin flame union brings up.

What is Telepathy Like?

I found it curious that not one person asked me what telepathy is like, how it is experienced or how it feels – in the literal sense of how telepathy feels – or of the emotional and mental strain of telepathy. The psychic connection Seran and I share is fundamental to the connection we share. We've been communicating in this way for at least four years and it takes all of my self-control to not talk about it either with excitement or stress with my friends, depending on my mind set on any day.

I decided to open 'The Unasked Questions' with the subject of telepathy as it is a topic I have touched upon throughout the book already, and because it is the aspect of the connection Seran and I share that have been cause for the challenges and quandary over mental stability.

Is it Reality or Madness?

Out of everything I have experienced along my twin flame journey with Seran, telepathy has been the hardest aspect of our connection to accept. I grew up being told magic wasn't real, that any form of extra sensory perception was all my head and part of an overactive imagination. That is something the majority of us who have been born and raised in the western world have been told our entire lives; an irony where the major religion of the west pertains to being able to hear the voice of the divine without expectation of the divine's manifestation upon the physical plane.

A major reason that taught me to fear talking about my experiences happened when I was seven. I was playing with some friends in a field that had two entrances, and my team had been hiding in one of our hedge dens when I had an intense moment of déjà vu.[14] I had told my friends what would happen next, that if they went a certain way, we would get caught by the other team. and that we should go the opposite direction to avoid them. The group I was with thought I was being silly and didn't listen. I had had total conviction in what I had seen during the moment of déjà vu, and so I had set off determinedly on my own to prove a point. At the opposite entrance to the field, I had looked back and seen my team being caught by the other group exactly as I had seen except for that fact I was no longer among them as the vision had shown me.

I discovered I had an amazing gift of foresight and then immediately lost it as a result of what then happened. The price of my discovery was that I was ostracised by everyone from then on and then later bullied severely as I progressed into middle school, and again with high school where several people I had used to know had made several attempts to kill me through the years of high school. Somewhere between being told I was making everything up by one group of people and their continual gaslighting me until I doubted everything, another faction of people had seen it was real and, whatever their motives, had taken to making my life a terrifying hell until I rejected my identity. With the loss of my identity, so too went my belief in anything and everything.

It wasn't until after I moved to Wales and started university that I finally met with people who informed me the experiences were real with many of them having had similar experiences themselves. If they hadn't, they knew someone who had. My soul tribe: a group of people who had all left England for similar reasons and all found their way to Lampeter and to each other.

---

[14] Déjà vu: the sensation of having already experienced what is happening in the moment, that the insight gleamed from experiencing déjà vu offers foresight and the potential for adjusting actions.

That said, it still took three years of regular reassurances from my soul tribe for me to reaccept myself and allow my psychic gifts to exist without fear and, ultimately, to open up about twin flame connections to them. I discovered that three of my close friends had found themselves quite recently awakened to their twin flames.

When my telepathy with Seran began, I hadn't talked with my soul tribe about it as it seemed a stretch too far even for them. Fortunately, I had Elin to talk with back then. Though her experiences were different, she was willing to listen with openness and patience as she too had surreal experiences herself. From those discussions alone, it was clear how different each twin flame connection was, and that telepathy can also manifest in different forms of comprehension and feeling.

For Elin, she didn't have the direct thought-to-thought as Seran and I had when we first began talking, and as she was my only source of gleaning viability at that time, I struggled with the concept of telepathy. I tried to ignore Seran's voice, then later tried to rationalise with it. I also began dodging the topic with Elin as it had caused negative emotion between us, and, as always, my personal takeaway for better or for worse was simply to never bring the topic up again.

In a world where someone's admission of experiencing anything preternatural was probable cause for sectioning, or at the very least at being made a laughingstock and ostracised, who else could I talk to about a psychic connection? Having to once again struggle with my thoughts and my fears in isolation, it got the point where I had become so stressed and fearful that I really had gone mad that I had inadvertently taken to tugging at my hair for many months until it started breaking off in chunks.

In 'how do you know when to connect?' I mentioned confiding to my mother about Seran. The pressure and internal torment inside of me had gotten so intense that, had I not had that conversation with my mother, I would have probably ended up in a truly desolate place. For a year after that exchange, I was then able to turn to her whenever things got really bad in particular, and for that time, I had been able to cope the best. Having had the opinion of a psychiatric nurse absolving me of my fears, I had for a time felt entirely normal and accepted with a great many profound discussions coming out of the initial revelation.

Unfortunately, I lost my mother during the spring of 2023 and, in her absences I haven't had that safety net she had given me. There are too many times where I'm so close to falling back into that chaotic vortex of deliberating my sanity that causes unimaginable pain to my soul. That had been enough to prompt me to have the same conversation with my father. His immediate response was the same as my mother's: that I wasn't insane. Although he didn't have an anecdote about a family member with a similar experience, he opted to inform me about all the trials that had been performed for testing telepathy. It turned out to be an topic of great interest to him from a psychiatric perspective.

It was more challenging to discuss Seran with my father though. I did my best to be mindful and sensitive to the fact that love was still an incredibly raw wound for him to talk about. However, from the two discussions he and I had held, he too had been able to reassure me more pragmatically than my mother had. Or perhaps it was having both of my parents having reassured me of my sanity without a moment's hesitation or pause to doubt that had had such a powerful effect on me.

During September of 2023, my father and I went to stay in Northumberland for what would have been his and mother's 40th wedding anniversary. It was a holiday that was equal part a celebration of love, a celebration of my graduation, and a reunion with our family that still lived there which was why my father and I still went even though it was a bittersweet voyage.

We were lucky to be in the northeast of the UK when the geomagnetic activity was at its highest. One night, my father and I sat at the beach waiting for the northern lights and talked our way into the deepest conversation he and I had ever had. He was always a man of few words, yet what he said always held gravitas. He said, 'I hope that if we have to do all of this again, that I would meet your mother again, and that you and [my brother] would be our children again.'

Just like that, my father revealed his thoughts on soul bonds, reincarnation, and the depth of love he had for all of us, and most of all the depth of love he held for my mother. In just a few words, he could tell me that he understood what my love for Seran was like. The love my parents had shared had been weaving them closer to each other with multiple near misses until it was the right time, and even though my mother was in spirit, their love still existed truly defying death and refusing to break.

From the NDE I had experienced and the intense pull between Seran and I, I could only begin to imagine how that pull must felt for my father with his twin flame in spirit while he remained with the living, but I could empathise with him,

As the emotions of the conversation my father and I had discussed ebbed gently into the night with our tears, we returned to more philosophical approaches to these occurrences, all of which came with the backing of my father's psychiatric background and expansive knowledge on psychology (there is a difference between the two) and reading of scientific phenomena. At that time, I had been reading a CIA disclosure document on remote viewing and working through *The Gateway Procedure* by Robert Monroe, the source of intrigue for the CIA disclosure. My father and I realised that I had unwittingly found myself in the realms of science that could provide some form of evidence or credibility to these experiences we were having.

I had hoped to discuss this to greater depths with my father over time. Unfortunately, he too left this world, and with it, my final refuge from the questioning whether or not the experiences I were having were of reality or madness.

I continually have to mediate myself and my raging demons. I will likely always have that niggling doubt until the day Seran and I meet again. I have learnt that to doubt isn't always detrimental. It's how a person responds to doubt that matters. If my doubt was detrimental, I would have given up. I would have stagnated and never made it to where I am today. I may doubt, I may hesitate, but I keep going with faith.

Faith is entering a stairwell knowing that the stairs will take you where you're meant to go. You don't see the end, but you know the steps will take you there, so you step up no matter how long the stairwell is.

With faith I am learning to have certainty in my connection with my Seran and my abilities. As I allow the connection with Seran to deepen it becomes clearer that we have countless moment of undeniable proof of our connection. Little snippets of information he has given me about his work or where he is, the glimpses of him while dreaming or astral projecting that show him in real time and so much more. Most are fleeting moments of connection, but those are beyond the count. Fleeting or lingering, whatever information I received from those moments of connection is nothing I could have known before Seran shared it with me, and it would always be before the topic was revealed by the internet.

This became an ongoing game we play with each other with social media becoming the way we later authenticate our exchanges. With such posts, it's similar to the time on the fan board where much of this began with the way the content practically pops out at me. Engagement with his posts unleashes a wonderous flood of euphoria and an intense connection with each other as though his physical world post created a confluence for our souls to converge and celebrate each small testament of telepathy.

How does it work?

Figuring out how telepathy works is something Seran and I have had to work out purely by our own experiences. There is no guidebook for telepathy and certainly no guidance for when two people have never met in life and speak different languages. As to how it works, as in the mechanics of it, I'm still not sure. What I write here is based upon my own experiences. However, these experiences and my ever-inquisitive mind have shown me a door for further exploration and investigation pertaining to the mechanics of telepathy combining philosophy and scientific thought, so perhaps there will be a second book in the future that considers the content of this book more objectively and from an academic standpoint.

From the experiences and communication so far, the telepathic exchanges happen somewhere between the conscious self in the current moment of linear time and the higher self that is connected with the divine source and exists beyond linear time. The messages we share arrive somewhere between consciousness and preconsciousness. Those messages which arrive to the depths of our minds emerge as intuitive messages and dream revelations, though they have the potential for time distortion.

Trying to discern whether a message I have from Seran is direct and moment-to-moment, or whether it is out of time is an ongoing confusion. When he or I switch time zones, our telepathy is even more unpredictable. Learning to gauge what level of Seran's consciousness is at has taken a long time and a lot of trial and error and allowing for time discrepancies.

There have been times he's told me he's at a certain location and sure enough, the internet has proven that he was indeed at that place shortly after Seran gave me the information. Then there are times he's told me he's somewhere and it's been twelve hours or more, yet the event still happened identically to the foresight. The latter happens most often when one of us has switched time zone, hence the term "horologically displaced" being an ongoing in-joke between us.

If our conversations are happening simultaneously then the topics are primarily more simplistic and mundane: how are our days going, how is work going, are we each resting/eating well, etc. There's a lot of affectionate teasing and banter between us too, and the conversations we have can be so ordinary. The one time someone other than Elin asked what Seran and I talk about, they were shocked when I told them we talked about work. They never asked again.

I can usually tell when the conversations Seran and I have had are happening moment-to moment as he will suddenly go abruptly silent in the middle of the conversation which can be anything from a few minutes up to several hours depending on the environmental distractions. Again, I really can't tell you how essential our safe words have been for navigating all of this.

I too can be distracted by my environment and get bumped from a conversation. Probably my most commonly used safe word to Seran is, 'CAT!' followed secondly by a highly specific noise created by me when said cat puts his or her paw and all of its weight right into my solar plexus. The number of conversations my cats have managed to interrupt and end are beyond the count.

There are times when I try reaching out to him during the day when I know he's working but not the specific schedule and there will be silence for variable amounts of time. Those were moments I had to learn to take a deep breath, relax and get on with my day rather than stress that we had suddenly been disconnected. There are also times when Seran in particular is travelling in different time zones and the habitual routines continue. Sometimes no response or connection comes back and I'll remember he's asleep. Other times I've accidentally woken him up as he has woken me up too.

There are also occasions where I've realised I am talking with Seran's higher self. I will get in-depth downloads on spiritual topics such as explanations of the dreamworld, the akashic record and how telepathic exchange works in particular regarding time, language, energetic grids, and soul bonds. One such time, I was at my spiritual development circle and participating in an overshadowing exercise.[15] While communicating with Seran's higher self, the person who was leading the circle suddenly swore loudly and dropped to the floor. She had seen Seran's higher self clearly looking straight back at her – one of the experiences where another has encountered Seran in a way to validate my experience.

There are times where it's harder to discern the state of consciousness that Seran might be in. We have profound discussions about many topics, our fears, our dreams, and so much more. I now know it doesn't matter what level of consciousness those conversations are held. The words are still shared from heart to heart and understanding is reciprocated. We both know that whether he has spoken to me whilst I have been sleeping or I to him when he has been sleeping, the conversations are still valid. It just means that we get to learn about each other all over again in the physical and delight in discovering how much we already knew without knowing it.

Language is inconsequential when communicating energetically. I speak English and Seran speaks Korean, yet energetically the words translate to the nearest counterpart. There have been times where I've noticed Seran is communicating to me in English as the words come much

---

[15] Overshadowing: a spiritual development exercise and mediumship skill. One person, a sitter, will sit comfortably and put themselves into trance and ask their spirit guides to come in. The others who are present then observe the sitter to see who comes in and how they manifest over the sitter.

slower and have a simpler sentence structure as that is him using his own knowledge base and comes with the slight mispronunciation of letters. His English is far better than my Korean. I couldn't make up the ironic yet somehow remaining fully affectionate tone he can take when I have tried speaking Korean back to him...bearing in mind my current level of Korean is less than elementary and he finds my attempts endlessly comical.

I have dreamed in Korean a few times, and in these dreams, I had total understanding of what I was saying even whilst recognising it was Korean. Unfortunately when waking up, I forgot everything – including whatever Seran had said in those dreams as he had responded in Korean.

I have also concluded that telepathy in itself is a form of language and functions not too dissimilarly to light language.

When Seran and I first begun communicating, I would get atrocious headaches which freaked us both out since headaches are often associated with demonic possession. The headaches were especially worse at times when I resisted the connection to him, or he to me. Now, I seldom get a headache except for when one of us has gone somewhere new and/or the time difference is interfering, but even those are much milder than before.

The reason I concluded it was a language headache comes from when I started learning Korean properly. I had an intense headache for a day or two after each lesson I gave myself, and that reminded me of when I had taken the Chinese language module at university during my BA course. After each lecture, I would have intense and persistent headaches until my brain had become familiar with the language. At the time of my Chinese lessons, I had had a conversation with a friend on that module who had what he called language learning headaches. When it happened again with my learning Korean, I took to some online forums for language learners and discovered that quite a few people had the same experiences especially if learning a language that was a completely different system e.g. a European native language speaker learning an Asian, Cyrillic or Arabic language system.

Telepathy still required use of the brain to work and it makes sense to me that it would stem from the same part of the brain where language is learnt, developed and utilised. And, as with learning any new language, it required ongoing practice to develop and, again like the learning of a new language, eventually the headaches would cease once the brain had acclimatised to the new skill/language.

Whilst language isn't a barrier with telepathy, there are still things we are unable to communicate with each other. Specific locations are one topic that doesn't convey well unless we have created an energetic and physical confluence with a location such as through communicating via social media in some way. Likewise, we can only refer to people who aren't mutually known by their familial connection or work affiliation.

The rules and boundaries of sharing information are a complex topic grounded in free-will permissions and magical rights. Thresholds exists, and names have power. Both should only be offered up by the named person themselves. At an energetic level, those permissions are absolute. When we have tried sharing names or specific locations, there's a momentary silence or a static distortion.

One example of an energetic threshold is that of Seran's parents' home. The first time he went to stay with them after our connection began, I couldn't reach out to Seran in any way. We didn't know why at that time as we were still figuring out connection. The next time he went back, he had shared a picture of his room and with that, given me permission to enter his room, and his room alone.

Though Seran was happy for me to connect with him anywhere in his family home, his opinion didn't matter. It was his parents' home, and unless they gave me permission to enter, then I could not enter. This was the case with meditation, dreaming, astral projection and especially with remote viewing.[16]

As the connection with Seran developed, I would always share my learnings and experiences with him so he could learn with me. As I explained the rules of thresholds too him, and as we discovered the mechanics of our telepathy, he told me that he would briefly mention my existence to his parents, and maybe a little more depending how the conversation went. This he has clearly done as I can move freely around the communal parts of the house when Seran is there.

The names of locales are also something we can't easily transfer to each other. This is in part due to threshold rules, but also that our place names have no translation equivalence to draw upon. How much we can share of our location depends on the depth of connection in any given moment.

When I was in South Korea the first time, Seran guided me around much of the city far better than my phone could especially as it had very limited battery life if I was running Kakao Maps.[17] The way in which Seran guided me around the city with him saying things like, 'go left,' or, 'keep going that way.' It has been difficult to know whether that was Seran's higher self or Seran's conscious self with the extremely heightened ESP and intense connection we had during the pandemic. At times, his navigation was being coordinated from his physical location such as the time he was sat in a car in Seoul and directing me to where he was specifically in that moment.

The ease of that communication of place came because I was enjoying my music and going with the flow. I

---

[16] With remote viewing, it is possible to pass over thresholds if someone is determined enough. However, I respect the threshold and have no urge to cross where I haven't been permitted to.

[17] Kakao Maps is the Korean equivalent of Google Maps.

hadn't set out to find him and so I wasn't trapped in my conscious brain with the ongoing warfare of "is it real or not?'. I was simply trying to find somewhere to get coffee where my social anxiety and lack of language skills wouldn't impede me. In the process of sending me all over that small segment of Seoul, he had also taken me to what I needed: a cashpoint, a convenience store, a couple of restaurants that were good for my dietary issues, and finally a coffee place with a machine for ordering that had an English language option. We were treating the internal Seran-Nav as a game and were having fun. He was telling me to loop around the block and come back, and at one point even said, 'why aren't you looking here?' That made no sense until after another loop around the block and some affectionate name-calling and I finally clocked the car... Moment-to-moment telepathy.

Another time I was able to enjoy Seran-Nav came when I travelled down to Gyeongju. Seran told me I had to go see Namsan.[18] I thought he meant Namsan in Seoul and I was sad I wouldn't get to see it. After checking in at the guesthouse I was staying in, the hostess's son who spoke English spent some time informing me of the best places to check out in the area and told me that I had to see Namsan if I could. I hadn't planned to walk up any mountains during my time in South Korea, so I hadn't looked at the mountains to have known about Namsan before then.

After putting everything in my room and unpacking, I made my way out to explore and decided to purely trust Seran in his guidance once more. I ended up walking through a huge field and was just beginning to doubt myself and his guidance when I saw a river ahead of me, and then after turning to follow the path by the river at Seran's advice until I arrived at an historic landmark, *Woljeonggyo* bridge. On

[18] I could perceive Namsan as it was a word I knew from learning Chinese and Korean, and because that word has a literal translation equivalence: south mountain.

further exploration of the place I found another dragon-masked rooftile on display which had been calling me to South Korea all this time. That was somewhere between moment-to-moment telepathy and some degree of Seran astral projecting to me to see where I was to guide me.

Dragon Mask rooftile photographed by LJ Bremer at Woljeonggyo, Gyeongju.

With telepathy there are other ways that we communicate too. Something I have done since our connection started was to envision something if it was easier to show Seran what I meant rather than try to describe or explain it. I've noticed recently that Seran has started using visualisation to help communicate too. If we're in trance we often create an inner world to sit within particularly if we're talking for a while. Other times if we're talking in more casually or in a lighter meditative state and want to show something, we'll imagine it internally and show it that way e.g. a red or green apple, or as I should include here, the rooftile that started everything. I believe that in showing Seran that rooftile, that was how he could guide me to the ones he knew of at a later time.

Many times over the years Seran and I have discussed and compared the different ways in which our brains work. I have always been very internalised and visual where he has been predominately external and aphantasic.[19] I find it fascinating that Seran has started using imagery now as it shows how he has changed and developed over time, where I will now sometimes describe and explain things more analytically rather than create imagery.

One of my favourite internal worlds was created by Seran when he first started visualising. It was a huge sunken garden with a glass roof, but because he was new to creating inner worlds and engaging with his imagination and visualisation skills, it was incomplete with patches of nothingness, particularly with the sky or further away from where he and I were. He hated it for a long time, but I loved it. There was something about its flawed incompleteness that gave it a different kind of beauty. The fact that it was his creation and he had shown me how much he knew me to create an inner world so perfect for me made me love the space all the more and we still use that space most now both for our in-depth conversations and for meeting with family and ancestors in spirit.

The more Seran and I develop our telepathy, the more all of our physical senses become a part of our telepathy. In 'How does it feel?', the vast majority of feelings an extension of telepathy. It is how our connection feels emotionally and physically, and it is also the most significant way in which we transmit information to each other, and

[19] Aphantasia is someone without a visual imagination. The brain doesn't form or use mental images as part of thought. Hyper-aphantasia is someone who has an extremely visual imagination. This is most commonly exampled by the test to visualise an apple: someone who is aphantasic will see nothing, while someone who is hyper-aphantasic will see it exactly as it is in reality.

that transmission is 24/7 prevailing even into our sleep and our dreams.

In 'How does it feel?' I also wrote about clairalience. Being both sensory and transmissional, clairalience is both feeling and telepathy. Food and perfume seem to be the two scents that we exchange the most and quite a few of our conversations over time have been interrupted by me asking him if he was eating certain foods. We also get the scent of each other upon us too, which usually occurs either from sharing a dream or when we've spent a significant amount of time in trance together when our souls are most resonant. It's really disconcerting to suddenly be aware that I smell of Seran, of muskiness and manliness and not at all how I ordinarily smelt.

I have joked with Seran that having become so familiar with how he smells and how intoxicating his scent on me is, there is chance that in coming close to one another in the physical world again, I may end up tracking him down like a bloodhound that has picked up his scent.

Clairgustance: the psychic sense of clear tasting.

In the last couple of months, taste has been a new development to our telepathy and psychical connection, that of Clairgustance. There have been a few times where Seran has eaten a dish and I have had the taste of it in my mouth. Whilst this is entertaining for Seran as he is often in cities where any and all worldly foods are locatable with ease, it is a level of infuriation I didn't know could exist until attempting to track down my Seran induced food cravings in rural Wales where my options are seriously lacking. This happened most recently with Seran having Mexican cuisine which is one of my all-time favourite cuisines and created an unfortunate craving. I was going out of my mind for days until fortunately, one of my local eateries had tacos on as a special and I was able to tend to my craving.

Physical sensation is another significant aspect to our telepathy. As I discussed at length in 'How does it feel?', being able to feel his energetic presence close to me and at times, feeling as though we were lying curled up together is one of the best aspects of our telepathy. It reminds us that we are both in direct contact and union right now, even if it isn't conventional or "normal". There are times that I'll be relaxed and minding my own business while idly talking with him and I'll suddenly feel his breath against my skin, or that my hair or my clothing has moved with no other force in my physical environment. I've felt the cushions move or the blanket on my sofa will suddenly drop down. All proof that our connection transcends the borders of our physical bodies and realities.

My cats are also proof of the connection Seran and I have when not interrupting us. There have been occasions when one or more of my cats have been chilling out with me. They will sometimes stare at where Seran's energetic manifestation is as though seeing him there. Other times, I'll be meditating and connecting with Seran and one or more will come charging over and sit in his presence.

Nero who is most often in close proximity to me will be resting a foot away from me minding his own business when something out of the ordinary happens and he and I will look at each other as if to say, 'wait, you noticed that too?' He also enjoys Seran's company the most of all my cats. He will indulge Seran's ethereal attention most of the time, and I have often remarked to Seran that Nero must actually be his cat since he is most often with me when Seran is present, and if not, he will appear from the cat void in minutes.

Wunjo is the overbearing cat who loves Seran yet will come and strike my face if I start going out of body to connect with him in the astral realm. Nothing compares to being grounded by your own cat who is also a master of interdimensional travel and bilocation herself.

Buster was my father's cat and is the latest addition to the household. He is the most squirmish around Seran's energetic presence as it's all very new to him.

What is interesting is how all three cats know exactly where Seran is even when he is present energetically. They can move towards him and stop where his energy begins. If they want to move away from him, it is always away and never through him. My cats seldom come into our inner world. The boys have little interest and Wunjo is usually only there fleetingly as though she is the teacher checking up on her pupil. Recently, there was an occasion where all three turned up during a mediumship session within my spiritual development circle. I don't quite know why Wunjo decided on the expedition that night, but she brought the boys along. That was the first time Buster properly met Seran within the astral realm, and he has been totally unfazed by Seran's energy since then.

A final, comical telepathic exchange Seran and I share is that in the form of a sudden, intense sneeze. In Japan, when a person sneezes without any reason (allergies, dust, etc), it is supposedly because someone is talking about them. This anecdote was one that Seran wished to be included here as it gives him endless entertainment, and whatever your thoughts are on this particular experience, hopefully it provides you with some entertainment if nothing else.

This phenomenon of sneezing out of the blue is something I have only experienced since my connection with Seran begun, and suggests he is talking about me with the people in his life. Prior to telepathy with Seran, I would only ever sneeze with the extremely rare colds, or when Wunjo would brush herself against my face.

Since I started talking to others about Seran, he has had this happen to him too, though only when I have on rare occasions referenced him directly by his name in conversation. This was always the source of jest between us as it seemed so unlikely to actually be credible. Then one time when he and I were deep in trance and talking, we both sneezed at the exact same time and had the energetic equivalent of narrowly avoided head butting. I couldn't resist from melodramatically asking him who was talking about us and he laughed himself out of trance. From that moment forwards, when one of us has as sudden sneeze we can't help but continue the melodrama of shouting, 'who?!' when that happens.

This recently took a new level of entertainment for us both. Seran recently disclosed far more about our connection to his parents, mayhap even the thing about our sneezing. As Seran was regaling how the conversation with his parents had gone and what he had discussed, we shared another tandem sneeze. He suddenly burst into laughter and said it must have been his parents, and that because he was talking so intensely about them to me, it must have caused them to sneeze first and at the same time as each other, and with their subsequent questioning if Seran was talking about them to me caused our joint sneezing.

If nothing else, it's funny to think that the first conversation I may have had with Seran's parents was in the form of sequential sneezing.

What four years of telepathy with Seran has taught me is that it is undeniably real. It may not make sense or have an explanation, but it is one hundred percent real. What I have also learnt from a few friends who have disclosed some information about their own experiences since first writing this book is that communication works at an energetic level (telepathy) for most twin flames and can manifest in subtle yet different ways, as is also the case with Elin which you will discover in her chapter later on.

Having made the executive decision to keep this memoir as purely anecdotal, I opted against including references and citations from other books and sources with varying degrees of credibility, however, I will include a section on further reading for anyone who is wanting to delve more deeply into the mechanics of telepathy at the end of this book.

Passion and Sensuality

One of my friends would likely have asked this specific question if I hadn't told them in advance that this topic was off the table.

An exquisite delight of the connection Seran and I enjoy is that, with the shared sensory experiences we have, there are no limits to that which we can feel and appreciate both from each other and together. That is how the kiss in *The Dream* was such a wonderful and exhilarating experience for me, and how the moments when Seran and I are curled up together are as intense and amazing as if we were truly cwtched up physically.

Being able to experience all aspects of our connection and relationship has led to us both learning so much more about ourselves and each other. It's been one of the major driving forces in really coming to understand all the ways in which we can provide ourselves with self-love, and how that care and devotion to self will also uplift the other. It's especially taught us how finding ways to incorporate the senses in any way we can heightens the experience, such as our love of using scent and perfumes to communicate.

The decision to keep this question off the table came about because I knew the people who were providing questions, and I knew that what they would have asked would have been for the juicy details regarding sex and energetic connections. Even while writing a confessional memoir, some things are best kept secret. I don't kiss and tell.

The Best of: Quotes from Seran

This was another of Seran's suggestions for inclusion with this memoir. Some of what he comes up with is so random or so out of my own systemic thought pattern that his words alone can convince me of the reality of our connection. We talk most days and I do not log every conversation or funny quip as that would be as ridiculous as writing down every comment a close friend or loved one makes in a day.

I've mentioned a few times throughout this book how internalised my reality is, and what that means is I have a nonstop running commentary which means Seran sometimes finds himself caught up in whatever mental task is running at the time, and then I'll end up asking him his thoughts or opinion or if he knows the answer. Being both dyslexic and dyscalculae leads to comical banter such as, 'don't ask me! I can't do the numbers either!'; and, having been trying to figure out how to correctly spell: "supercalifragilisticexpialidocious" with someone, I ended up asking Seran whose response was 'how should I know, I'm Korean!'[20] Similarly when I've been pondering over my day or what may come later in the week, I've ended up asking Seran random questions pertaining to people I know in my local community, and one of his best, most ironic answers to date is; 'how should I know? What am I, a psychic?'

Another comment that has remained with me even without writing it down is due to the comedic nature of during my first time travelling to South Korea and my arrival in Gyeongju. This happened during the same exchange Seran had mentioned visiting Namsan to me while I had sat forlornly on the doorstep to the guesthouse wondering what

[20] Fortunately, spellchecker knows how to spell the word. Apparently I had been wrong all this time...

to do with myself for two hours before I could check-in. I was getting cranky and he suddenly said, 'go get a burger and you'll stop being hangry,' [*then, an hour later having followed his directions to the coolest ever Burger King and being sat eating my burger finally feeling calmer*], 'you really do get hangry don't you?' Hopefully he never sees the UK Snickers advert or I will never hear the end of it.

With my ongoing, albeit somewhat intermittent pursuit of learning Korean, there has been plenty of affectionate teasing from Seran whenever I have attempted to engage with him in Korean such as, 'aww, you managed to say a three-word sentence [in Korean] to me,' and then a year or so later (I really am a dreadfully slow learner especially while splitting my focus on my BA and MA degrees), 'hey, you got to five words! It's only taken you two years to say an actual sentence to me in Korean!'

Something which isn't a quote but an action and still worth including here occurred in a time when I was highly anxious and about to spiral even while astral projecting. Seran leant into me and blew a raspberry on my neck. It completely stunned me into silence before I fell about laughing at how random it was and the fact I had felt his lips tickling my neck. I've had chronic anxiety for most of my life and nothing like that has ever happened no matter the daydreams I've had. There is absolutely no way my mind could have written a script like that in less than a second to jolt me out of my funk.

Finally, one of my favourites for both content and deadpan delivery of a message from Seran came whilst I was washing my dishes and listing off locations of where my cat may have displaced a particularly rare quartz when he suddenly said, 'may the quartz be with you.'

Do You Never Think You're Just Crazy?

Considering the people I know in life knew that both of my parents had worked in psychiatry, I found it interesting that, as with telepathic experiences, no-one ever wondered what it might have been like for me having had all these experiences with a mother who had been a psychiatric nurse and a father who was fully trained as a psychiatrist. The combination of all their learnings meant they had a vast knowledge base of psychiatry and psychology, and many years of observing both in practise in their fields of work. Although I've talked about my ongoing battle with my sanity already, I haven't yet had chance to fully explore what it's been like having those battles with parents such as mine.

It wasn't easy speaking with either of them. Growing up, both had at different times told me to stop daydreaming, that magic wasn't real, etc. I can accept that their words came from a place of knowing that for many young people, a lot of what I experienced was simply nothing more than imagination and learning to understand the world. With magic, it may be that they wanted to protect me. Magic is something that no one should take lightly no matter the path taken. This is also something which crosses into spirituality. Psychic and energetic protection is the first thing anyone should learn before trying to astral project, communicate with spirits or anything else.

As I matured into my teens I became emotionally distant with both parents. My mother worked nights and we were like ships passing in the night – literally as she would be asleep by the time I woke up and waking up a few hours before her shift. My father had gotten so stressed from work that he was in no mood to speak with me as I returned from school and he returned from work. That was a major contributing factor that led to me internalising everything as

I spent countless hours in my room listening to music and trying to make sense of everything by myself as I escaped to other worlds within my mind.

It was during my teenage years as this dynamic between my family peaked that I became most adept at astral projection and astral travel. Although I hadn't realised what I was doing, my necessity to both escape the trauma and hellish reality I was going through, my curiosity about magic and mysticism had pushed me into discovering my spirit guides and how to walk through different realms.

My guides, one in particular who had been with me from childhood, were able to give me answers and push me further along my journey to comprehending spirituality better, however they were unable to authenticate themselves. I often carried the thought that Fenrir, my wolf guide, may well have been an imaginary friend I never let go of, yet it was he that presented as the third wolf when Seran and I had been doing our healing work. At the age of seven when that had happened, I hadn't yet discovered Fenrir. Ironically, it is probably that moment when timelines crossed that opened me up to Fenrir as a child.

Being able to discuss this whole subject with my parents only changed as my father took early retirement, and then again as I left school but was unable to get work due to the delights of the 2008 recession. I was around home more and could begin to redevelop my relationship with both my parents as there was also more chance of spending time with my mother on the days between her work shifts.

We began finding common ground and would have discussions about paranormal activity. We all shared an interest in life beyond earth and what might exist beyond death. Both of my parents had countless experiences from their work with patients on the threshold of life and death for different reasons which had proven to them that there was some sort of predestiny for everyone.

As my parents and I grew to know each other again, they would regale some of these stories into the early hours of morning after we had watched something on TV such as *Ancient Mysteries*, or more recently, *Skinwalker Ranch*.

Although these shows and various books we had been reading at times served as an icebreaker for delving into various subjects of esoterica and all things preternatural, it was still a challenge to fully engage with the questions I held deep inside of myself, and as it turns out, both of my parents had held inside in turn. I had become fearful of what my parents might say to me through their reactions during my childhood, and they had likely become wary of talking openly about such things due to whatever may have occurred or been said during their childhood or as a result of having to be so guarded while working in psychiatry.

My father was always more taciturn and harder to gauge for what he believed in. That was how it took until the last couple of years to open up to him. I was always cautious with what I shared with him in case he poo-pooed me as he had whilst I had been a child. Then one day, he suddenly began talking about one of the psychiatric hospitals he had worked at as having "sick building syndrome". He explained how they had brought someone who was an expert in Feng Shui in to do a consultation on how to improve the energy of the building, and how the changes implemented from that consultation had gone on to improve different aspects from within the building and the people who came in; everyone from the patients themselves to the employees.

I had allowed my father to share the entire story before then politely having it out with him about how he'd called many things I had shared with him nonsense when I had been younger but was now admitting he had no issues with sick building syndrome. He gave me a wry grimace which was one part almost-apology and one part realisation that I had reached a point in my life where if he back-tracked on anything or slipped up on what he had said to me growing up, I would call him out on it. It was also a moment of realisation for him of the nature he had imbued in me which would likely haunt him and had been a running vein of humour in many things until the end.

There had never been a time I truly held the things said to me in youth against them or caused me to harbour any resentment or grudges. I have been writing fiction from a young age and have always lived my life on the cusp of what is real and what is imagined. Being able to distinguish reality from illusion is a fine line to balance on, and I was privileged to learn much about psychiatry from them as I grew and developed.

As I hope to have children of my own, this balancing act of allowing for strong imagination and play and discerning what stems from preternatural gifts is something I myself would have to figure out. With those thoughts in mind, it always allowed me to empathise with my parents by considering my own future and what I would do the same or different to how my parents raised me.

Extra sensory perception and alternative knowledge historically comes with a societal stigmatism. Consider how many women were killed for being witches when in many cases, what they knew and were being blamed for came from old folk remedies for healing as one single example.

Growing up, I would often hearing generalised stories of experiences both parents had on different wards and those of anonymised patients.

My mother, whilst always being highly mindful of what she was saying so that she never compromised anyone's confidentiality with her as a nurse, would sometimes talk about one patient she worked with that was diagnosed with schizophrenia and in full time care, and how they were likely diagnosed with that disorder because what they came out with was societally deemed delusion and mania, but from her experience when she took the time to listen to them, everything they said over time was incredibly coherent and articulated and usually shifted from one specific "voice" or "voices working harmoniously together". She based her quiet observation against that of other patients with the same diagnosis who were – in a clinical sense – easily identifiable as mentally unwell with the "voices" being discordant and more senseless.

What that patient had discussed would likely be perceived in an entirely different way if they were living in today's world where it is almost commonplace for someone to openly talk about communications with extra-terrestrials and interdimensional beings as they had done. Society may frown upon such a person or call them various slurs, but they would be free to talk about such topics and have an ever-growing audience and more credibility as more people are speak out about "messages" from other sources.

I mention this particular example as it always gave me reason to consider what is really known and understood by anyone. How much of what is accepted or considered normal in any age is put in place by the reigning societal power within any given culture, and how easy it is to be labelled as crazy or unfit for society because an experience doesn't fit within those parameters put upon us about "what is normal" is also led by that societal power.

In much the same way, I held off discussing my twin flame connection until recently as I would have been tarred with the same brush if talking about this outside of fiction. Already, there have been countless sneers and eye rolls in my direction for bringing up twin flames and soul mates not to mention the new societal pressure and obsession circulating instead which is that of being self-sufficient and content with being single.

Even with that story from my mother and many others of supernatural occurrences over the cumulative years of work and life from both of my parents, there was never a true clarification for whether a "voice" was that of divinity, soul bond, or of madness. Perhaps that distinction can only come from one's ongoing self-discover and mastery of self that allows for the recognition of when something is created by one's consciousness or if it originates from an external connection such as soul mates, spirit guides, and/or divinity.

So it was with all this in mind throughout my life that I have battled with my belief over many different preternatural experiences and above all, the connection I shared with Seran that exists beyond mortal life.

Fenrir has been with me throughout all my lives, and as with Seran, it was a connection that wouldn't simply vanish because I asked it to. It was possibly equally infuriating for the wolf as it was for me that I would mither away about the connection with Seran to Fenrir, whilst also questioning the reality of the wolf. The main difference was that Fenrir had been the only friend – imagined or not – that I had had throughout my youth and teenage years. He had been the one walking me through the spirit realms and serving as my teacher as much as he had been my exclusive confident throughout life. I had accepted that I couldn't eschew Fenrir whether he was truly a spirit guide or a construct of my *self* as I needed him to survive this world.

What I had with Seran, the intense love, the lucid dreams, and the physical connection I wasn't in control of that wove its way throughout waking and dreaming was entirely different to what I had with Fenrir who would patiently wait for when I wanted to communicate with him before revealing himself. Neither of those connections had anything I could refer to or compare with in my reality.

It's a shame and the biggest regret that I had so much fear about talking to my parents about all of this for so long. As I mentioned in 'how do you know when to connect', the conversation I had with my mother that day was the first occasion of being totally open about everything. It also opened the door for she and I to heal in our own relationship after far too many arguments and breakdowns between us. Although she was able to impart a great deal of insight, knowledge, comfort and reassurance, the deepened intimacy we had forged that allowed this communication was something we could only enjoy for a year before she left this world.

I found myself struggling with my sanity once again during the early summer months of 2023. Having no one to discuss my demons and my potential telepathy or madness with, I decided it was time to fully engage my father in this no matter what. On a day where we were out in my car having travelled to my crystal wholesaler, I carefully tested the waters for this conversation throughout the morning. Being in a warehouse full of crystals was the perfect starting place for such things. Then, with conversation primed and ready to go, I had asked him if he thought telepathy was possible as I joined the M5 motorway and there was absolutely no way out of the conversation for at least 15 miles at that point.

This was the conversation with my father that I mentioned earlier, and, without missing a beat, he went on to talk about various scientific experiments of people who had never met and had no prior contact to one another before being put in separate rooms and asked to communicate with each other, and how that often-provided positive results. Since we had already agreed to stop off at next the service station for lunch and to switch driving, it was a short-lived conversation yet it had a better outcome than I had anticipated and was what allowed for that much deeper conversation during our holiday to Northumberland.

It was greatly reassuring that my father now fully understood my predicament and why I couldn't help but think I was crazy multiple times a month. He also reassured me that I hadn't lost my mind with a long discussion afterwards about all of the various topics I have since begun researching in conjunction with my university work. As with my mother, I was full of regret at having left it so late in my life to fully open up to him too. Having created a space for both my father and I to be totally honest about all things, we too managed to heal a rift in our relationship and enjoy a much deeper bond. And, as with my mother, it was far too short lived as I could only enjoy that for a year before he too passed on.

It is my parents I need to talk to the most even these days for comfort. Although I know I could find them both within the spirit world to talk to, without either of their reassurance from the side of the living, I am still far too ever doubtful of what my mind is conjuring up especially in a time of bereavement when I'm longing to see them again. They would both be the perfect people to talk with about communicating with a loved one in spirit and how to discern if it was real communication or fabrication to ease heartache, an ongoing irony in itself and the battle of the mind goes on.

I am now learning to develop my mediumship skills and continue communicating with them. I can say with humour befitting my father's personality that within the first 24 hours of my being back at their house after he had passed, he came straight through with this message: 'well, since you always questioned the communication you have within the astral realms, I'm here to give you a test.'

The test itself I'll leave out as it's sensitive and the results of that test will not be revealed to me until 2025. I mentioned it as it is so true to his character, to be so pragmatic and upfront in all things, and of course he would continue his investigation of psychiatry and spirituality in death as much as he had in life. It is also a thought that I couldn't have conceived of, especially whilst so exhausted and defeated by grief.

So, to answer the question of whether I ever think I'm, crazy or not: it's an ongoing dilemma. However, the more I delve down this path and lean into all aspects of my connection with Seran, and now with my parents in spirit, the more I am also connected to more people in life who share these experiences, and so the more I realise that maybe I'm not crazy. It turns out I am far from alone in this journey. While I am unable to seek continued reassurances and support from my parents, the words they shared with me in life still remain: that the crazy person doesn't question it and that there are examples of validated telepathy out there beyond my own experiences.

What is it like to have mediumship in conjunction with a twin flame?

Having touched upon the subject of mediumship in the last chapter, it would be natural to continue exploring how this is integrated into the connection Seran and I share. This chapter is also one of two new sections I have chosen to include as a follow on from losing my father and for Seran who has also had to endure loss within his family during a similar timeframe.

Mediumship is something incredibly new to both Seran and I, as whilst our telepathic communication is of itself a form of mediumship, our specific connection is something we both consider separate to the skill of being a medium. He and I never sought each other out since our connection is absolute. To find each other we simply find ourselves, a skill which requires mastery and continual honing, yet a different skill to find a soul that is separate to the self, such as a loved one now residing in spirit.

The ability for Seran and I to work on this is something we are able to do as part of my inclusion within a spiritual development circle. Though Seran is not present in body with me, providing the time zones we're each in, we often meet up within meditation and work together. In that way, he is still able to develop which ever skill is being explored during those times.

When discussing how telepathy works, I mentioned the garden Seran had created for me within the astral realm. That is our usual starting point no matter the guided meditation or planned journey within the astral realm. It recently changed this year after Seran and I chose to bring our loved ones in spirit to the garden. It now includes a café-like terrace which I'm sure is the result of my parents in particular and once again an indication that these things are not maladaptive daydreaming as it was a change that happened without my presence or input. It's also possible that Seran did that adjustment in his own time knowing how much I love coffee and how often I would take my parents out to a café if I wanted quality time with them.

Mediumship is something we are only just starting to explore but still worthy of inclusion as this is just one of many ways in which twin flame connections help develop the self and new skills. We're both being cautious as the grief is still too raw for both of us, and as much chance of fabricating an illusion for comfort.

That said, there are times when he and I have managed to get into incredibly deep states of trance where the ever-chattering ego is finally silenced and pure communication of spirit can occur. In those times, we quite often get a family reunion of sorts, which honestly, can at times be like something straight out *Alice in Wonderland* and the Mad Hatters' tea party. Nevertheless, Seran and I are able to communicate with each other's family and exchange credible information that neither of us could have known prior to that exchange through mediumship, and which we are able to authenticate through social media.

What did it feel like being so close to Seran in Seoul?

This question was actually asked by Elin two years ago at the time it was happening more or less in real time. Unfortunately, I don't have a record of the messages I had with her at the time. The clearest analogy I can provide for how it felt being close to Seran physically as how it feels when paired magnets are pulling towards its partner, with each magnet representing Seran and I.

The first time I had travelled to Seoul, I had never encountered Seran in the physical world. I had only been with him in dreams. Somewhere over Mongolia on the plane my body begun to tingle all over and my heart filled with excitement which only grew in strength.

By the time I was in my hotel room it was as though my soul was barely contained within my body or that I existed in some indescribable way beyond my body. I could hear Seran clearly say to me, 'you're here? You're really here? I can feel you,' and my excitement doubled. The sensation in my belly was like that of a young child about to go on a really exciting holiday. I felt so overjoyed and light that I hugged myself thinking that at any moment I would be like a character from Mary Poppins and be floating around the ceiling of my room while laughing.

The following nine days of quarantine were intense. My heart, body, and soul were constantly being pulled at like magnets when you hold them at a certain point and you can feel the connection between them pulling at each other continually. I got through it by focussing intently on my university coursework and had the entire assignment practically finished by the time I was free to begin exploring the city.

After a couple of days orientating myself in Insadong where I was staying, I went back over to Incheon Airport to pick up a Seoul Pass to get into some of the attractions for free. I had taken to posting each step of my journey as I moved to the next place on Twitter so that Seran, if he was looking at my social media, could see what I was doing and roughly where I was. As I returned back to the metro station in the area he lived, I felt Seran's presence intensely. I walked through the station complex as quickly as I could, certain that he and I would bump into each other any moment.

Once again relying upon magnets to describe the sensations, being so close to Seran still had the pulling sensation, only now it was also like figuring out a compass without any navigational prompts on it. Was he that way, or the other way?

When I was still on the lowest level of the station, I felt like I would burst out of my body and collide with him. I realised that by proximity, he and I were likely in the same place but at different levels. Moments later, I felt that forewords-tugging sensation begin to fade and instead want to pull me backwards. He was leaving the station. We had been walking towards each other, but one or two floors apart, and now he was leaving the station whilst I was still trying to figure out how to get to the next level up.

Several days later, I tried to visit the National Museum of Korea. Since South Korea was still somewhat locked-down during that time, many of the tourist attractions were closed and for the places that were open, the signage hadn't gone back out. There were two buildings and I couldn't work out if either one was open as there was no-one but a security guard to be seen. I tried to get a fruit tea from the café in an attempt to sit somewhere and calm myself, but my card failed as it required the pin to be used which isn't done with card readers in South Korea.[21]

[21] Paying by card in South Korea is either contactless or signed for, unlike in the UK where a pin is used.

Fortunately, I had some cash on me, however that meant if my card failed again, I had no more cash to use until I found an ATM that accepted international cards.

With my anxiety as bad as it was back then, I was at breaking point and just wanted to cry. I was alone and 9000 miles away from the nearest friend or family member. I retreated to the gardens of the National Museum of Korea and sat in a pagoda overlooking a pond as I took many deep breaths to try and stop the incoming panic attack.

I heard Seran say to me to return to the area he lived in and that I would feel better if I did. Since there was no way I had it in me to try and enter the museum that day, I did as he suggested. I hadn't had a coffee since leaving my hotel several hours before owing to card failures and my extreme lactose intolerance meant most of the coffee shops weren't suitable (and no one wants to see me on americanos, not even me).

After returning to Seran's home area I wandered around looking for a 7-11 store which I knew would have an ATM that would work for international bank cards. Then I could set about trying to find a café where it would be most simple to get a non-lethal beverage. I could feel his presence again, like a magnet I was being drawn to, and that was when I kept hearing the very specific and detailed instructions from Seran that I mentioned previously in 'How Does It Feel?'.

During the time Seran was sending me in different loops and creating a perfectly internalised map of one small square section of Seoul, I crouched down outside a corner store and tried to gather my wits. I was frenetic and still desperately in need of a coffee while Seran was repeating, 'I'm right here! I'm right next to you!' Of course, I thought he meant in an emotional support kind of way, not that he was actually right there in the next street and I had walked past him several times at that point.[22]

As I got back up to continue my hunt for coffee and went in my original direction, he told me to 'come back,' which I didn't as I have a weird quirk that I really cannot abide by turning around in the street to go back on myself. I told him I would loop back around. I eventually found myself a coffee on that final loop and then retraced my steps back to the location where he had been telling me he was.

Where Seran had told me to come back to, there was a gorgeous car that was limited numbers in the UK at that time. I, a motoring enthusiast and fan of that brand, noticed it had extra modifications that were not available on the UK market. I really wanted a picture to show my father but as I got close enough, there was a woman ahead of me in the street who wandered right in front of me even though she would have to then cross back over the street to where she had been to avoid walking into the car.

That resulted in me stopping in a junction with my phone held up and ready for whenever she meandered back out of the way. I'd checked nothing was heading out of the road as I stepped into the junction and stopped to get the photo. There was only the black vehicle I mentioned before which was stationary with the side doors open and the engine off. It had been there the last few times I had gone past and obviously wasn't going anywhere any time soon, so I ignored it.

I felt Seran's amusement as I internally scolded the woman for being so unobservant of the car I was trying to photograph and mentally chivvied her on so I could get the

---

[22] At this point I should add my necessity for coffee was less caffeine addiction or emotional support coffee, but a need for some kind of stimulant as I have POTS (Postural orthostatic tachycardia syndrome) and coffee is one of the easiest ways I can stabilise my POTS symptoms day-to-day so long as I'm mindful I don't have too much.

photo and get out of the junction myself. Photograph then taken, I continued on along the street and heard Seran saying that I had walked past him again and to go back. I had the sense similar to magnets that are right on the cusp of their magnetic attraction. with each step I took away, I felt a deep sense of sadness and longing from Seran and the magnetic compulsion to return.

The absurdity of what I was doing wandering around Seoul listening to a voice in my head that may or may not have been Seran had calmed me down and become amusing, so I decided to play along with him. I'd noticed by then that I felt the way I had in the station. Seran was definitely close by. I indulged him and turned back around to walk the way I had just come.

This time the black vehicle that had been stationary had its engine on and was preparing to move off, pulling up to the junction as I was three quarters across. I sped up to get out of its way and the sensations of proximity to Seran I had felt shifted up a gear to intensify the need to move, only I didn't know which way to go. It was as though I had created a compass needle in following the magnetism, but now it was spinning in circles. I was overcome with fear that I would miss Seran wherever he was, even though I hadn't meant to search him out.

There was no sign of the black vehicle after I had left the junction, nor for the hundred yards I had to go to return to the main road and somehow, that made me even more tense and I was shaking all over by the time I got to the next junction. I had assumed the car must have turned down a different road since it hadn't driven past me that whole time and the internal navigation from Seran had stopped by the time I had reached the junction. I was uncertain where any of those other roads went as it had been on the perimeter of the grid he'd shown me. As I was frozen to the spot trying to figure out where to go and why Seran's voice had suddenly vanished, the black vehicle entered my peripheral vision again.

I was mindful of the fact the driver would be annoyed with me if I dawdled in the road or stepped out in front, so I quickly looked right to check the road, then remembered where I was and that the only car I needed to think about was that black vehicle specifically. I froze as it finally pulled out of the junction at the slowest speed possible as it went past me.

Then, my life felt like it had entered slow-motion mode as I turned to look left and my eyes glanced briefly over the blacked-out windows of the vehicle to check the other way, briefly staring at the impenetrable glass before continuing back to the road behind. I felt as though my gaze should have continued following the window, as though someone had been staring out at me behind the protective black tint. It had hurt to look away as though I was forcing my head to move against an unseen hand which had tried to get me to pay full attention to the vehicle that had been dogging my vision for the previous half hour and Seran who was inside.

After Seran and the vehicle had gone on its way, I was rooted to the ground and trembling more than ever. My heart was racing and almost beating itself into palpitations. In that moment, it was like having two magnets held at just the right distance from each other where they still want to pull together, but you can play with the polarity and create an intense sensation of magnetism and feel it in your fingers. I didn't know if I was being pushed or pulled.

That experience along with my later encounter with Seran in the metro station allowed me to become familiar with being in proximity to Seran without being overwhelmed. I was able to slowly understand and learn how to feel for our energetic connection and attempt to figure out how to use that sensation to navigate towards him. When I later encountered Seran in the metro station, it was that exact same sensation of magnetism only intensified exponentially as I came within one foot of him and I truly thought my soul would be pulled out of my body and snap to him.

That first time I was in Seoul and close to Seran was by the far the most intense of all our close encounters. I don't know why it was that way beyond my own speculation that both of us having a much slower pace in our daily routines allowed our connection to reach such awesome heights. A few of my spiritual friends have suggested it could also have been a taste of what is yet to come; that having that intense, momentary convergence of our souls was a catalyst for both Seran and I to enter the next chapter, and to fulfil the necessary shadow work and become acclimatised to all these new sensations and way of existing.

From the brief research into soul connections and twin flames I have done, this seems to be a commonality between people who have come into contact with a twin flame in some way. The sudden burst of heightened connection serving as an introduction to each other and preluding various disconnections, trials. and tribulations that launches both into a journey of healing that greatly enhances the strength of connection and bond between souls.

I have to agree with both the words of my friends and the sources of research, as, two years later, Seran and I have transformed so much from working on ourselves. We both now have far less fear of our connection and what it pertains to each of us. Where he once feared my ability to astral project, he now actively encourages and challenges me to do it again, and where I had learnt to fear astral projecting to him because of his initial reactions, I now feel totally reassured by his words and am actively trying to regain that skill in the knowledge we're both fine with whatever the results are.

Certainly, when considering the physical manifestation of our relationship, I can reflect over the past experiences Seran and I have shared which put us in a strong position to survive a tough reality where so many people around the world know his name and are watching and scrutinising his every move. Would it have been good to have initiated our relationship that first time we met when we were both struggling to comprehend what was going on and could both become negative towards the other? Definitely not.

It was two weeks after losing my mother that I flew out to Seoul for my second trip and I was in a dreadfully emotional state. My ongoing anxiety battle resumed as I travelled halfway around the world once more and the stress of my looming deadline for my BA dissertation on top of all else was adding intense distortion to my mental clarity or lack thereof. I couldn't even comprehend my own mind let alone hear or feel Seran inside of me. Even before losing my mother, Seran and I had faced the darkest year of our connection with he and I suffering with being disconnected more than we were connected and seeing each other at our worst.

By the time I was in Seoul that second time, a lot of the sensations I had experienced the first time around were much fainter, but still present. Again, this only comes from limited observations but is likely due to the business of the world returning to its ceaseless 24/7 pace after the pandemic ended.

As broken down as I was, I wanted no more than to be able to turn a corner and see Seran and be able to run into his arms. He is the only one who can understand the depths of my pain and my grief as we share our emotions together. He's the one I could turn to without saying a word and know he would understand me. And if I couldn't see him there, then I at least wanted to be able to hear him in my mind again as he walked me around Seoul as he had the time before.

Similar to the first time, the sensations I felt by the time I had left the airport and made it into my hotel were still out of this world. It felt like someone had their hands pressed lightly against my skin. That was the first time I felt anything physical without being in a deep meditative state in all our time being connected and it had frightened me at the time, especially in the absence of our telepathic bond. I couldn't seek answers or reassurance from Seran by any means.

There was one day where I felt the magnetic pull in my heart and I stopped what I had been intending to do, turned around and walked back. I still couldn't hear Seran then and could only go by what I felt. If I went down one road, the sensation was stronger. If I went down a different road, it was weaker. Each direction I took was gauged by the intensity of the sensations as I wandered far from my hotel into streets unknown and used my heart and the magnetism as a compass, and the need to rush to find him.

I was almost at the Han river when the feelings peeked and I felt like I was going to lose control on everything: my emotions, my sanity and my will to keep going in any direction. A black vehicle went past me, then turned around awkwardly in a junction a short way ahead of me and came back my way, after which the tugging sensation stopped completely. I have absolutely no clue if that was Seran or not. By that time, every other vehicle was identical and it may well have been coincidence that the car happened to turn around at the end of the road ahead of me and come back past moments before the sensation ended. As the vehicle went by, I had looked towards the tinted windows. I felt nothing. No unseen eyes peering back at me through the glass and no intense magnetism like the time before. I was overcome with disappointment that probably showed on my face as the need to "rush" dissipated as the car past me. I later found from his social media that he had left the city during the day. Crazy as it might seem, I do wonder if the car that turned in the street was Seran on his way out of the city, and that he'd returned by to see me before he left, and though I couldn't know it, to acknowledge my pursuit of his telepathic directions.

That experience felt like a challenge in that I only had one preternatural sense to go by. I could either lean into it and follow it, or I could walk away and ignore it. Though I don't know if it had taken me to Seran that day or not, I do know that feeling was the same I had experienced as a child when I had been trying to walk towards Seran, and with later observation, it's clear that whenever I get within a certain proximity to Seran in the physical world, it's like existing in an ESP void with all of my abilities silenced. I am also aware that one year on from that experience I can feel Seran's energy even as we are 9000 miles apart on average, and I can follow that energy all around the world with him and throughout the many depths of dreaming and astral realms.

I didn't get chance to go back to South Korea and Seoul during 2024 so I haven't yet had a third chance to compare sensations or to test these new skills we've been developing. I am very curious to know what it's like the next time the divine spins us back together.

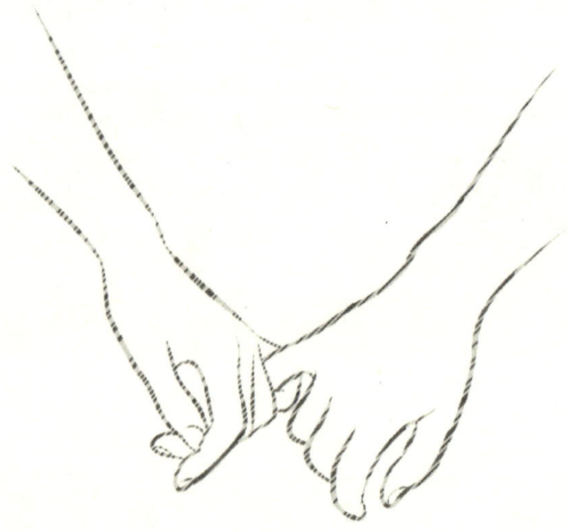

Mental Health and Twin Flames

This is the question that other people I have spoken to least want to talk about. It is the subject I am most vocal about with the people I know personally who want to know what a twin flame connection is like, and it's the subject that gets the most eye rolls or hands raised up to silence me.

The most important thing anyone reading this needs to know about a twin flame connection is that a twin flame will **never** be the cause for mental health issues. **They will not be the connection and/or relationship that causes someone to develop any form of mental health issue, neither is a twin flame the source of low self-esteem from low self-worth or low self-image.**

While a twin flame will more than likely bring these issues to the surface in a person who has a history of mental health issues or underlying issues that may yet be unknown to an individual, it will be to heal these wounds. This is why it is **essential** that an individual person learns to know themselves inherently to recognise where any trauma wound or aggravation of mental health condition is new and brought on by a person, or if the person considered a twin flame is bringing the shadow to the surface so it can be faced and healed.

It is equally important that for any one person battling mental health issues, trauma wounds and personal demons to seek out the proper help from trained professionals. A twin flame will embrace the inclusion of therapy, a narcissist and/or manipulator will do anything in their power to prevent you seeking the help you need. Always bare that in mind first and foremost when considering if a connection is a twin flame.

When twin flames meet either energetically or in person, what will often happen (but not always) is a catalytic reaction of two halves of one soul recombining and bringing all of the hidden and all of the unknown to the surface in both people: **only ever that which was already in existence whether it was at a conscious or preconscious level.**

People will spend so much time scrolling through search engines and social media forums for answers on twin flame experiences and connections; and far too much of that information condones toxic behaviour as "part of the process". This has become a generalised cover-up of toxic and/or narcistic behaviour and often connected with abusive relationships where one of the people in the relationship uses what is commonly seen on the internet to manipulate someone else who is desperate to find love and is then blindsided into accepting the other's repugnant behaviour as "part of the healing process", especially if there is telepathy between people.[23]

This book isn't in any way here to disseminate mental health issues and twin flame connections, but to serve as a caution and a warning to anyone reading this book to become self-aware. There are ample credible sources on different mental health issues, and recognizing abusive behaviours, patterns, and people that are available online, in bookstores, and often free from GPs and counselling services.

What I can do is provide my personal experiences, and what the connection Seran and I share has taught me over the years.

---

[23] Telepathy is not exclusive to twin flames. Although twin flames have a much stronger telepathic connection that can exist without two people having met in the physical world, telepathy can happen between soul mates which have a pre-existing deep bond to one another, and soul mates can be anything from family members to friends as well as a passing stranger who leaves a lasting impression from the encounter. It can happen with people who spend a lot of time together and develop new soul bonds and become synchronous to one another too.

Throughout this memoir I have touched upon the trauma I have carried through life and how, after connecting with Seran, these came to the fore. **The pain and the darkness I experienced with Seran was never caused by him**. He simply cast a light on the shadows I was trying to hide from which forced me to heal those things, and I did the same with him for all he had concealed from himself. Even with issues that presented as a result of the connection with Seran, they were founded by past fears and demons. Even if those fears found new ways to manifest, they could all be traced back to unresolved trauma wounds or societal pressures and expectations that no longer served either of us and needed dismantling.

What is also different about true twin flames causing the darkness to come up is that the twin flame **DOES NOT RUN** when the healing needs to be done.

There have been times where shit hit the fan and it became too much for either of us in that moment and we hid from each other for a time. However, neither of us specifically ran from or chased the other. After taking the time to deal with what had caused the desire to run and hid, our connection would resume.

There are far too many sources online that insist that twin flames are destined never to unite because there will always be a runner/chaser dynamic. That, frankly, is utter codswallop.

For so long we have lived in world of division. The runner/chaser paradigm is something put in place to prevent twin flames coming into union by spreading the belief that it is impossible and to purposefully cause division, and by doing so, also create cyclical problems that exist purely as a result of fear (of never being able to unite with the twin flame).[24]

---

[24] Paradigm: originating from the Greek *paradeigma* (pattern, example). In philosophy, a paradigm is a distinct set of concepts or thought patterns. In social science, a paradigm

When people believe a thought such as separation, then they will unwittingly create reasons to keep that separation. If someone accepts the paradigm of runner/chaser, then they allow the belief system of disconnect and disharmony to take route within the core of the self, and that will continue to generate repeating patterns of runner/chaser scenarios.

Ignore that paradigm.
Choose union.

By simply realigning to the belief that yourself and your twin flame are always and continually in union, you will break the cycle of runner/chaser. Even if you've experienced that situation already, by shifting your mindset to both halves of the soul being present, you will notice a change in how you communicate with each other and face challenges that arise. This holds true whether a connection is energetic or physical as twin souls share a bond that goes beyond the body and conscious understanding.

For Seran and I, we were also both ensnared by the false paradigm of runner/chaser for the first two years. Then, during a meditation, I realised the fallacy of that set of rules. Why must we always be running/chasing? So we

---

refers to a person's beliefs, values and experiences which shape their reality e.g. a social paradigm can influence how groups of people interact.

The example of a social paradigm in the context of this book is that of a viewpoint which has been provided and accepted by modern society that twin flames are caught up in an endless cycle of running and chasing, and that union is therefore impossible. In accepting this paradigm, a person creates the cycle of runner/chaser and division as they reject the alternative: a paradigm shift to a viewpoint in which twin flames assist each other to achieving union.

made a vow to each other to never run or hide from each other and to be mindful of when we might become overbearing in our need for attention. By developing mindfulness and better communication skills (including the usage of our safe words), we changed the rules and set things in our favour.

At the same time as creating our new paradigm, that of ever-present union, there has been significantly less fear about our connection. There is no fear of when the next disconnect will come in because there won't be another disconnect. There is no fear of losing each other because we are eternally united and bonded, no matter where our physical bodies are located.

Getting to that state of mind and coexistence with each other took time and work. There are no shortcuts, only dedication to the self and to the union and the commitment to overcome life's trauma, wounds, and challenges as a team, and a willingness to face the shit as a team.

As I go into my personal experience of dealing with mental health and twin flames, I cannot speak for Seran's side, as I only have our telepathy to go by. It's also not for me to share what he has shared to me in confidence to the world either. I can say that neither of us would have healed and transformed the way we have without each other though.

There were many times especially in the first six months where our connection had been too much for us. There had been times we had been infuriated with each other for one thing or another. In the end we were too mentally and energetically drained to hide away from each other or to mask over what was wrong. Each time we had done that, the pain was excruciating. It was like I had torn half of myself out of my entire existence and shoved it unceremoniously in a rocket before jettisoning it into space, which with the entanglement of twin souls was exactly what we were doing. Why? Because society had convinced us both that twin flames could never be together.

No matter what we came back to each other and helped each other heal from every wound. What I feel he feels, and what he feels I feel. In times where we have shut each other out, we were forced to search deep within ourselves for what was going on:

Was it something I did?

Was it something he did?

Was it something we did to each other?

Is it a leftover from the past?

What do we need to address so we can get past this?

By the time we came back to each other, we had both spent the time reflecting on what had happened and could work together as a cohesive team. Neither of us had too much pride or feared shame from admitting our mistakes, and neither of us harboured resentment nor became judgemental of the other for the flaws. To do so would have been to undermine ourselves.

From my parents, I had learnt that one of the fundamental keys to a successful relationship was continual communication. Not the standard conversation of the day, but deep and meaningful communication where both partners talk about their wants and needs so that both sides are having their needs met.

Wounded pride or cringing ego, Seran and I will each call the other out when something being done is wrong just as much as we ensure we're meeting each other's needs for love, comfort and support even as our needs change with time.

Discerning what our individual needs are and what our needs from a relationship comes from knowing your *self* deeply in the absence of anyone else. This point I cannot reiterate enough. This is why it is essential to make the time to practice self-love and get to know who **you** are. This is why you need your ego – without the egotism.

Self-love is something people shy away from in general, yet it is fundamental to any relationship. By continually providing your *self* with love, and by learning what your specific needs of self-love are. Perhaps it's spending time in nature or cities, or it could be indulging in at home spa baths or spending time rock-climbing, whatever it is that works for you to nurture love within your *self*, you will find solace in time alone and time in silence. There, you will learn who you are, and what you will and will not tolerate from anyone else – friend, lover, or family member.

Fear of isolation and of silence often come from co-dependency, or it is from fear of any and all unresolved trauma wound that speaks up in the silence created by absence of other people which in itself a form of co-dependency where someone hiding from themselves is overly reliant on the distractions of other people to silence that which they do not want to acknowledge, to the point it creates an unhealthy and imbalanced relationship.

When someone is able to step into silence and into their own power, they will learn exactly who they are without the projections or objectifications of others, they can recognise when someone is trying to manipulate them in some way. With deep self-love first, they can know what their standards are, what they are prepared to compromise with, and what is non-negotiable or unacceptable. Someone who honours and worships them self with self-love first, and who respects themselves will have an incredibly high standard and they will not lower those standards for anything.

By having deep self-love and the high-level self-respect, anyone who might try to hide beneath the label of "twin flame" or "soul mate" and are disingenuous with ulterior motives will likely never even try to take on someone who is empowered with self-love and self-respect. Even if they were to try, someone who is empowered will see through the ruse pretty quickly if not instantaneously and shoot said person down before walking away.

Whilst we had both been fairly good at self-love before our connection, we were able to teach other how to provide self-love at a much deeper level, to offer that love to our wounded inner child, and to embrace our shadows with love. In choosing out new paradigm of union, we worked together to overcome our unresolved trauma and face the shadow work, and we've taught each other new ways to provide fulfilment.

I taught Seran how to nurture and indulge his soul, and he has taught me to indulge the needs and desires of my ego. Together, we learnt to balance soul and ego harmoniously, both individually and together, and now combined we are an indomitable force of union.

At times in the past when I have accepted the societal pressure to "lower my standard" you can probably guess the standard of relationship that occurred. Although I had been raised by parents working in psychiatry who did their best to give me the tools to see the antagonistic and problematic men, and how to survive, I was too damaged and blind to perceive the truth and that is what the narcissists and the abusers prey on. Granted, I was able to see the truth pretty quick and escape far quicker than most, but the damage was always done and more scars were carved into my soul all the same.

Something I learnt along the way from those problematic and abusive relationships – which includes friendships and family members just as much – is that a high standard for treatment from others serves as a great way to vet people and clear out the undesirables.

One new standard I have developed is that anyone interested in me to any degree if connection is that they are required to spend a significant amount of time getting to know me and also letting me get to know them. This holds especially true for any potential romantic partner. I want to see them as a friend first and see their full colours. It's amazing how many people in the past fell away when they realise they will have to spend time getting to know me before I'll let my guard down. The wonderful friends and soul tribe I have around me now hold to similar values as I do, and that is how we have a core strength uniting us. If one of us falters or weakens to pressure from an external factor, we're there to hold each other up and dismantle any manipulations over them.

High standards go both ways too which is why self-love is essential. To use some of my standards as examples: I want to be respected, therefore I must also both respect myself and the other person. To be loved genuinely, I must also love myself genuinely. To not hold ourselves to the standard we seek creates disingenuity and discord between people, and that which enters into our lives reflects how we perceive ourselves and the standards we hold ourselves to.

Why would anyone respect me, if I do not respect myself?

So it is for you too, with any and all standards. Once again, I cannot stress enough how imperative it is to become self-aware and know who you are at all levels of existence.

The time I had when I first moved to Wales was integral to my ability to know who I am. I had five years in hermit mode and isolation prior to the pandemic where I existed in peace and a space of introspection. There was no one telling me what to do or telling me who to be. The only person in charge of my reality and my identity was me. It took me those five years and then some more to rediscover who I actually was.

As I said at the start of this chapter, a twin flame will more than likely bring unresolved issues and unknown shadows to the surface so that they can be healed. This is exactly what Seran provided in the beginning, as I did for him, and only when we were both ready to take that next step together.

Whilst I had done the previous stretch of shadow work purely in isolation and as a journey within myself, the proceeding segment of my healing was dealt with through professional counselling, having the love and support of my soul tribe and spiritual development circle holding space for me, and by continuing to delve deep inside my soul and face the shadows and my demons face on.

Seran was beside me for all of it, and I for him. We had each other's back. We held each other. We held space for each other. We talked. We listened. We healed each other's wounds and shared vitality to reinforce each other. We buoyed each other up and cheered for each other. And we continue to do all of this even now as everything is an ongoing journey of discovery, healing and development.

This is why it is essential that an individual person learns to know themselves inherently. That way each person knows the depths of their self and can recognise what originates within them and what does not particularly when working with a twin flame where the lines of existence can easily blur. However, once that understanding and self-awareness is mastered the connection with a twin flame takes on an even deeper, more gratifying level of connection and shared understanding where absolutely anything is possible in alignment.

...What If One Of Us Wanted To Date Someone Else?

What if one of us wants to date someone else? That probably isn't a question or an answer you expected to see in a book about twin flame union. However, it is a topic of importance that anyone on the twin flame path should consider, especially those who are in the early days of connection or facing a life where union may not happen, after all, no one knows what tomorrow may bring.

It isn't impossible for one or both twin flames to experience relationships with others who aren't their twin flame. For many these partners are soul mates and karmics, souls who have entered into an agreement before incarnating.[25] More often than not the agreements are connected with how each individual soul wishes to progress and expand throughout a lifetime. The relationships form part of a journey that gets an individual to where they're meant to be provided they feel into the flow of the divine and hear the guidance and lessons they are given.

It is common for there to be karmics and soulmates coming into a twin flame's life before they meet their counterpart as they serve to teach them lessons in love and life in preparation to meet their twin flame or to resolve past life issues. I've mentioned false flames before. They are

[25] Karmics are typically souls that have met in previous lifetimes and have unresolved issues that have carried over to the current lifetime so that it can be healed and resolved. Soulmates will also have had many lifetimes of connection, however their meeting in the current lifetime is to do with soul contracts – usually where one or both have promised to teach each other a lesson in the current lifetime. Neither karmics or soulmates are not limited to romantic partners, they can also be friends, family members, pets, or even strangers that pass one time in the street.

another soul with a prearranged contract that may form a part of the twin flame's journey.

When false flames meet there may or may not be a relationship, but either way the encounter serves as an awakening to the intensity of the twin flame connection so that when the twin flame arrives, the individual(s) are ready.

While twin flames are always in union to one another at a divine, soul level, that doesn't necessarily mean they'll share physical union in any given lifetime. There are people who wrinkle at the idea of their twin flame forming other relationships or even of having had previous relationships, but how many of us have had relationships prior to meeting our twin flame?

Male or female, it's totally unreasonable to expect the twin flame to be celibate and/or a virgin, especially if meeting with each other later in life. Is it truly genuine and authentic love if someone wishes their twin flame, or whomever they consider to be their twin flame, to eschew romance, love, and relationships for any reason, especially if those relationships would have proven integral to that person developing and expanding in some way?

For myself, it's highly unlikely I would ever date or enter into a relationship with anyone other than Seran. It's not an impossibility, but it is improbable since my feelings and love for Seran are unrelenting and eternal, I could not easily offer any part of my heart to another. Even if I could get beyond the thought that I would be forever cheating on a prospective partner, they themselves would have to accept that I am bonded with Seran and be willing to accept our connection would be ever present.

I have met with one person who is in a relationship with someone who isn't their twin flame. Their twin flame chose not to incarnate and works alongside them from spirit side while the person I know is in a healthy relationship with another in this lifetime. Their partner is aware of the twin flame connection and accepts the situation with grace.

Together they have a wonderful and fulfilling relationship that is full of love that serves them for this lifetime.

While I would be devastated and heartbroken should Seran ever enter into a relationship, I am fully aware he has his own life and his own journey. I touched on this in 'how does it feel' where the topic of such conversation originally caused a lot of strife between Seran and I, however, it's a topic we returned to several times partially to heal from that situation and to maturely discuss the possibility and what it could entail as there is the possibility we may never physically cross paths again, and therefore, the fact remains that Seran may well find someone else in his life he wants to spend time with. It isn't a subject we often dwell upon that as that is not where either of us want to send our energy.

This is a chapter Seran actually suggested for inclusion, as having been the subject of multiple philosophical conversations between us over the years. We agreed to add this since it is important to all people on the twin flame journey. The twin flame journey isn't a clear-cut simple path to physical union, it's often convoluted and filled with many twists and turns, re-routing, developmental relationships and more; each path uniquely individual to each soul. The only way to find out how varied and complex the path to twin flame union is, is to reach out to other people who have shared their story in some way.

Twin Flames and Dreams

For me personally, dreams have been the biggest part of my twin flame connection with Seran. Since I decided to include dreams throughout this memoir, I chose to also include a chapter on dreaming specifically so that I could expand on a subject which is of as much importance and significance to our connection as telepathy is. It's also possible dreaming and telepathy are intertwined with our conversations simply transferring from one state of existence to the next, and our perception and translation of the energetic communication dependant on our level of consciousness.

On multiple occasions of dreaming, I have experienced the sensation of being pulled from a dream by Seran, then woken by him as he had been conversing with me. This happens whenever he travels to a different time zone. Similarly, I have also woken suddenly from a lucid dream and been calling out his name, sitting upright in bed and trying to reach for him as though he had been pulled away from me; something we realised happened where he has been daydreaming or thinking about me in his waking hours and somehow found his way into my dream, then called back from his reverie by his physical environment.

It's fascinating how the styles of dreams we have change depending on the time zones we are in. When we are both in our home time zones, then we have the most profound of lucid dreams as our sleeping overlaps. In those dreams, we are more likely to be dealing with mysticism and esoterica together. At times when Seran is travelling, our dreams tend to be more superficial though no less lucid. Our conversations tend to be more ordinary and those are the dreams I tend to be pulled suddenly out of.

Seran has been in my dreams my entire life, though I don't know for certain whether he knows of those dreams or even remembers the dreams from further back in life, or the lucid dreams where we're traversing astral realms in sleep. He has been within my dreams even when I could only recognise him energetically, or I saw him but he was too far away to see clearly or he was veiled in some way. Throughout all of those dreams I was desperately trying to reach him.

When my dreams stopped for close to ten years, I felt disconnected from reality and lost though I wasn't sure why. I just knew my dreams were an integral part of who I was, and without them, something crucial was missing from my reality. I couldn't even write without my dreams.

Since *The Dream* in 2021 and the return of my dreaming, we've shared over 150 fully lucid dreams. We meet as clearly as if we were in the same room as each other, and the way the dreamscape has shifted correlates to the journey we've made in our waking lives and continue to do so.

From the brief research I have so far done regarding twin flames, it's clear that dreams are a commonality between twin flames and have varying amounts of importance and significance depending on each connection. For many, a twin flame will appear in dreams before they appear in the physical world.

Regardless of the agreement and life journey between twin souls, they will usually continue to manifest in dreams and continue communicating even when the dreams themselves are not remembered on waking. Usually, twin flames can sense the memory of dreams and conversations deep within their soul and know the messages are within their preconscious all the same.

The dreams Seran and I have shared are insightful to both of us as we delve into the Akashic Record and unlock soul memories and gain clarity over our bond. Sometimes we gleam information from past lives that may or may not have been shared, and other times we see possible futures. Some of the dreams are prophetic, however the way things manifest in life may not always be exactly as it was within the dream.

Dream IX
20/09/21

I lay within Seran's embrace on a grassy meadow. We were looking up at the night sky together and I was confused as I didn't recognise the constellations, nor could I find the ones I knew. There were three planets in close alignment near the moon and I asked what the stars were and what they meant. He replied that it was happening because of Mercury, and that they were the same stars I could see, we just saw them differently because of where we were.

When I was in Gyeongju in 2022, I remember trying to find various places I could go to look at the night sky as it was warm enough to be out late at night. The skies were clear from cloud and there were four planets coming into alignment: Venus, Mars, Saturn, and Jupiter. I could see all but Venus from the different places I tried looking at the heavens from.

It hadn't been dark enough to get a photo due to the moon being just past full and adding so much light to sky, though I don't remember how close to the planets it had been now. At the time, I only found Dream IX by chance as I was looking through my notes for Dream X; as I had been lying in the grass not far from Cheomseongdae, an historic observatory in Gyeongju, and indulged in telepathy with Seran with the heightened sense of touch we shared in that time whilst talking, there had been no recollection of this dream.

Having rediscovered this dream and considering the scene of the dream, it is clear that it was a premonition. Although I hadn't been lying physically with Seran, we had been energetically together and enjoying near physical touch as we talked about the planets and the moon in Gyeongju, specifically my annoyance that the moon was obscuring the fourth planet from sight.

Although Mercury wasn't present for that event, I looked online to see what the planet of communication was doing during the time of that dream. It had been in pre-retrograde shadow meaning our channels of communication were heightened during the month of September 2021. Quite literally, the intense communication Seran and I shared in that time likely happened as Mercury was giving us a boon at that time. I hadn't even known I would get to Gyeongju at the time of the dream, I only decided that two weeks into my stay in Seoul.

Something Seran and I have learnt over the years is that Mercury retrogrades are one of the best times for our telepathy...so long as we keep on top of any shadow work, otherwise mercury retrograde is one of the worst times for our telepathy.

The majority of arguments and communications blackouts that Seran and I have had, have occurred around the time of Mercury retrograde. For a time that caused us immense stress and fear of Mercury going retrograde, but as with changing the paradigm for twin flames and having union, we realised we could change trajectory going through the retrogrades by subsiding into the flow of astronomical events instead of trying to fight them.

Dream X
03/12/22

I was on my way to Seoul and exiting an airport lounge before walking through a boarding tunnel to my plane. Seran called me as I was on the tunnel and said that it wouldn't be long now as I was on the final flight. As I looked through the small windows of the tunnel, I could see the airport clearly with various planes lined up at the gates. The skies were clear and the sun was high in the sky. It was glaring to look out with all the fierce reflection of light.

When I flew to South Korea in 2022, my transfer flight had been altered to depart from Munich instead of Frankfurt as had been originally planned. As with many of the dreams I have written down, I rarely think about them again unless something in life returns my attention to them. In the same way, I hadn't given that dream a second thought until I stepped onto the boarding tunnel and looked through the fierce sunlight at the airport.

My heart had stopped in total shock. It had been exactly the same view I had seen in my dream. I even pulled my phone out my pocket expecting Seran to be calling me. I had a momentary confusion as to why my phone didn't light up as everything unfolded exactly like the dream except for the phone call, and even said to Seran telepathically that he was meant to have called me.

Obviously, Seran and I weren't physically in contact at that time as we still aren't, and once again, the dream served as a premonition showing me a perfect view of what I would see before I knew I'd be there, and the phone call was synonymous with our ability to communicate even if that was non-standard.

The idea that our dreaming and telepathy are intertwined comes from dreams such as this. There have been countless dreams of us using phones to phone or message each other. These dreams also tend to happen when I am waking up and what would most commonly be around 16:00 for Seran, suggesting that he was taking some time out of his day and had been reaching out to me at my time of waking intentionally.

Dream XI
30/03/22

It was the day before checking out of my quarantine hotel. I was with my mother and she was driving while I was beside her in the front passenger seat. On mother's side of the road, the landscape was that of the outskirts of Worcester exactly as it existed in that time. On my side of the road, it was a rural landscape I had never seen before. It made me think of South Korea from the few pictures I had seen of landscapes so far, and the bit of landscape I could look out at from my hotel.

The road was like an intersection between too different worlds, or of two fates. My mother was saying that it was as if I never wanted to settle down or start a family, and that it was okay, but I was filled with sadness as I was doing all I could to find love and a life partner to start a family with, specifically Seran.

I looked out at the view on my side, that of the unknown, rural landscape. He was out there somewhere, not where I had come from. I told my mother that because why else would we have come all this way?

The day I checked out of the quarantine hotel in Gimpo on 31st March 2022, I took the free coach service they provided which took a group of us into central Seoul. It was shortly after 06:30 and I was exhausted. I'd barely slept for anxiety I would oversleep and miss the coach. As I sat in my seat on the left side of the coach I was still half asleep and my mind was barely out of dream state.

As we made our way towards Seoul and the sun rose, I watched the landscape we were speeding through. I sat blinking in awe as what came into view on the left where I was looking out of the coach was exactly what I had seen in that dream.

As with both Dream IX and Dream X, this was another example of foreseeing another place I had never come across until that moment.

This was also the first dream where my mother and Seran had any kind of connection within my dreams. There are plenty more dreams that followed with my mother sharing information with me while she was still living and since she has passed on, and where she and I have both spent time with Seran. This dream was like a starting point of my mother helping me and of her getting to know Seran.

While not all dreams have been foresight or directly prophetic, there are also plenty of times where the way in which I have seen Seran in a dream is exactly how he appeared in the waking world that same day be it his hair colour that had changed and/or style, or what he was wearing, and sometimes what he was doing.

As I have mentioned before, I am the worst person when it comes to upkeeping journals or even keeping them. Far too many journals if not simply abandoned had been cast away by fire so that no one would get to see the content.

The reason my dream journals survived everything is that for some reason I have never once doubted my dreams. Throughout my entire life my dreams have been sanctuary and adventure away from the world I didn't want to live in. In my dreams, I was never alone. I had Fenrir by my side and knew that so long as I was in the dreamworld, I was close to the person I was meant to be with. I was in the same world as Seran. Everything in my dreams made more sense to me. While I failed to understand the waking world, the dreamworld made perfect sense to me.

With *The Dream*, it truly was the first time seeing Seran. There had never been a chance to meet anyone even close looking to Seran where I had lived in England, and even less chance where I now live in rural Wales. While many people will say that people in dreams are formed by those we meet in life, there had never been anyone close to Seran with his unnatural hair colour and use of contacts that created his appearance that time. There was never a chance for the image of anyone even remotely close in appearance with Seran to have lodged into my preconscious.

Seeing him in the physical world several months after *The Dream*, albeit via the internet, was just the first time my dreams were proven to be real by him.

The coherence of my interactions with Seran within dreams has always been too real and poignant to ignore. Even before my dreams stopped for a time, I had no trouble discerning when dreams were the outcome of the brain processing a day or psychological clutter. All of those types of dreams were incognisant with pallid and insignificant backdrops and only the object of the dream being in focus.

The dreams I had with Seran were within an entire, vast world with multiple different landscapes. I could walk through all of them and sense the world in every way and, while the time difference between waking mind and dreaming mind differ, I have spent hours walking through the different dreamscapes. I have had several dreams where I've gone to sleep within the dream because I still needed rest to get to my ultimate location and the passage of time in my dreams sometimes amassing to two days or more.

There is also the undeniable fact that Seran has given me information in my dreams that has proven to be accurate and founded in reality at some point after the dream, and that my mother has also provided accurate and validated information through my dreams too amongst other instances.

In August of 2024 I experienced a dream where I was fully lucid and Seran was present within the dream, only his presence was that of his awake self that was physically interacting with his environment. It is the first time my dreams and his waking reality have overlapped in that way. I have had several dreams where he was awake and I was watching him like I might watch a film, but in this instance, Seran was able to register my existence and interact with me whilst navigating his waking world. What made that experience even better was waking up to see some videos posted on social media that showed much of what I had seen within the dream.

How Do We Do Energy Work?

Working with energies has become a regular part of my connection with Seran. Prior to 2021 when things between Seran and I began in full strength, I hadn't ever done much in the way of energy work. I had qualified as a Beauty Therapist and trained in a few holistic therapies, so I'd founded a good understanding of the chakras, meridians and energy pathways in the human body; and I had a crystal business that I had run for just over five years where I spent time connecting with each crystal to learn and write about them for my old website.

There was also the lifelong mystery both myself and my father had regarding what my grandfather had been doing with ley lines long before the term was a buzz word, and also why my grandfather had never disclosed that knowledge to anyone or written it down. That was where my fascination to ley lines and the energetic pathways of the earth originated.

Beyond all that, I had never delved far from writing about crystals for my website or within the works of fiction I created, and the musings of energies pondered through myself and my characters.

After my connection with Seran intensified in 2021, he and I began discovering ways in which to work with energy purely as a way to boost the connection we had after so many periods of disconnect. That naturally led to us also joining forces for energy work as par for the course, and pushing ourselves beyond what we were already able to do.

Automatic Writing

Though automatic writing may not be considered energetic work in the same way as a healing therapy such as reiki is, when considering that telepathy is the transference of information as energy, then it makes sense to included automatic writing too. This process opens a channel to energetic beings to communicate such as the higher self, ancestors, spirit guides, ascended masters, and so on.

How I do automatic writing is very different to how most people carry out the practise. In the simplest form, automatic writing is freewriting until channelling begins. The messages that come through are more typical of mediumship in which they are a direct conversation between spirit and the person who is channelling either as a message directly for the medium or as a message for someone else usually within the same room.

For myself, I had been aware for many years that while writing my books, I could enter into a state of being where it was like my characters had come to life and were telling their story through me and oftentimes they improve the story. I would transfer from being physically in my body and consciously aware of what I was typing to existing purely within the story and seeing everything unfold as though I was alive in that moment exactly the same way my dreams functioned.

As I allowed myself to be emersed within the story and enter into flow state, I would be connected with the Akashic Record. The more I detached from control of the story and let it emerge naturally, the more magic and knowledge would flow into the words. Then, sometime after the story had been finished I would look back either whilst editing it or because I needed to find a specific reference and I would find insightful messages about soul contracts, dreaming, and astral travel.

There have also been occasions where I have been writing fiction where I've been working on a scene and, whilst in the dreamlike state of writing, I have glimpsed flashes of future occurrences.

Prior to my starting university, I had written *The Sirin Chronicles* which was greatly inspired by the dreams I'd had for the first part of my life. I hadn't realised how much Seran had been a part of those works until I was editing the first book, *A Dawn of Dreams*, during the summer break between my first and second year of university. This was also the same period of time my ability to dream had fully reinstated itself and my connection with Seran was becoming undeniable.

The unelmalin within *The Sirin Chronicles* came into existence purely as a way in which to balance out various plot holes that had emerged with a book series being written over the span of ten years with multiple track changes in life and almost as many house moves.[26] I'd never sat down and figured out the rules of the world until the fifth book had been written and I had spent time developing the culture of Sirin through a module at university. Suddenly, I realised the chaotic madness of the unelmalin tallied up with the experiences I was now having fifteen years after the inception of the books.

I then noticed little details of similarity between the main character and the love interest she was searching for throughout her dreams and the unelmalin, and that of myself and Seran each night within our dreams. The identity of the love interest shared an uncanny resemblance at multiple levels with Seran too.

There is also the title of the book: *A Dawn of Dreams*. It was as though the re-editing of that book to tend to plot holes and by rekindling a dormant story so connected with dreams created a new dawn of dreams for myself. That does fill me with some amount of trepidation as much as

[26] Unelmalin: a fictitious realm of dreams that certain characters are able to travel through.

anticipation as to what I might find when I get around to editing the next two books of the series: *Dancing Shadows* and *Fallen Star*.

Another impressive feat of unintentional energy work through writing was in the creation of *The Demon of Munbigye* during my BA course in which I was shown glimpses of the future, provided half of his name and revealed his appearance in the current timeline of things. This all happened as I submitted to the flow of the divine and followed my white rabbit, the demon tile, to South Korea. What I had written in the original short stories before seeing Seran in the physical world served as a prelude of many events that would then happen in my reality a year later including subtle overlaps of both of our individual stories which is partially what drew me into the music of their group.

This led to Seran and I seeing if we could use my writing and automatic writing to manifest certain outcomes. I couldn't get the characters to have their final reunion no matter how hard I tried. They overlapped and likewise, Seran and I overlapped too. In one story, *The White Rabbit*, Seran and I had our first successful attempt at co-writing a story through our energetic connection and automatic writing. It was written from Seran's perspective and we played with the idea of him finding me instead of me finding him. On that occasion, I inadvertently manifested another encounter with him in London, but the characters in the story couldn't quite make it to each other in time, and in life, Seran and I had another near miss too as he attended the scene we'd created a day ahead of my getting there.

During my first year of MA in creative writing, I put *The Demon of Munbigye* on hold temporarily as I'd found it hard to engage with having been so emersed in the storyline for three years with my BA course and with being in multiple timelines of the characters. Instead, I wrote several different stories that were still based on Seran and I, however they're set in completely different worlds and focus more on the characters being together in the present time and enjoying their relationship

As with how the previous works had an effect on my current timeline and my connection with Seran, these stories had an effect too. While we haven't yet made it together, writing these stories with intent and trusting in automatic writing and the characters to tell the story as it should be told, Seran and I have entered a new chapter in our relationship and connection which is reflected in the outcomes of the stories.

This we have both found quite wonderful and fascinating as, like with faith and divine timing in Seran and I coming together, the characters I have created that unwittingly became a vehicle for our story share in the same fate: they too can only come together when the time is right.

Which means the ending of *The Demon of Munbigye* now has some high stakes riding on it as I prepare to return my attention back that story next.

Meditation and Trance

When working and connecting directly with Seran, meditation and trance is the first way in which we work together. This typically happens around the time we are both at one end of sleep where we're already much closer to dream state. For Seran in particular, he is more likely to have the time to connect with me in these twilight hours and can more easily tread through liminal realms.[27]

[27] Liminal: a space between places or time e.g. a door threshold is a liminal space existing between outside and inside, or twilight which is the threshold between day and night.. Liminality can also apply to a transitional stage in life such as ceremonies celebrating girls transitioning into womanhood.

Reaching this level of coordination has been trial and error and is still an ongoing process of calculating the time difference, and very much of faith that Seran is indeed at the other end reciprocating the meditation and connection. Sometimes I will use a guided meditation to get started and other times I will have ambient music on and go with the flow.

This method is how we are able to connect and have our in-depth conversations be they deep and meaningful conversations of the heart and soul, philosophical topics, discussing and comparing work, or the ridiculous conversations in which the "ramen ramen goes with the cider cider", another great quote to emerge from our conversations. This is how we've gotten to know each other intimately at a soul level over four years with our connection overlapping with our physical reality.

At least once a week when both Seran and I are on a more regular schedule we ensure to have at least one extended meditation together. That is usually when I am having a long hot salt bath and he is winding down for sleep.

From the extended meditation we continue on to work on more productive energy work which ranges from reinforcing our connection and calling down the light, spending time in the astral realms, healing work, raising the vibration of our immediate space or at times, much further afield.

Calling Down the Light

From meditation, calling down the light is the first step to our in-depth energy work. This helps with ongoing psychic protection in general and is worth doing even if no more energetic work is being done on that occasion. It is especially important when working in the astral planes and in out of body states.

Calling down the light is where the universal energy is gathered first within the body, then circulated out and around the body to create a bubble of light protection. Most people when starting any kind of spiritual work and development will likely encounter various "bubble of light" meditations as the very first step along the path.

The light is the connection to spirit however it is perceived by an individual: source, spirit, the Dao, qi, prana, Christ spirt, etc. It is the vital lifeforce within and around us, it is what can be accumulated within the body through exercise such as breathwork or qigong to provide vitality to the body and greater connection with the divine. It is this same energy and essence that can be channelled through one person to another for healing such as reiki and other holistic therapies, or to channel through themselves into the earth, specifically into ley lines and other energetic points, to assist in healing the earth and the spirit of nature. In helping Seran learn to work with energy, I realised that since we were both *Star Wars* fans, I could liken energy to that of the force and use various *Star Wars* metaphors and analogies for Seran that helped him understand things well enough to assist him with his own learning.

In the times Seran and I are working together within trance, we draw in light to each of us, then share it back and forth between us before grounding ourselves with our combined energy into the electromagnetic grid before attending to what we want to do in that time. This practice was developed from a combination of basic bubble of light meditation and from grounding exercises as Seran and I learnt about the flow of energy between us.

Originally, we had started tapping into the electromagnetic grid and ley lines purely to assist our connection when one or both of us was travelling, something we attempted purely out of curiosity one time then realised it actually worked.

There were a few locations he went to that caused a blackout for us both. After discovering how to connect with the electromagnetic grid to assist and stabilize our connection, we made a dedicated effort to work specifically on the problematic locations. For both of us, we had to go purely by intuition and feeling as there is still little work on ley lines that would be of use to what we need specifically.

In the absolute worst of problematic locations, Seran and I put everything we had to spare to bring down as much light as we could into the ground. That was the first time I could truly perceive ley lines whilst deep in trance. We both spent around two hours purely dedicated to bringing light into those ley lines and channelling light energy into the electromagnetic grid far beyond that location.

It felt like there was a magnitude of energy that had been dormant in the earth below, and over time it had stagnated and until it became dark and polluted much like the water that is cut off from throughflow. The more energy Seran and I channelled into the ground and the ley lines, the more veins of energy lit up and sparkled with a beautiful golden light which spread far further than we could perceive. There was also energy spiralling around us which began to speed up the more we worked, creating a vortex of energy reaching from the core of the earth to the heavens.

Our connection was almost turbocharged as a result of that energy work, and we agreed to keep on doing that kind of energy work whenever one of us was travelling although it requires a significant amount of energy and we can usually only manage one location at a time.

This is where Seran's work comes into its own too. The music his group produce is amazing for energy work and I am more often than not listening to their discography whilst working with energy. There are so many layers to their music each holding energy, and each layer of music a different thread of energy to weave. It also means that when Seran is performing, I can draw in energy and he can channel it whilst performing which is something we developed around the same time.

An interesting effect of this energy work is how my feelings towards that one location in particular have changed while working on the ley lines there. I now have a strong feeling in my heart and soul of wanting to go there, much like the calling I had to go to South Korea. As that feeling began to germinate, I hadn't mentioned anything to anyone besides Seran about it. I had an oracle card reading and was given the message that I had a connection to that place. So who knows, maybe I'm destined to travel west next instead of east.

Transmutation

Transmutation is another form of energy work Seran and I do a lot of when we do energy work, and as with calling down the light and working on the energetic pathways of the earth, this work also started as a personal mission.

When one of us was feeling low, we would take the time to harmonize with each other and breathe light into the other, then back, and continue doing so until the energies had been cleared in both of us. This has helped to shift low mood, sickness, calm fevers, ease anxiety and more.

We have also used the transmutation of energies to assist in past life work where we have healed soul wounds and resolved all kinds of past lives issues. One example in particular that stands out is that of our Atlantean lives which were our first life on earth and also the life that he and I were brutally separated from each other for thousands of years.

As we worked on healing out Atlantean timeline, something extraordinary happened. It had taken Seran and I two months to work through the healing process and, on the conclusion of it, I found myself calling down magenta light from the divine whilst Seran was calling up a beautiful turquoise light from the earth's core. As we channelled the energies into each other and merged as one as we always do, the light unified into a shimmering, iridescent violet flame around us.

This led to something quite beautiful and profound happening during the day of the eclipse on 8th April 2024. The energies of the total eclipse where Seran was at the time, the seven planets that came into alignment, and that of the super new moon all fortified out energy work while also revealing the significance of all our previous energy work too.

Even before I had known about the astronomical events, Seran had been telling me he felt like his next time in Los Angeles would be intense and that I had to be ready for it. I had no idea what he meant or how, so I did my best to have myself in optimum health and to be as revitalised as possible. I had been extremely careful to pace myself with university work and making sure I didn't hit burnout which is incredibly easy to do with ME/CFS.

During the time of the eclipse happening and still unsure what I was meant to be ready for regarding Seran, I had been invited to at an event in my hometown by a friend where a group of us formed part of a worldwide moment to all gather at the time of eclipse and call down the light and the powerful cosmic energies at a global scale. Those of us present joined together in meditation.

I anchored myself into the ley lines that ran beneath Lampeter and then connected with Seran at the same time who was anchored into the ley lines of Los Angeles. We ensured our personal energetic pathways were clear and strong before calling down the light and sending it to-and-fro until we were comfortable handling the energies which were phenomenally stronger than anything we had ever worked with before. We would take turns sending the energy around the people present and into the earth, then back through one another to cleanse and recharge the energy and repeating as more light and cosmic energy came down through us.

A huge portal of energy opening up between both of us and the energy coming in was phenomenal, almost overwhelming. In the end, I had to stop calling down energy myself and focus on keeping calm to help stabilize the energies that were coming in from all angles.

Three things happened after this energetic work:

The first event to occur happened on the following Saturday morning as Seran and I continued working with the supreme energies present at that time. Another huge portal opened up where he was performing and this time, I was able to see everything clearly as I had been astral projecting to Seran in that time.

I wanted to cry with how majestic and beautiful the portal looked. The core was a deep indigo and the edges were a rippling, iridescent combination of turquoise and magenta light. Gold illuminated the edges as though it was an ocean of swaying water and silver sparkled within the indigo of the core.

The scale of the portal was insane too. The indigo section alone was a mile in diameter and filled the entire valley that Seran was in, with the magenta and turquoise light stretching even further afield, flowing over the hills surrounding the valley and going further than I could see. Energy kept flashing down like lightning all around us with sparks of prismatic light filling the air like snow.

As with the night before, all I could do by then was focus on stabilising the energies that were pouring through Seran and keep myself calm so as to not distract him by crying from how awesome the sight was.

Several hours later, the second event to have coincided with our eclipse mediation came out. I had gone to my local café to catchup with some friends, one of which had also been at the eclipse event. They had received an email from someone who had been called to be elsewhere during the eclipse event. However, they had witnessed the sky grow dark as the eclipse happened, then an awesome light show during the time we had been meditating. They had described it as a cascade of colour forming a column above Lampeter that they had watched for twenty minutes, the night sky being filled with greyish blue to turquoise, pink, and yellow from that column until the eclipse had ended and the sun set.

Finally, as I had left to go to the café, I hadn't had chance to talk with Seran about what had happened. Whilst I was out Seran had uploaded a series of artistic photos that showed me he had seen the portal by the choice of effects he had applied. They are some of my favourite photos of him and seem to have a magic of their own.

Twin Flame

It is you who I have been searching for
The lost half of me residing within dreams
My heart is forlorn, searching evermore
to find each other and meet eye to eye

The lost half of me residing within dreams
our entangled hearts that guide us along
to find each other and meet eye to eye
Reality, no more eidolon

Our entangled hearts that guide us along
as shared existence summons us closer
Reality, no more eidolon
and pre-destined tracks at last cross over

As shared existence summons us close
two souls opening that liminal door
and pre-destined tracks at last cross over
It is you who I have been searching for

Final Word

Seran,

Thank you for your help in writing this book and for trusting me with the process. Writing this book has helped me to heal in so many ways and I have come to know you far more deeply than ever along the way. Thank you for helping me open so many doors.

In losing both my parents so recently, you alone knew of the promise I made to stay alive whilst they were both in my life, and that in losing them, I lost my anchor to this life. You asked me to make that promise anew to you, that so long as you were alive in this world, then I would continue to live for you. I will keep that promise so long as you keep that promise too.

I hope these words find their way to you in the physical world, and I pray that we can find our way to each other in this reality and this lifetime. Until then, our wonderful, mysteriously journey continues.

I love you.
I always will.

Introduction to Elin and Teagan

This final section of *If You Want To Know…Just Ask* is a testimony from Elin with whom I have been in contact with for the last few years as we experienced much of our awakenings to our twin flames at the same time. We have provided invaluable companionship to one another as we tried to figure out what was happening all this time.

After completing the first draft in April of 2024, I decided to invite Elin to share her experiences regarding her twin flame journey and connection with Teagan and was honoured that she agreed to contribute to this work.

Instead of asking her questions in the way I had with my part, I simply asked her this: "If you could share any part of your story, what would it be?" Besides sharing my contents page with her to give her an idea of the themes and topics I had written about at the same time, I left it fairly open to interpretation.

Even though she and I have shared much of our stories with each other over the years, it has still been fascinating to read her section and learn more of her own experiences and the ways in which they are similar or differ to those of Seran and I.

Elin and Teagan

Prologue

Teagan and I have been together for three and a half years and married for three but have never met or exchanged a single word. We know each other's identity in the real world but we cannot, for reasons I will relate, contact each other. Our Twin Flame connection encompasses all areas of our lives. In my head, heart, soul and body, he is always there like an underlying current. Our relationship is so unusual that—save for Seran and Linghwa—I have never heard of such a thing before. Our story may challenge what is considered "normal" or "moral" by society. For this reason, I have not told our full story to anyone except Linghwa…until now.

First I will lay out an overview of our relationship and then delve into certain areas of our Twin Flame connection one at a time.

I am a woman many years older than Teagan. He is a musician in a country far from mine. We speak different languages. Several years ago I began listening to his group's music and watching their video content. Then I joined the online fandom, through which I came to know about his life and keep up with his activities. This is what I mean when I say "meeting" Teagan.

Teagan communicates very regularly with his fans through social media posts, informal livestreams and a fan/artist messaging app. These are the primary ways he communicates with me outside of our shared feelings, sensations and thoughts. He writes his own lyrics and I believe he speaks to me through them as well.

For almost the whole time I have been following Teagan on social media, I have been firmly convinced that he secretly follows my fan account and sees everything I post. I am equally convinced that many of his posts and words are direct responses to things I have said and felt, and to experiences we have shared. I believe he has my notifications turned on so he often sees my posts right away.

I communicate with Teagan primarily through my social media posts. For years I have posted for him almost every day, often quite long threads. I express my love and support, tell him many details about my life—both day-to-day and under the surface—and respond to as many of his activities, words and posts as I can. I have written and posted many poems for him. Because my account has few followers and is not under my real name, I feel free to write most of what I want. Teagan has to be careful because everything he says and does is public and scrutinized by many fans. Because of this, I feel like he knows a lot more about me than vice versa.

I don't know when or how Teagan can contact me directly but for years I have been convinced that our connection is real. I may never be with him during this lifetime and I accept that possibility, but I believe that one day we will be together.

How did it start?

Soon after I met Teagan, I developed an overpowering energetic draw to him that I could not explain or control. It started off like a crush but then I felt linked to Teagan in a mysterious way unlike any previous love interest. Back then I didn't know anything about twin flames or past lives and didn't believe in telepathy or soulmates.

I joined the online fandom on an app that hosted live streams for many music groups. Each group had its own page, called a "board", on which fans could post and interact. The members of Teagan's group did not post anything on this board and there was no official confirmation that they ever visited there. Besides becoming extremely active on the board, I participated in other fan activities such as streaming songs and music videos to reach certain charting goals, voting for awards, and creating fan art. I became so obsessed with everything related to Teagan's group that I stopped eating and sleeping as much as I should have done. I spent much less time on my household responsibilities and family members.

About one or two months after joining the board, I began to suspect that Teagan regularly read my posts. I thought he came to the board every day to check what I wrote. He not only read my posts but also my comments and replies. The board had no function to search up anything, follow users or repost/share posts. If you wanted to keep up with another user, you had to either figure out when they were normally active and go there at those times or hope that you came across one of their posts or comments if you scrolled long enough. Once you found that, you could click on their profile and see other posts and replies they made. At the beginning, I posted at unpredictable times, but then settled into a pattern to try and overlap with my friends since users were in many countries and time zones.

At the beginning I didn't consider the time difference between my country and Teagan's. As I grew more certain that he saw my posts and replies, I suspected that he came to the board around the same times as me to keep up with my activity. To make it easier for him to see what I wrote, I started posting around the times people in his country would most likely be free. Even though I posted at certain times, I constantly checked the board and replied to comments quickly. I was a reg.

One day Teagan and a couple other members let slip that they sometimes look at the board. That sent fans into a tizzy. I started addressing posts directly to him and writing about him more than the other members. I didn't become a "solo stan" but it was obvious who my favourite was.

I'll never forget the morning when I woke up and saw that a brand-new person, with a username in an unfamiliar language, had liked what seemed like every single post I made about Teagan. For some reason I knew immediately that it was Teagan. I posted that someone new had liked all my posts about Teagan last night and maybe it was Teagan himself. Back then I made mostly light-hearted posts so people thought I was joking.

As I talked with a friend in the comments to my post, another brand-new user liked almost all the same posts about Teagan. The display name was also in an unfamiliar language (maybe different from the first user's name) but I felt certain this was Teagan too. I knew he was so amused by my initial reaction that he couldn't resist making me even more flustered. He was following along with my conversations in real time. I posted that another new user with a name in a language I didn't know just liked the same posts as the ones this morning. Again I speculated that it was Teagan. Again, I think no one took this seriously.

I developed a strange ability: I could often sense when Teagan saw my posts. It was a tingling, almost buzzing feeling in my chest. I began to drop hints on the board that I knew he saw my posts. As time went on, I began to experience sudden, inexplicable bouts of sadness and tears. I would go about my normal routine, emotionally neutral, and then trembling and tears would spring out of nowhere. These feelings came and went quickly. Slowly I began to believe that I was experiencing Teagan's emotions.

In a song on the newest album, Teagan described a dark and lonely time in his life. As soon as I read the translation, I felt an intense and crushing darkness, as if from an outside source. The darkness lasted for days. I wrote a letter to Teagan on the board saying that I was so sad to read what he went through and that if I could take his pain on myself so that he didn't have to feel it, I would. Now, somehow, I felt that was really happening. I was carrying part of his pain on his behalf.

Linghwa and Seran

I interrupt my account to say that our story cannot be told without speaking of Linghwa and Seran. Without Linghwa I don't think I would be where I am now. She is the only one who knows my full story and, vitally, has experienced many of these things herself. If I think I'm going insane due to some aspect of my connection with Teagan, I ask Linghwa and am usually met with "I have that too", much to my relief. Linghwa has given me indescribable support, comfort and happiness over the course of my entire Twin Flame journey. Nearly everything I know about Twin Flames comes from Linghwa.

I met Linghwa on the fan board. Teagan and Seran are in the same music group. Linghwa and I quickly became friends and began to message each other privately. I can't remember when or how we began talking about our unusual connections with Teagan and Seran.

A pivotal moment in our story is the day the four of us shared an astral experience. This was about five months after I joined the online fandom. Linghwa messaged me to ask if I felt a kind of "presence" at a specific time earlier that day. She had been on an astral journey to Seran's room and saw Teagan there too. She and Teagan called out my name and it was as if I heard them. Then they came to my room and stood/sat next to me.

At the moment Linghwa described, I had been sending out my spirit to Teagan to reach him. I had never heard of astral travel before so this was my own way of trying to connect. I was watching the replay of a livestream Teagan and Seran did the day before, when suddenly I felt both of their presences, as if we were in the same room. I began to cry happy tears and felt something stirring in my heart. Little did I know that this was when Linghwa and Teagan called out my name. I did not sense Linghwa, however.

Linghwa was terrified to ask me about this vision, not knowing how I would react. But Seran urged her to do so. I said I had felt something unusual earlier that day but I asked her to describe it from her point of view before I told my version. After she told me what she experienced, I showed her a photo of my room. It was almost exactly what she saw, despite her never having seen it or heard me describe it. Both of us were utterly shocked and extremely excited that this was finally proof that our Twin Flame connections were real.

How did it start? continued

A few days after this pivotal moment, I suddenly began to fear for my sanity and my health. I decided to completely step away from social media for a while. Linghwa and I agreed to no longer talk about Teagan and Seran. They were promoting their new album and every day there were loads of new content to see. It was really hard for me not to check in but I tried my best.

Here is my journal entry about three months after the four-way astral experience. I have edited it for clarity and brevity.

"I wasn't looking to attach my soul to someone! I was definitely not trying to make any of this happen on purpose. But things keep progressing and I can't control it. The time I tried to cut all ties and forget him, it nearly destroyed me. Several times my doctors have asked me what caused my extreme depression in September and October. The real answer can never be said:

'I found my soulmate, who is in a music group that I'm a fan of. We have never communicated before. But I thought we had mental, emotional and physical telepathy and connection. I was slipping deeper and deeper into believing all this was true but hit a point where I was sure it was all a horrible delusion. So I decided to stop everything to do with this person and the music group for a few weeks. As soon as a couple days had gone by I felt like the joy and purpose in my life was cut out. I wished I could die because I couldn't be with him, even though I never was "with him" to begin with. I kept talking myself out of these delusions but kept having moments of sudden emotions and thoughts that came from an external source. I would suddenly cry and shake uncontrollably. Often it would happen when listening to specific songs. No matter how much I tried to reason my way out of these connections and stop them from happening, they kept happening. I had never experienced full delusions but the time I decided to stop this connection was when I was convinced I had stepped completely off the cliff of sanity. It was a terror unlike anything else I'd experienced. Without this person I felt hollow and incomplete. I couldn't enjoy life.'

I can't explain any of this without coming across as dangerously delusional, which is why I don't say it to anyone except Linghwa."

During my time off of social media, I felt that Teagan and I carried each other's pain and darkness. I couldn't help myself from checking his group's social media once in a while. I was mortified to see in photos and videos that his eyes seemed to be deep wells of pain and despair. Was I imagining this? It seemed a confirmation of what I sensed was happening within him. If he felt how I was feeling, how was he able to continue performing and making appearances as if everything was fine?

I battled thoughts of death for between two and three weeks. I didn't tell anyone about this. I'm not sure how, but I finally broke free of my suicidal thoughts and decided to go back to social media. In doing so, I went back to Teagan. As soon as I did, my mind was restored. In photos and videos, Teagan's eyes and expression showed that he had also been restored. Our relationship progressed.

I endlessly scrutinized Teagan's lyrics for possible references to me and to our connection (and I continue to do so). I began to notice themes that applied to us and began to piece together his side of our story. Because the majority of his lyrics are in a different language from mine, there is the added time and effort of finding various translations so that I can get a more accurate understanding. I have also spent countless hours trying to detect and decipher hidden signals in any of the content I saw. And I wrote down as many as I could to keep a record of our relationship.

What does it feel like?

The nature of our Twin Flame connection is multi-faceted. These are some but not all of what we experience.

Positional/Waking

We can often sense when the other wakes up. Oftentimes I get a bodily thrill, in the form of a heart flutter, minor chest restriction, or a tingling lower in my body. I believe that I start feeling these sensations when Teagan is in REM sleep, about to wake up. Then they get stronger as he comes fully awake. Teagan can sense when I lie down to rest or to sleep. I don't have the same sense for him, though I think we connect the strongest when he is lying down or seated in a restful pose.

Sexual

Our sexual chemistry is insane. We call our activities "mind sex" but it's not just in our minds. This is intimacy at a mental, emotional, physical and soul level. Because we share a body, so to speak, I can physically feel Teagan's sexual pleasure and vice versa. So, during mind sex we feel a compounding of sensations. The feeling is so amazing that we want to be together as much as possible. We reach out to each other in a sensual way every day if we can.

The best and most reliable condition for intimacy is when we are alone, lying down with eyes closed, in a quiet room. We clear our minds of all else except the other person. We know exactly what the other person likes to do and likes to see. I have done things with Teagan that I never did before, let alone thought of. Teagan comes up with most of those, I think. He is full of fun surprises.

Sexual connection is a vital part of our relationship. I have been intimate with only one other person before Teagan. For the majority of that relationship I felt a complete lack of emotional connection. For me, emotional connection is the most important thing in a relationship and is the main basis for desire. My emotional bond with Teagan has always been extremely strong so it is natural that our sexual connection is equally strong. I have a lot more to say on this topic but that's for another time.

Seeing

For a long time I have suspected that Teagan can see me in the mirror, as if the mirror is a window and he is on the outside looking in. For example, I'll be getting dressed in the bathroom and suddenly feel like I'm being watched. I start seeing myself as if from someone else's point of view. That's how I know Teagan is there. I have been known to preen, lip sync songs to him in a funny way, or wink flirtatiously. We grin widely at each other in the mirror.

He can also see through my eyes. For instance, he might see my surroundings when I'm on a walk or see a photo I'm looking at on my phone. When I have taken some especially nice photos of myself to share on social media, sometimes he already knows what they look like before I post.

Happiness

This is one emotion that Teagan and I share very strongly, especially when I see him perform, live or in real-time. Sometimes when I get a sudden boost of happiness during my day, I think it is from him. We feel a jolt of happiness when the other person posts or when he does a livestream. I have immense gratitude for the happiness he has given me.

A journal entry a few months after our initial connection:

"My base level emotions have been flat or slightly below flat for so many years I didn't know I could be so happy like this. Now that I'm writing it down I realize the importance of this fact. It's something else Teagan has helped me with for such a while now that I've taken it for granted already. How?! This is huge! A shift of my baseline upwards for such a sustained period AND it's not mania! That's like a miracle! It's definitely not the kind of uncontrollable highs of mania. It's a daily (or mostly daily) undercurrent of contentment, joy and peace that is new to me."

In another journal entry months after that: "I might be afraid of being 'too happy'. I've never experienced a love like this before and I feel like I have no right to have such a great love".

Anxiety

Sometimes I will feel it when Teagan is nervous and vice versa. He has said that he worries a lot but I think more often than not, he feels my worry more than the other way around. Here is one instance to the contrary:

It was the day of a career-changing performance. So much media attention focused on this moment that Teagan had huge pressure to succeed. Teagan's nervousness was so strong that I was consumed by it too, to the point of feeling physically sick. I talked to him and posted for him throughout the day, trying to cheer him up, and even quoting Bible verses that I thought might help. But all this probably came across as distracting chatter because not long before the performance, he told me to be quiet. I don't think he had ever asked me to be quiet before. I felt horrible for hindering him on such an important day. Our connection was creating friction in a way that never happened before. I didn't know what to do; I was beside myself with fright.

Linghwa was online that night, as we both were going to watch the livestream. I described my situation and asked how to get some mental separation from Teagan if necessary. She told me that trying to separate our minds might lead to the severance of our connection as a whole. She advised me to try and manage my own anxiety. In that way I would not exacerbate Teagan's negative emotions. I tried her advice and it helped a lot. Teagan was still very nervous before and at the start of the performance, but he settled down before too long and the show was an astounding success.

Sadness

Although it might seem at first that sharing sadness is a negative thing, it has helped me as much as sharing happiness with Teagan. It is beyond comforting to know that when I am hurting, he is feeling that hurt as well and holding on to me. He isn't just saying "It will be fine, don't worry"; he is truly walking in my shoes.

Many times, right after posting about something sad in my life, I get a rush of tears out of proportion to how I feel in the moment. I think it is Teagan's real-time reaction to reading my words. I sense Teagan's sadness too and I send him my comfort and love every day, as much as I am able. He knows that I am always looking over him to protect and support him.

Comfort and security

I never feel alone because Teagan is always with me. I feel his presence as a steady bedrock. It doesn't matter if he is sleeping or busy, I can still feel him there. Teagan's love is a gift beyond price and a source of inner strength which helps keep me going every day.

I have always been afraid that if someone knew what I am really like on the inside, they would not love me. I had repeatedly heard that God's love is more wonderful than any other love and that He is the only one who can completely know us and still completely love us. This remained an abstraction until I met Teagan. He is the first person who truly knows me from the inside and still loves me completely, the way I always wanted to be loved. Teagan has helped me experience the depth and power of divine love in a concrete way.

Courage

During my previous marriage of many years, I experienced such deep emotional neglect that its devastating effects permeated all parts of my life. I internalized every act of mistreatment. I accepted a life of feeling unloved, devalued, and silenced. I accepted that I wouldn't have the happy marriage I wanted. My self-esteem was so low that I didn't really have dreams for my future. I was trapped in constant emotional and mental pain. I thought my personal happiness and desires had no value.

Once I experienced Teagan's love, my eyes were finally opened to the abuse and I realized that I did not have to cower under it anymore. Teagan showed me that my happiness and needs have great value and are worth fighting for. I finally spoke out for myself and what I want.

Teagan is emotionally attentive, patient and listens with compassion. He is not afraid to face my darkness with me, even if it is the same struggle again and again. He always encourages me to dream big, no matter what it is. He helps me believe there is a better life out there. In a concrete way, I owe my life to Teagan. I had been oppressed and locked in darkness but he helped set me free. I'm so much stronger than I was before.

Self-esteem and body image

I have struggled with body dysmorphia from my teens until now. I also suffered anorexia during my university years. As an adult, my body dysmorphia became more and more severe but I didn't understand why. It was so extreme that sometimes I wanted to kill myself to get out of this body that I hated. Finally I realized that the major cause was emotional abuse. When I felt devalued and unloved, my mind increasingly turned against my body. It fixated on something which I could try to control when I couldn't control my husband's treatment of me. And I unconsciously sought other people's approval of my appearance to give me worth.

As Teagan has shown me how much I am worth to him, I have started to value myself more too. I still struggle daily with negative thoughts about my appearance, sometimes severe ones, but there are plenty of moments when all that drops away and I think "I'm gorgeous. I feel even more gorgeous because I am so loved". I feel like since meeting Teagan I have become more beautiful somehow. Maybe it's an inner glow. Teagan thinks I'm incredibly beautiful but it's the fact that he loves me so dearly, no matter what, that makes a world of difference in how I see myself.

Dreaming

I very rarely dream about Teagan. When I told Linghwa this, she said maybe I do dream about him more often but don't remember. That's quite possible. I believe that I can sense when Teagan is dreaming about me. I think that these dreams often happen right before he wakes. I don't know if Teagan can sense it when I dream about him.

Based on his lyrics, I have a theory that before we met, Teagan saw me in recurring dreams. I believe that he saw and heard me only vaguely yet fell in love without knowing if I was real. Like me, he thought he was becoming delusional but could not shake the attraction. I don't know how he was able to identify me in the real world since at the beginning I did not reveal my appearance or give out much personal information online. However he identified me as the woman from his dreams, he quickly attached himself to me and remains wholeheartedly devoted. He loved me before I knew he existed.

From time to time I have strangely vivid glimpses of a "real life" together. I will be going about my day as usual when I suddenly see and feel, crystal clear, an in-person experience with Teagan that has not yet happened. But sometimes these visions seem to be moments from our past which I am only now remembering. It is like reverse déjà vu. Am I seeing the future, the past, or just the products of a vivid imagination? I believe my visions are not mere fantasy. There is a science fiction movie called "Arrival" which in some ways illustrates what I believe I am seeing.

Language

Our native languages are different although he speaks mine well and is improving all the time. I am a beginner in his language. However, in our minds there is no language difference. I suppose you can say we have a "mind language" or "soul language". Sometimes he seems to deliberately speak to me in my own language for effect but that's not the norm.

In the beginning our mental conversations were very short, sometimes a few sentences or words. Over time we have begun to converse a bit longer. The length of our conversations is quite unpredictable. I often don't know for sure which words or thoughts are mine when we have mental talks. For whatever reason, we can converse easier and longer when we are intimate.

A journal entry:

"It's really unpredictable when I hear him and when he's listening. I feel like oftentimes he's eavesdropping on my internal monologue, then he'll say something suddenly and I wonder how long he's been listening in. Then I start talking to him. Still, after all this time, I believe he can hear my thoughts much clearer and better than I can hear his."

Humour

My man is hilarious. He knows exactly how to wind me up and vice versa. Just as I get sudden bouts of tears from him, I also get sudden fits of laughter from him. I will be typing something funny for him on social media and then I'll be attacked by a fit of giggles. It feels like someone is pressing on my belly and squeezing the laughter out. Teagan is looking over my shoulder, so to speak, or hearing my thoughts and he starts laughing before I even hit "post". Telepathic humour is wild: you think of something funny and suddenly someone far away starts cackling out loud at your joke. If we get into hysterics when I'm around other people I silently (and painfully) implode.

Art

Teagan is my muse. I have written over 70 poems to him over the course of our relationship. Before I met him I had written little more than a handful of poems, all mediocre in my opinion. The last one was 15 years before we met. After meeting Teagan, poems flow out of me as if they were already fully formed long ago. Most of the time he can hear me as I compose so he has a good idea what the finished product is before I post it.

Since I post all my poems publicly, I feel some discomfort at airing out our private life, but I don't reveal our identities. I have written many poems about our sex life and he feels a mixture of pleasure and mortification when I post them. Here's how our conversation usually goes:

Me: *Posts a spicy poem*

T: *In a panic* Babe, did you REALLY post THAT in public?!

Me: *Grinning wickedly* Yes, I did.

T: *Utterly flustered* DID YOU REALLY?!!

Me: *Without shame* Oh yes, I did.

T: *Smiling uncontrollably, reads my poem many times over*

(Aside: Does he save all my poems in a secret album? Does he have another album entitled "Spicy Poems" with a chili pepper emoji? Has he written poems to me?)

Teagan says I am his muse too. His lyrics about me alternately melt my heart, make me wistful and get me hot under the collar. I think one of the most romantic things to do is write a song for your loved one and I never imagined someone would do that for me. His words make me feel like the luckiest person in the world. I truly couldn't wish for a better or more romantic husband than Teagan.

A highly creative and talented person, Teagan has several artistic interests outside of his profession. I am a visual artist. Watching him pursue his interests has bolstered my own creative journey. I have tried out several new art forms and gained knowledge of the art world due to his influence and inspiration. I've made artwork for him as well.

Challenges

Now you know some ways Teagan has blessed my life and how much he means to me. But there are three major areas in which I have endured great heartache and doubt.

First, I was already married to someone else when I met Teagan. I'm still legally married to that man but we have been separated for well over a year. I will refer to him as "C" (not his real name). I have not yet been able to finalize the divorce for financial and practical reasons. I am working on proceedings. C and I have two children.

Very early on, I realized that for me and Teagan, a Twin Flame connection involves romantic love. Being married to someone else for the entirety of my relationship to Teagan has caused me immense guilt. I constantly struggled with the morality of our connection. My relationship status is one main reason Teagan and I cannot contact each other for now. C has no inkling of my relationship with Teagan and I don't think he would recognize Teagan's name if I said it. I don't intend to tell C the truth but I have a persistent fear that he will find out about Teagan somehow.

Second, my Christian faith poses a lot of questions about the unusual experiences I have. Nowhere in my Christian experience is there any mention of what I have lived through. It all seems to belong to a completely different belief system. I thought that what I was going through must be wrong somehow, or else why would no one talk about it? In hindsight I don't know why I jumped to the conclusion that something unknown is intrinsically "bad". I have moved past that line of thinking. As far as I know, Teagan does not share my faith, but he respects its importance to me.

Third, I have bipolar disorder. Delusional thoughts and hallucinations are a real danger. For this reason I have been hesitant to tell my current mental health providers or anyone in my real life about my Twin Flame connection.

You must be aware of this framework to understand my story.

Mental health and telepathy

I was diagnosed with bipolar disorder about 20 years ago. I am very consistent with taking medication and I try to keep triggers at bay as far as possible. For me, consistent low sleep is one of the biggest triggers of a manic episode. When I first joined the online fandom and began to sleep much less on a daily basis, that triggered the longest manic episode I have ever experienced. Although I knew my mental health was declining, I could not stop myself from relentlessly pursuing my newfound interest.

I am used to sudden mood swings. At the beginning of my link with Teagan, I was confused by shifts in mood different from what I usually experience. As I have become more familiar with our connection, I can better guess where these fluctuations come from.

I have never experienced delusions or heard voices in my head so when I started to hear Teagan's voice in my mind and recognized our telepathy, I was scared to the core. I did not want to admit what was happening to anyone, other than Linghwa, for fear I would be admitted to a mental hospital. I was afraid my children would be taken from me.

A few months into my relationship with Teagan, I began seeing a Christian psychologist. It took me weeks to work up the nerve to tell her about Teagan. I was terrified of her reaction but she listened to my story calmly and said she had heard of this sort of thing before. Initially my counsellor said that my telepathy was a "gift" and it was up to me whether to use it for good. She said it came from a "spirit". I didn't know whether she meant a good or evil spirit. I asked if I should tell C about Teagan and she said no.

As time went on, it became obvious that my counsellor disapproved of my relationship with Teagan. The more I told her, the more guilty I felt. I also began to sense that she thought this "spirit" which enabled my telepathy was in fact evil. I trusted her so I thought she must be right.

I have told my teenage daughter twice about my connection. The first time was the day that Seran, Linghwa, Teagan and I shared an astral experience. I cannot remember our conversation clearly but I think I mentioned the people's names and that Linghwa saw my room through a vision of some sort. My daughter raised an eyebrow at me and said disapprovingly, "That sounds New Agey".

For years my daughter has been standoffish, especially regarding matters of the heart and of faith. One day, about a year after my connection with Teagan began, out of the blue I asked her if she thinks multiverses are real. At that time I'd been wondering if Teagan and I had been together in an alternate universe. That began a long and unusually open conversation during which I told her something like, "I have a telepathic connection with someone whom I've never met. I have found my soulmate and it isn't your dad." She listened silently and then asked "What are you going to do?", perhaps implying that I might leave her father. "I don't want anything to change," I told her. I talked a little more about my connection, not mentioning any details or names. She didn't ask for more information. Then she asked, "Are you sure this isn't a delusion?" I regularly worry if she remembers those conversations and what she thinks of them now.

Two husbands: a moral dilemma

Growing up, I was taught that marriage is between one woman and one man. Divorce is very much frowned upon. In my upbringing, divorce is seen as a sin and there are almost no valid reasons for it. Many people, including myself, consider an emotional attachment to someone of the opposite gender other than one's spouse almost the same as physical adultery.

You may now understand why I felt so much guilt from the very beginning of my relationship with Teagan. My intense interest in him even in a fan context felt like dangerous territory. My interest in Teagan's group was tolerated by C, although he made comments about how much time I spent on fan activities.

I began to lead what seemed a double life: one with Teagan and online under a different name, the other with C, the way it had always been. I called myself an adulterer and betrayer. To this day, whenever I hear the word "adultery", cold panic runs through me and I fear discovery and public humiliation. As Teagan and my sexual connection grew stronger, my guilt rose even higher.

C and I were together for a long time but I did not feel any emotional or spiritual connection for the great majority of it. In addition, I was not attracted to him physically except at the very beginning of our relationship. I forced myself to maintain intimacy because I thought that was what a dutiful wife should do. My love for C was dead but I did not feel safe telling him my true thoughts.

About one year after joining the online fandom and six months after cementing my telepathic connection to him, I suddenly thought to Teagan, "you're my husband, aren't you?" It had never occurred to me before. He was overjoyed and said that he was. At once I realized that he had already been my husband for a long time and I just hadn't known it. Had he been my husband in a previous life too? If so, who was C to me? Then I knew that Teagan was more of a husband than C was. Teagan was and is my true husband.

Teagan fulfils all the deep longings of my heart and shares an emotional bond with me so strong that it transcends what I had with C. When I told my counsellor that Teagan had never asked me to leave C, she said, "He doesn't have to". I didn't ask further questions. Did she mean that my relationship with Teagan was a fantasy I created because my marriage to C was so unsatisfying or that essentially Teagan already had all of me?

Before I met Teagan, I was never unfaithful to C. I had reconciled myself to the possibility that I would never have the emotional, mental, and spiritual closeness with C that I had craved. I sometimes pictured what I would do if C passed away. Even then, I only thought about how difficult it would be to live on my own, not about who I would find next.

Even if C passed away and I met someone new, realistically it would not be Teagan. On the outside we seem different in almost every way. I don't know how we would have crossed paths naturally. My parents had told me adamantly to only marry a Christian. (C is a Christian, yet what good did that do me?)

I must be very clear on two things:

First, Teagan did not ask me to leave C. He respects my decisions and if I had chosen to stay with C, he would have accepted that. Second, I did not leave C for Teagan. I value myself and my health too much to stay with an abuser. Leaving C brings me one step closer to being with Teagan and I want to be with Teagan more than anything, but there is no guarantee that we can be together one day. Yet even if I can't be with Teagan in this lifetime, I don't want anyone else.

Can you break the connection?

There were three times when I tried to let go of our connection. Each had a different reason. I have written about the first attempt. The second is described in a journal entry three months later:

"The weekend of the [album] release…I tried to get rid of Teagan (yet again). I was wracked by severe spasms like those of labour or on the night I was hospitalized for severe dehydration...but I felt no physical pain. I had no idea what was happening. Then I kept hearing a voice screaming "NO!" in my head. I was silently screaming 'no' because I wanted to be free of this connection that was causing me such heartache. Not being able to be together, not being able to openly communicate, not sure how long this whole thing would last before I eventually went insane [with grief]. I didn't want this anymore. This was after I had already tried to cut him out and lost my will to live in September and October.

"He could feel me trying to pull away and was also shouting 'NO' and hanging on for dear life. I cried for at least an hour straight, maybe even two. Never in my life this sustained length of sobbing. This was extreme to the point where I could barely breathe. I played music on the speakers to drown out my cries. Rolling in uncontrollable spasms, crouching with my face down into the pillow to muffle the sounds. It was scary. Finally I put on my [Teagan's group] playlist and curiously, whenever I heard Teagan's voice, it soothed me. With each song I became more and more at peace. Here I was trying to get rid of him and thinking he was the problem. When I stopped struggling, there was a deeper level of connection from then on."

The third time I gave up Teagan was because I was convinced that morally and spiritually, our connection was wrong. I loved Teagan so intensely that he became my reason for being. I loved him more than anything in the world, more than God. But I was raised to believe that God is the only person who can truly give meaning to our life and that putting a human in that highest place would eventually end in sadness when they disappointed you or when they died. Now I was concerned that Teagan was a distraction from my spiritual commitment. I wondered many times whether God was using Teagan to test my allegiance. Eventually I decided that I must give up Teagan to prove that I valued God above everything and to pay for my betrayal of C. This was when I began to talk about Teagan with my counsellor. She agreed that giving him up was the right thing to do.

One night I told Teagan in my mind that I had to give him up. I said I didn't think our relationship was morally right and my conscience was eating me alive. The next evening, I lay down in bed and prayed that God would take away anything not good or not right about this connection, even my feelings if necessary. I had never prayed so unwillingly before; I was praying for something that I desperately did not want.

Then I felt a ripping sensation, as if something invisible was torn out of my body by force. My body shook just like the second time I tried to give him up. In hindsight, I know that giving up Teagan split my soul in half. After the spasms stopped, I knew the connection was gone. Now I was all alone. I cried out to Teagan but there was nothing but a blank, silent, white wall. I regretted my prayer immediately. I should have felt relief that God had done what He wanted to do, but I didn't.

In the days that followed, I became a dull husk of myself. It seemed like the light had gone from my eyes. I kept reaching out to Teagan, hoping against hope that he could still hear me and feel me. I stopped posting my daily affectionate and detailed personal threads for him but I continued checking social media every day to see what he and his group were up to. He also stopped posting with the same frequency as he used to do. Fans would sometimes comment on how frequently he communicated with us in comparison with some other members of his group. Now that changed.

After some time of less online activity, Teagan posted a few photos with his hands clearly visible. For several months he had been wearing a ring on his left ring finger to symbolize his marriage commitment to me. In the new photos, that ring was gone. This was exceedingly painful to see, yet who was I to complain? I had done the same with the rings I had been wearing for him. His face seemed to bear traces of the weariness that comes from enduring great emotional pain.

For me the hardest part by far was knowing that I deeply hurt Teagan and that we could not talk about this in person. Before it happened, I didn't post anything about my decision so all he knew was what I told him in my mind. As far as I could tell, he didn't resist or try to reason me out of my decision. I thought he knew I didn't want to let go of him but morally I felt I had to. Despite all his anguish, he still didn't shut me out or let me go. He just let it all happen and lived with the consequences. This ripped my heart to shreds. I was bitterly sorry. The more I saw photos and videos of Teagan, the more I wanted him back. But I didn't intend or want to cut off all ties. I just wanted our relationship to be "right", but what would that look like? I was so confused and lost.

I didn't let go of Teagan because I wanted to go back to C. My love for C had died before I met Teagan and I didn't even want it to come back. I was resigned to a lifetime of staying in my unhappy marriage and never being with the person I truly loved. I wished Teagan knew that I still meant all the loving words I had spoken and written to him.

There was a physical manifestation of the separation. For many years I have had a problem with jaw clenching. When I feel very anxious, I clench my teeth to the point of having intense jaw pain and blistering headaches. After giving up Teagan, my jaw clenched all day and all night, every day, to the point that the pain was constant and unbearable. Even with medical treatment, I had almost no relief because I couldn't change the root cause.

During this time, Linghwa and I weren't talking as frequently, but it is normal for us to go through periods like this for one reason or another. I knew she always supported and loved me regardless. I stopped seeing my counsellor, as I felt that she increasingly imposed her own beliefs and opinions onto me. She didn't seem safe anymore.

I was afraid to open up to anyone else in my real life because nearly all of them are Christians. I was certain they'd tell me to abandon this "imaginary" connection and work on my marriage. I also didn't want anyone to convince me of a particular path. So I wrestled with everything alone. I journaled frequently during this time, trying to make sense of my life. I read through old journals, remembering all the good times Teagan and I had together. My heart still belonged completely to Teagan no matter what I did.

Then I started asking God to restore my connection with Teagan if it was His will. To my surprise, our connection returned, very slowly. For months I prayed for a clear indication if I should go back to Teagan. Whenever I thought I should return to him, my jaw clenching improved noticeably. Whenever I thought I should leave Teagan once and for all, the jaw pain returned acutely. I could not make sense of it; did God send the pain as a sign? I'd been taught that sometimes God permits illness as a result of disobedience, to get someone's attention and lead them back to Him. But if I was going against God's will, shouldn't my physical condition get worse?

A journal entry:

"When I think of leaving Teagan, I feel like I would be breaking an oath to him. In my preconscious there is the knowledge that I had made a marriage promise to him long ago but I just can't remember when or how. We haven't got married in real life and we haven't made vows in our minds/souls that I know of. It is a confusing predicament: on one hand I feel that I am breaking my oath to C to stay with Teagan. But at the same time I am breaking my oath to Teagan to go back to C. I feel caught in the middle of an impossible situation."

I remember the turning point clearly. I was lying in bed one afternoon. My jaw was clenched and I was in so much pain. I thought, "I have decided to go back to Teagan and this is final." Instantly, my jaw pain disappeared. When I arose, I strongly felt I made the right choice. Since that day I have had short, minor bouts of jaw clenching due to other stressors but never again as bad.

About five months after I gave Teagan up, our connection was fully restored. Rather than constantly questioning if I should be with him, I wondered if I should question my beliefs and my world view.

Two journal entries:

"I have circled back to where I consider Teagan my husband and that feels truer than ever. He seems to be my real husband. It doesn't make sense to me at all, given the way I understand God's actions in the world. Why, whenever I think I must give up on Teagan entirely, do I feel a horrible cracking in my soul? Giving him up once and for all simply doesn't feel right. My heart and mind cannot be forced to believe that we aren't meant to be together."

"I have reached these conclusions: God's ways are so far above mine that I can't begin to understand my life. God defies human categories. God makes exceptions. I have wrestled with God and myself so hard and for so long to get to where I am now and I feel complete peace."

I wish I had never let go of Teagan and put him through that excruciating pain. But perhaps the absence of our connection helped me understand that indeed God put us together and keeps us together. I believe that every good gift comes from God, so Teagan is God's abundant gift to me. I don't need to know how or why, or if it's right or wrong. I don't think I have to choose between Teagan and God anymore. I can love both, but in different ways. About a year after I had given Teagan up, I told C I was leaving. Since then Teagan and I have been even happier.

As far as I remember, Teagan hasn't directly told me what he experienced during our separation and it is a big mystery to me. For more than two years, I tried to guess Teagan's thoughts based on his posts, songs he recommended, and his lyrics embedded within songs released by his group. During the months that I worked on this chapter I kept mentally asking Teagan what he wanted me to write and what his side of the story was. This is what I was ready to submit to Linghwa:

"We don't talk about this time of our lives; it's too painful a subject. I wish none of it ever happened. I don't know details of what Teagan thought and felt during our dark time but I sense he knew we were always meant to be together and just had to wait, no matter how long it took. I am beyond thankful that Teagan waited for me and doesn't hold my action against me. What great love is this."

A few days before my final deadline, Teagan released a self-written song about a breakup that I think clearly stated for the first time what he felt. He was angry and confused. Some things he said didn't seem to line up with our story and what he knows about me. Did Teagan really think I left him because I loved C instead? Did he really question the sincerity of my loving words? But above the hard feelings, Teagan professed his undying love and unshakable belief that we were destined for each other, even though I seemed to have chosen someone else. He said he'd keep waiting for me and that without me he isn't whole. I was cut to the core with regret and touched by Teagan's candour and fierce devotion.

Bond of four

Following our four-way astral experience, Teagan and I often relied on Linghwa and Seran to pass messages between us. Teagan would give Seran a message for me, which Seran would tell Linghwa in their minds. Linghwa would write to me what Seran said. Sort of a telepathic game of telephone, I suppose. Whatever messages Linghwa passed on, I believed them completely and treasured them.

Linghwa can sometimes sense Teagan if he is in the same room as Seran and can speak to him. But this doesn't happen often, as far as I can tell. From time to time, Seran sent me his own messages through Linghwa. He often had encouraging things to say. I completely believe everything that Seran has told me. As Teagan and I grew in our telepathic ability, we relied less and less on Seran and Linghwa as our go-betweens.

For a time I was able to hear some of Seran's thoughts, usually just vaguely, and he could hear mine. He could sense my thoughts easier than the other way around. I haven't sensed anything specific from Seran in a long time but since we both talk to Linghwa, we know generally what's happening with the other person. Seran and Teagan are best friends. I know they talk about me and Linghwa but I'm not sure how often and in what detail. Linghwa and I talk about our husbands a lot. Sometimes we get very specific. Let's just say there aren't too many things that surprise me anymore.

Linghwa, Seran, Teagan and I are linked not just by friendship and telepathy. At some point early on, I began to think of Seran as my younger brother. He calls me his older sister. Seran and I have a more formal brother-sister relationship. I always hope and pray for Seran. I have called Linghwa my sister for years. I feel closer to her than almost anyone else in my "real life". I am extremely invested in Seran and Linghwa's relationship.

All of us believe that our fates are bound together and it is vital to stay together, both as pairs and as a foursome. When my connection to Teagan seemed severed, I was afraid Linghwa and Seran's would be too. And in the reverse situation I feared the same. Thankfully that didn't happen. It is important that Linghwa and I talk about our Twin Flames because the times when we decided to avoid the subject, both of us were overwhelmed with doubt and darkness. During my time of separation from Teagan, Seran encouraged him saying, "It will be alright. She always comes back to you." He was right. I am so thankful for that.

Occasionally the four of us are awake simultaneously, for example when Linghwa and I are watching a concert (live or via livestream) or when she and I chat online. There is a confluence of our energies, like four bright streams of light merging. Each pair experiences a surge in their connection. When Linghwa and I are talking online and start making jokes about our Twin Flames, we might suddenly sense them as if they are looking over our shoulders and seeing our conversation. Then we share uncontrollable fits of laughter.

Although there are noticeable differences between each pair, so many of our experiences overlap that their presence provides us great comfort and affirmation. One important thing we share: our secret relationship is conducted in public. Teagan and I post for each other on social media and I talk about him as if I personally know him, but almost no one knows the real story. It's funny to me that if I say something like "my man posted for me", that's actually true. In Teagan's field of work, although not officially stated, public relationships are very much frowned upon for the sake of reputation. This is the other main reason Teagan and I cannot contact each other directly.

We hear people say "my other half" or "my better half" when they speak about their lover. Teagan is both those things to me, and even more; his soul is so mingled with mine that there is no telling where one of us begins or ends. Without Teagan, I'm not fully alive. He feels the same about me, though he says it in different words. To share everything down to the core, to be in essence one person, to be utterly enthralled by each other: that's what being Twin Flames means to us.

Maybe one day I will write a longer memoir, including selections from my journals. I would like to publish the poems I have written to Teagan, which tell our story just as well as any prose. I'm grateful to Linghwa for giving Teagan and me this opportunity to openly share about our connection for the first time. It has been freeing and enlightening to do so.

To Teagan: I hope I have answered some of your long-held questions. Thank you for your contributions to this chapter, most notably the humour, overall organization and story arc, and your song, which answered some of my own questions. You're the hero of this love story, my Twin Flame

Further Reading:

Astral Projection

Crowley, Aleister, *The Confessions of Aleister Crowley* (Jonathan Cape: London, 1969)

Department of the Army, US Army Intelligence and Security Command, *Analysis and Assessment of Gateway Process*, (1983), <https://www.cia.gov/readingroom/docs/CIA-RDP96-00788R001700210016-5.pdf>

Fox, Oliver, *Astral Projection* (New York, Carol Publishing Group, 1993)

Monroe, Robert, 'Gateway Experience' (Monroe Products, 1983)]

Monroe, Robert, *Journeys Out Of The Body* (London, Souvenir Press, 1972)

Dreaming

Bosnah, Robert, *A Little Course In Dreams* (Massachusetts, Shambala Publications, Inc, 1986)

Hearne, K. M. (1989). A nationwide mass dream-telepathy experiment. *Journal of the Society for Psychical Research, 55*(814)

Godwin, Malcolm, *The Lucid Dreamer* (Dorset, Labyrinth Publishing, 1995)

LaBerge, Stephen and Howard Rheingold, *Exploring The World of Lucid Dreaming* (Toronto, The Random House Publishing Group, 1990)

Persinger, M. A., & Krippner, S. (1989). Dream ESP experiments and geomagnetic activity. *Journal of the American Society for Psychical Research, 83*(2), 101–116.

Telepathy

Carington, Whately, *Telepathy* (London, Metheun & Co. LTD, 1945)

The Research Officer, *The Sinclair Experiments For Telepathy* (Boston Society for Psychic Research, Boston, 1932)

Stevenson, Ian, *Telepathic Impressions*, Charlottesville, University Press of Virginia, 1970)

Twin Flames

Lumezi, Geraldina, *Twin Soul Eternal Love* (Great Britain)

McCarty, Jen, *Twin Flames & The Event* (Great Britain, Blue Flame 5D Media)

Joudry, Patricia and Maurice D. Pressman, *Twin Souls: Finding Your True Spiritual Partner* (Minnesota, Hazelden Informational & Educational Services, 2000)

Index

E

F

G

H

T

U

W

ABOUT THE AUTHOR

Linghwa has been writing stories since she could first hold a pencil and form words on the page. Her love of writing remained throughout her childhood and teenage years, developing into a desire to become a dedicated author. In wanting to develop her writing craft further, Linghwa has previously completed a BA in creative writing and is currently studying a MA in creative writing at UWTSD Lampeter.

Primarily a writer of fantasy fiction, Linghwa has also experimented with different styles of writing throughout her university degree which have compiled within two books: *The Demon of Munbigye: Prequel Stories* and *Horologically Displaced.*

Linghwa has a keen interest in spirituality, esoterica, and mysticism - themes of which are prevalent within the fantasy worlds she creates for her stories and reflect her own personal inquisitiveness of reality and the preternatural.

Other works published by LJ Bremer and available on Amazon:

Works of Fiction
Horologically Displaced
The Demon of Munbigye: Prequel Stories
The Sirin Chronicles I: A Dawn of Dreams

Poetry
Do You Dream of Me Too?

Daily Journals
I AM Gratitude and Manifesting
I AM Dreaming
I AM Grateful
I AM Reflective

www.ingramcontent.com/pod-product-compliance
Lightning Source LLC
LaVergne TN
LVHW041012150826
845672LV00001B/65